£50
'07

F E

45604

European Solidarity

STUDIES IN SOCIAL AND POLITICAL THOUGHT 16

STUDIES IN SOCIAL AND POLITICAL THOUGHT
Editor: Gerard Delanty, *University of Sussex*

This series publishes peer-reviewed scholarly books on all aspects of social and political thought. It will be of interest to scholars and advanced students working in the areas of social theory and sociology, the history of ideas, philosophy, political and legal theory, anthropological and cultural theory. Works of individual scholarship will have preference for inclusion in the series, but appropriate co- or multi-authored works and edited volumes of outstanding quality or exceptional merit will also be included. The series will also consider English translations of major works in other languages.

Challenging and intellectually innovative books are particularly welcome on the history of social and political theory; modernity and the social and human sciences; major historical or contemporary thinkers; the philosophy of the social sciences; theoretical issues on the transformation of contemporary society; social change and European societies.

It is not series policy to publish textbooks, research reports, empirical case studies, conference proceedings or books of an essayist or polemical nature.

Recent titles in the series:

Social Theory and Later Modernities: The Turkish Experience
Ibrahim Kaya

Sociological Beginnings: The First Conference of the German Society for Sociology
Christopher Adair-Toteff

Multiple Modernities, Civil Society and Islam: The Case of Iran and Turkey
Masoud Kamali

Varieties of World-Making: Beyond Globalization
edited by Nathalie Karagiannis and Peter Wagner

Cosmopolitanism and Europe
edited by Chris Rumford

European Solidarity

EDITED BY NATHALIE KARAGIANNIS

LIVERPOOL UNIVERSITY PRESS

First published 2007 by
Liverpool University Press
4 Cambridge Street
Liverpool L69 7ZU

Copyright © 2007 Liverpool University Press

The right of Nathalie Karagiannis to be identified as the
editor of this work has been asserted by her in accordance
with the Copyright, Design and Patents Act 1988.

British Library Cataloguing-in-Publication data
A British Library CIP record is available

ISBN 978-1-84631-080-5 cased

Typeset by XL Publishing Services, Tiverton
Printed and bound in the European Union by
Biddles Ltd, King's Lynn

Contents

Part II: Contemporary Boundaries of Solidarity in Europe

List of Contributors

Schirin Amir-Moazami is currently a Research Fellow at the Europa-Universität Viadrina in Frankfurt/Oder. Her research focuses on the ways in which Islam is dealt with in European public spheres, and on gender issues related to Islam in both the Muslim world and Europe. Relevant publications include: *Politisierte Religion: Der Kopftuchstreit in Deutschland und Frankreich* (transcript, Bielefeld, 2007); 'Muslim challenges to the secular consensus: a German case study' in Frank Peter and Barbara Thériault (eds), *Islam and the Dynamics of European National Societies* (*Journal of Contemporary European Studies*, 13.3, 2005); 'Reaffirming and shifting boundaries: Muslim perspectives on gender and citizenship in France and Germany' in S. Nökel and L. Teczan (eds), *Yearbook of Sociology of Islam*, 6, New Brunswick and London, Lit Verlag, 2005.

Thomas Fiegle is Assistant Professor in Political Theory at the University of Potsdam. His recent publications are: *Von der Solidarité zur Solidarität: Ein französisch-deutscher Begriffstransfer*, Münster/Hamburg/London, Lit-Verlag, 2003; 'Das Gesetz der Gesellschaft: Der Solidaritätsbegriff in Frankreich und Deutschland im 19. Jahrhundert' in Wolfgang Bock (ed.), *Gesetz und Gesetzlichkeit in den Wissenschaften*, Darmstadt, Wissenschaftliche Buchgesellschaft, 2005; 'Die Verzeitlichung des Ethnos. Zur Begriffsgeschichte von Volk' in *lendemains: Etudes comparées sur la France/Vergleichende Frankreichforschung*, vol. 125, 2007.

Nathalie Karagiannis is a Fellow of the Provincia Autonoma di Trento at the University of Trento. Her recent books are *Varieties of World-Making: Beyond Globalization* (ed. with Peter Wagner), Liverpool, Liverpool University Press, 2006, and *Avoiding Responsibility: The Discourse of EU Development Policy*, London, Pluto Press, 2004. Related articles and book chapters include: 'Solidarity within Europe/solidarity without Europe' in *European Societies*, 9.1, 2006; 'Multiple solidarities: autonomy and resistance' in Nathalie Karagiannis and Peter Wagner (eds), *Varieties of World-Making:*

Beyond Globalization, Liverpool, Liverpool University Press, 2006; 'Die Gabe der Entwicklung' in Max Adloff and Steffen Mau (eds), *Reziprozität*, Frankfurt, Campus Verlag, 2005; 'Towards a theory of synagonism' (with Peter Wagner) in *Journal of Political Philosophy*, 13.3, 2005; and 'Preceding "global responsibility": autonomy, knowledge, power' in Michael Davis et al. (eds), *International Intervention*, New York, Sharpe, 2004.

Steffen Mau is Professor of Sociology at the Graduate School of Social Sciences, University of Bremen. He works in the fields of comparative welfare research, social inequality and European integration. His books include *Welfare States: Construction, Deconstruction, Reconstruction* (ed. with Stephan Leibfried), Cheltenham, Edward Elgar, 2007; *Vom Geben und Nehmen: Zur Soziologie der Reziprozität* (ed. with Frank Adloff), Frankfurt am Main/New York, Campus, 2005; *Gerechtigkeit und Verteilungsprobleme in modernen Gesellschaften* (ed. with Stefan Liebig and Holger Lengfeld), Frankfurt am Main/New York, Campus, 2004; and *The Moral Economy of Welfare States: Britain and Germany Compared*, London/New York, Routledge, 2003. His articles include: 'Die Politik der Grenze: Grenzziehung und politische Systembildung in der Europäischen Union', *Berliner Journal für Soziologie*, 16, 2006.

Senadin Musabegović, a journalist, poet and soldier during the war in Bosnia, is now Lecturer in Aesthetics and Social Sciences at the University of Mostar Džemal Bijedić. His publications include: *Udarci Tijela*, Sarajevo, Oko, 1995 (poems); *Odrastanje Domovine*, Sarajevo, Svjetlost, 1999 (poems, translated into French as *Grandissement de la patrie*, Toulouse, N&B, 2002); 'Pourquoi les rats agitent leurs moustaches' in Francis Buep (ed.), *Carnets de Sarajevo 1*, Paris, Gallimard, 2002; 'La pelle du paradis' in Martine Paturle, Patricia Urrea-Carette and Jean-Marc Urrea (eds), *La Paix en toutes Lettres*, Arles, Actes Sud, 2003; 'Circle and present' in Bo Strath and Ron Robin (eds), *'Homeland', Poetic Power and the Politics of Space*, Brussels, Peter Lang, 2003; and *Rajska Lopata*, Sarajevo, Zoro, 2004 (poems).

Claus Offe is Professor Emeritus of Political Science at Humboldt University, Berlin. He taught at the universities of Bielefeld (1975–89) and Bremen (1989–95), and has served as Visiting Professor at academic institutions in the USA, Canada, the Netherlands, Austria, Sweden, Italy and Australia. His fields of research include political sociology, social policy, democratic theory and transformation studies. His recent English-language books include: *Varieties of Transition*, Cambridge (Mass.), MIT Press, 1996; *Modernity and*

The State: East and West, Cambridge (Mass.), MIT Press, 1996; *Constitutional Design in Post-Communist Societies: Rebuilding the Ship at Sea* (with Jon Elster and Ulrich K. Preuss), Cambridge, Cambridge University Press, 1998; and *Reflections on America: Tocqueville, Weber and Adorno in the United States*, Cambridge, Polity, 2005.

William Outhwaite is Professor of Sociology at Newcastle University. He is the author of *Understanding Social Life: The Method Called Verstehen*, London, Allen & Unwin, 1975 (second edition 1986); *Concept Formation in Social Science*, Routledge, 1983; *New Philosophies of Social Science: Realism, Hermeneutics and Critical Theory*, London, Macmillan, 1987; *Habermas: A Critical Introduction*, Cambridge, Polity, 1994; *The Future of Society*, Oxford, Blackwell, 2005; and *Social Theory and Postcommunism* (with Larry Ray), Oxford, Blackwell, 2005. He edited *The Habermas Reader*, Cambridge, Polity, 1996; *The Blackwell Dictionary of Twentieth-century Social Thought* (with Tom Bottomore), Oxford, Blackwell, 1993; *The Blackwell Dictionary of Modern Social Thought*, Oxford, Blackwell, 1993; *The Sociology of Politics* (with Luke Martell), Cheltenham, Edward Elgar, 1998; and *Defending Objectivity* (with Margaret Archer), London, Routledge, 2004. He is currently working on a book about European society.

Mihnea Panu is Assistant Professor in the Sociology Department at Wilfrid Laurier University, Canada. His current research looks at the relationship between power, truth, subjectivity and the governing of reproduction in the USA.

Raluca Parvu currently teaches at Wilfrid Laurier University and UOIT, Canada. She was previously a Lecturer in the Department of Sociology, Oxford Brookes University, and taught undergraduates in sociology departments in the universities of Surrey and Sussex. Her research interests focus on the reconfiguration of the social, and identities in post-Communist contexts, including issues of representation and possibilities for identity negotiation in Eastern Europe as framed by the relationship with 'the West'.

Herwig Reiter is Research Fellow at the Graduate School of Social Sciences, University of Bremen. His work focuses on issues of youth, work and unemployment in Europe. Recent publications include: 'Youth in the labour market: citizenship or exclusion?' (with Gary Craig) in Harriet Bradley and Jacques van Hoof (eds), *Young People in Europe: Labour Markets and Citizenship*, Bristol, Policy Press, 2005; and 'Past, present, future:

biographical time structuring of disadvantaged young people' in *Young – Nordic Journal of Youth Research*, **11**, 2003.

Armando Salvatore is Reader in Social Theory in the Department of Social Sciences, Humboldt University, Berlin. He is editor of the *Yearbook of the Sociology of Islam*. Among his most recent publications are: *The Public Sphere: Liberal Modernity, Catholicism, Islam*, New York, Palgrave Macmillan, 2007; *Religion, Social Practice and Contested Hegemonies* (ed. with Mark LeVine), New York, Palgrave Macmillan, 2005; and *Public Islam and the Common Good* (ed. with Dale F. Eickelman), Leiden and Boston, Brill, 2004.

Peter Wagner is Professor of Sociology at the University of Trento. His research interests have taken him from the historical sociology of the social sciences, to an intellectual/institutional history of European societies, to attempts at developing a social and political theory of modernity. Peter Wagner's previous publications include *Theorizing Modernity*, London, Sage, 2001; *A History and Theory of the Social Sciences*, London, Sage, 2001; and *A Sociology of Modernity, Liberty and Discipline*, London, Routledge, 1994. A book tentatively titled *Modernity as Experience and Interpretation* is forthcoming with Polity, Cambridge.

Acknowledgements

The editor would like to acknowledge an EU Marie Curie Grant, which contributed greatly to the preparation of this book. In this context, she would like to thank William Outhwaite for his kindness and understanding. She would also like to thank Gerard Delanty for his helpful suggestions and his encouragement, Anthony Cond for his availability, Thomas Roberts and Jonathan White for their editing and translation respectively, Bo Strath for his generous help with organizing a related event at the EUI in Florence, and Peter Wagner for his invaluable support.

Introduction: Solidarity in Europe – Politics, Religion, Knowledge

Nathalie Karagiannis

In the context of two recent, important events for the nascent European polity, the concept of 'solidarity' was revived and placed centre stage by two major thinkers of our time, effectively initiating a wider debate about Europe (Habermas and Derrida, 2003). The first event was the launch of, preparation for and, ultimately, failure of the European Constitution. The second event was the largely Anglo-American war in Iraq that began in 2003. Both of these set Europeans thinking about what it is that makes them European, and though the second event made clear the Europeans' wish to distinguish between Europe and the USA, the first showed that this demarcation did not necessarily correspond to a unified self-understanding among Europeans. Despite this divergence, the term 'solidarity' and, specifically, 'European solidarity' was widely used, and was probably meant to designate both empirical reality and normative commitment on the part of Europeans.

These two occasions were not entirely detached from a wider re-launching of the concept in other areas, such as development cooperation, humanitarian aid and social policy. However, the growing resistance to neo-liberalism as a dogma and as a social reality in Europe (where no erosion of public finances earmarked for social expenditure could be observed) has also increasingly used 'solidarity' to rally supporters and sympathisers to its cause. It is in this resistance that one can locate the major social transformation of our time: the opposition between institutionalized forms of solidarity, and solidarity expressed in new social movements. This highlights the tension created by solidarity in an exemplary way. Institutional forms of solidarity have long been accepted as legitimate expressions of the common social feeling of belonging: the nation state is the most obvious example. Solidarity expressed in and by social movements represents a novel expression of a common feeling of belonging that is not encompassed by traditional institutional forms (the

1

expression 'institutional forms of solidarity' is slightly misleading, as 'new social movements' are now solidly institutionalized too). These two broad forms of solidarity confront one another: institutional forms of solidarity principally aim at cooperation, whereas more recent forms of solidarity aim at dissent and conflict; and the former have social order as their main objective, while the latter pursue disorder or the breaking of the previous order.

This transformation is intimately connected to the one really novel feature of solidarity today: the intensification of its multiplicity – or, in other words, the ever-increasing number of solidarities. The existence of multiple solidarities is by no means new. Indeed, this can be shown with recourse to a definition of solidarity that is sufficiently broad to encompass the various situations it covers, while at the same time specific enough to avoid confusion with society or the social. Such a definition runs as follows: solidarity is the periodic specification of social bonds in a political perspective. Throughout different historical experiences, rather than presenting concrete content or even a particular form of social dynamics, solidarity is a *politically committed re-specification of the social*. This means not only that solidarity is that which allows the very (and varying) definition of the social, but also that throughout different historical experiences it has given a political spin to the social, by translating the social into political terms; in other words, such a definition allows for the (always political) articulation of the social.[1] One consequence of this definition is that solidarity's chronological oneness is not sustainable in the face of historical evidence: different solidarities predominate at different times. It also means that several ties of solidarity – several specifications of the social – struggling against each other in the context of competing political projects can indeed co-exist.[2] The European continent and the nascent European polity are examples par excellence of this tendency.

Nevertheless, it seems that the frequency with which the concept is encountered does nothing to ease the suspicion that it is a mere buzzword, not only because it does not have any practical implications or correspond to any social reality, but also because it is too often drawn upon without consideration for the theoretical questions it raises. This book, therefore, intends to make the theoretical aspects of European solidarity clearer, and to specify its socio-political implications.

---

1 A theoretically secondary but crucial conclusion that needs to be drawn from this definition is that solidarity is as expandable as the political will for it, rather than being a scarce resource (as it is often conceptualized). However, the objective and the effect of the institutionalization of solidarity in France has also been convincingly shown to be a depoliticizing 'third way' between liberalism and Marxism (Donzelot, 1984).
2 Simmel's (1955; 1971) multiple group belongings can be brought close to this conceptualization.

Any conceptual–historical exploration uncovers at least three roots of the concept: politics, religion and knowledge. Thus, firstly, solidarity is usually understood to be a social issue, and its cohesive and inclusive nature is assumed to be antithetical to the political, which is characterized by dissent, deliberation and decision-making. However, solidarity also happens to be a political project, in the sense that it becomes an object and objective of debate and contestation, and also in the sense that it becomes an aim despite internal conflicts in the polity. Indeed, if it is widely accepted that institutionalized forms of solidarity in liberal democracies aim at both economic redistribution and cultural recognition, it is often less clearly theorized that the references to the economic and cultural aspects of society have political consequences, and that they are themselves part of ongoing political projects (see Chapter 7).[3] Overshadowed by the erosion of the European welfare state, and the globalizing tendencies of financial capital and multiculturalism, such political projects take new forms. Placing this political aspect of solidarity in its historical context inevitably brings to the fore the question of the role of colonialism in the construction of European nation states. In general terms, it raises the question of the post-colonial world, the solidarity between its inhabitants despite their unequal positions within it, and the solidarity within ex-colonial groups and ex-colonized groups (see Chapter 12).

Secondly, modern solidarity is frequently understood to have religious origins (see Chapters 3 and 4). In fact, the tension between the religious, and therefore – it is assumed – traditional roots of solidarity and its presence in secularized contexts has given birth to some of the most renowned works on the concept. For instance, Durkheim's (1973) reading of the passage from tradition to modernity by means of the transition from mechanical to organic solidarity is also, for this thinker, a reading of the passage from religion to secularization.[4] However, in the European context today, the road from a religious to a secular understanding of the social bond does not appear to be quite so straightforward.[5] The current making of a European identity certainly owes a lot to a sense of European solidarity that is promoted, notably, by European institutions (see Chapter 8). If this European identity is, as a result, a secular one, less 'institutionalized' understandings of what it means to be a European include religious solidarities. The debates around the inclusion of

---

3 Solidarity in the guise of economic redistribution, on the one hand, aims at an egalitarian society. Cultural recognition, on the other hand, has as its objective the acknowledgement and respect of cultural difference. For these formulations, see Fraser and Honneth, 2003; for a reformulation, see Fraser, 2006.

4 See also Brunkhorst, 2005 and Stjernø, 2004.

5 See Michalski, 2006.

a Christian reference in the European Constitution or, more significantly, the debates around and within European Islam are highly illuminating in this regard. In the case of European Islam, solidarity may characterise both the *umma* and also the European-ness of those who belong to the *umma* (see Chapters 4 and 11).

Thirdly, the role of solidarity as the keystone of social science disciplines is largely due to Durkheim's central use of this concept (see Chapter 5). Durkheim was strongly influenced by debates centred on issues of common interest in France, and himself strongly influenced the view that a science which took society as its object was needed at the end of the 19th century. The involvement of the concept in the evolution and subsequent development of the discipline established 'solidarity' as one of the most significant theoretical concepts of the 20th century. Indeed, after the birth of sociology, 'solidarity' thrived as the disciplinary characterization of the social. However, as with every discipline, this meant imposing reductionisms and sacrificing complexity for the sake of order (see Chapter 6). Thus, if the concept is to be seen as that which intellectuals propose as a rallying reference point and a necessary policy – following not only Leon Bourgeois and Jürgen Habermas but also, perhaps unexpectedly, the European Union's think tanks – then solidarity is the top–down catalyst necessary to hold society together (Donzelot, 1984). On the other hand, if solidarity is seen as the ushering into historical existence of the masses (Papaioannou, 1998), or the working classes, or the 'global' social movement, then it is also conceptualized as the re-actualization of the French Revolution's bottom–up concept of 'fraternity' (Sewell, 1980): in this case, privileged knowledge comes from the grass roots (Santos, 1995).

Four problematized features of solidarity

Growing out of these complex roots – the religious, the political and the epistemological – and spreading out in multiple forms, solidarity, and a fortiori European solidarity, remains surprisingly unproblematized when used in both political and theoretical discourse. With the common aim to shed more light on its ambivalent aspects, the chapters of this book all, more or less explicitly, address at least one of the four features of European solidarity. These features are either not usually acknowledged or, when they are, they remain unproblematized. These features are:

1 the issue of inclusion/exclusion;
2 the elusive nature of the centre of solidarity;

3 the issue of inequality; and
4 the simultaneity of commitment and belonging.

As a matter of common sense, we see inclusion as the first quality of solidarity. According to this commonsensical view, solidarity federates; that is, it makes social things come together and then hold together. However, perhaps more paradoxical is the widely observed fact that such inclusion entails exclusion. The universalist–particularist dynamics of European nation states are the most obvious example. Is exclusion always the price to be paid for the creation of commonality by solidarity? Different answers that may be given to this question, ranging from an acceptance of exclusion as the inevitable fate of solidarity, to the quest for an all-inclusive solidarity. Thus, any theorization – other than cosmopolitan – of human rights, and in particular the right to asylum and migration, has to concede that there is a limit to such practices. Beyond that limit, wherever it may be situated – not only geographically but also in terms of the conditions of entry and so on – there is exclusion from solidarity. Similarly, the ways in which existing socialism and, more generally, totalitarian societies were built are also particularly telling in this respect. Total inclusion meant that any deviation had to be corrected by a programme of simultaneous exclusion and inclusion in prison, and re-education (see Chapter 2). This problem is also acutely evident in different conceptualizations of the religious and the social, most notably in the case of Islam and Europe.

Traditionally, solidarity federated previously separate elements around a specific core of values, ideas or reified categories. Western Christian solidarity, for instance, federated around entities such as 'God' or 'the Church'. Working class solidarity was created around the central category of 'the workers', French nationalism around *une certaine idée de la France*, etc. These core categories have increasingly been challenged; but, at the same time, references to solidarity are still crucial in socio-political discourse. In other words, a normative commitment to solidarity as a value and a practice is on the one hand upheld, while on the other hand there is a recognition that this solidarity no longer has fixed points of reference, such as 'God', 'the workers', or 'the French'. Against the background of the invisibility of God in a republican, European Islam, or the dissolution of a fixed subject, a commitment to a novel type of solidarity is claimed. This novel solidarity admits to having no fixed core (see Chapter 6). Whether this paradoxical normative pursuit can in the end bear fruit (or indeed be coherent) is by no means certain, but it is clear that it can be socially observed. This is quite different from the observation that solidarity always installs a third term in the middle of the relationship between two other terms, only in order to overcome this third term. According to this view, 'God', 'the Church', 'the workers' or 'France' are not the central categories of solidarity, but constitute conceptual steps that, once taken, transform things that *must* hold together into exactly this (Karagiannis, 2005).

The third problem of solidarity is the problem of equality/inequality, equality being one of the fundamental traits of the received view of solidarity, together with reasonableness/rationality and abstraction. Thus, Arendt (1990) sees solidarity as including in the same community the oppressed and the non-oppressed, the exploited and – one assumes – the exploiters, the wealthy and the poor. Yet although solidarity may well aim to overcome inequality, as Arendt wishes, solidarity can only exist where there already is inequality (for related issues, see Chapter 9). Only if there are rich and poor can solidarity be inclusive; only if there are oppressed and oppressors can there be a dispassionate community; only if there are less powerful and more powerful classes can there be class-based solidarity. This feature of solidarity is present in its rare artistic representations. While 'charity', an ancestor of solidarity, is abundantly present in paintings as a rather plump, often breast-feeding woman (Starobinski, 1997), artistic representations of solidarity as such are rare. Such representations are most frequently encountered in socialist art. The raised fist, or the worker's body, often made up of many small bodies, shows that 'all [are] in one, and one [is] in all' (see Chapter 3). Images of charity always clearly represent the asymmetrical relationship between the giver and the receiver: the woman feeds children or, in the extreme case of Roman charity, her old, weak mother or father. It is note-worthy that representations of solidarity in the socialist artistic tradition are no less asymmetrical in the relationships between the constituent parts and the whole.

Fourthly, there is a hiatus between solidarity as a commitment or a value – that is, as something that is pursued – and solidarity as 'belonging', 'belongingness' or 'we-ness', something that is already there (see Chapters 5 and 7). In this sense, we are dealing with a different sense of solidarity when it is attached to particular world views about the good life, to autonomy and to freedom, and when it is viewed as endangered, dissolving or emerging. In the first case, solidarity is seen as the attribute that will keep the good polity together, and thus as an expression of the belief in the future of this polity as polity (see Chapter 1). In the second case, solidarity is seen as that which, having adequately described a social situation, no longer does so because the situation has become undescribable in social terms (see Chapter 10). The move from the second to the first case is always necessary before a new sense of 'belonging' can be ascribed to the social.

The exploration of these features is a necessary step towards the re-conceptualization of solidarity in a way that makes sense to the current social world. Such a step, therefore, taken against the background of the current social world, assumes that solidarity is inadequately conceptualized and that the current social world differs from previous situations. However, the manner in which the current social world differs from previous situations resides in none of these features. Indeed, as we saw above, the only novelty in current solidarity is its intense or intensified pluralization: that is, the systematic transformation of solidarity into solidar*ities*. Why then point at these features, if older and newer forms of solidarity are likewise characterized by them?

These features are united by their clarification of two things, one political and one theoretical. The first is that solidarity is a creator of social tension. The received understanding of solidarity holds, by contrast, that solidarity is a purveyor of social smoothness, harmony and order. Durkheim's conceptualization is the most evident reference here, where anomie is social chaos and disorder, and – situated at the opposite pole of the social – solidarity brings together various functionally differentiated social elements into one highly efficient machine. Critiques of Durkheim have pointed out that anomie also presupposes some social organization (Lockwood, 1992). More importantly for the purposes of this paper, the 19th century transformation of revolutionary fraternity into workers' solidarity, which Durkheim had witnessed, was certainly not aimed at the establishment of social order: or, if it was, it was at most orientated towards the distant, post-revolutionary future, following the disappearance of the bourgeois social order to which this solidarity was opposed. The confrontation between institutionalized forms of solidarity and solidarity as expressed in social movements is a similar type of tension.

The second commonality that these features have is that solidarity is inescapably ambiguous, signalling at almost every level at which it is examined (or through every feature) one thing and its opposite. In this sense, these features must be made into problems: not only because they address socially problematic situations, but also because they give theoretically problematic answers.

The few examples that I have very briefly alluded to refer to current forms of solidarity that are recognizable by all. It is clear, for instance, that while all forms of gender, religion or ethnic solidarity are characterized by both inclusion and exclusion, some of them are more intensely oriented towards exclusion than others. Similarly, every study in post-Marxism or post-structuralism deals in more or less nuanced ways with the problem of the elusive centre of the social bond. The same goes for the ambiguity between 'belonging' and the commitment that inhabits almost every form of social association – to such an extent that no form of social belonging is nowadays presented without its 'politics'. It could therefore be said that a major part of social theory is preoccupied with these four features without acknowledging their relation to solidarity. Part of the problem they represent can thus be solved by recourse to a systematic re-conceptualization of solidarity. It is only the third feature, equality, which remains problematic: untangling the various threads of this problem is, however, beyond the scope of this volume.

Reconceptualizing and recontextualizing European solidarity

The chapters in this book are all characterized by a stance of puzzlement vis-à-vis the multiplication of European solidarity, and by an understanding that one or more of the above four features of solidarity is problematic. In a certain sense, therefore, all the chapters engage with the same question: how is it possible to keep referring to 'European solidarity' when it is not one thing but many, and when deeper analysis reveals an unsurpassable evasiveness?

Two possible answers to this question would have structured this book along the lines of the preceding sections of this Introduction. The first answer would have privileged the breaking down of the social world into the political, the religious and the epistemological. It would have had the advantage of establishing a traditional form of clarity, but would have overlooked a complexity in solidarity that all chapters attempt to make evident. The second answer would have focused on the four problematic features. This would have had the advantage of originality, but would have limited the reading of each chapter to one of four headings. Hence, the reader has now been given the above *grilles de lecture*, while remaining able freely to interpret, first, a historically informed theory of the concept and, second, the contemporary boundaries of European solidarity.

The first part of the book is a historically informed exploration of crucial theoretical problems that solidarity has posed in the past and poses nowadays.[6] The more explicitly political version of the question of solidarity was developed during the 19th century within Europe's foremost political theory, liberalism, and its later version, individual liberalism. Peter Wagner starts out with the observation that the commitment to solidarity as we know it today

---

6 The Greek and Jewish precursors of the concept are beyond the scope of this book. For related overviews from different viewpoints, see, for instance, Ludwig, 2002; Brunkhorst, 2005; Karagiannis, 2006.

arose in response to the socio-economic consequences of the growing prominence of individual liberty in the aftermath of the French Revolution. Therefore, the principle of solidarity can be seen as historically secondary to freedom, at least in the language of familiar political philosophy. He argues, however, that there is no compelling conceptual reason to give priority to freedom, but that freedom and solidarity can more fruitfully be seen as co-constitutive of each other as political commitments (Chapter 1). At the other extreme of liberal individualism, 20th-century European totalitarianism heavily relied on a rhetoric of solidarity that subordinated the idea of individual freedom to a closely-knit society. Taking the example of Goli Otok, a former prison in Yugoslavia, Senadin Musabegovic problematizes the ambiguity of practices of solidarity, which aimed both at excluding and including those who dissented from the Communist regime. The (imposed) rhetoric of solidarity between the prisoners and the state is here shown to be co-extensive with the organized use of violence. Its main aim was to undermine previous solidarities between former fellow combatants (Chapter 2).

It is uncontested by now that the various religions of the European space played fundamental roles in the emergence of the concept of solidarity. During the crucial period in which French notions of 'solidarité' emerged, and before the usage was consolidated, the concept had other, conservative, Christian roots. Seeing in the Gnostic tradition two versions of solidarity – one positive and the other negative – Thomas Fiegle argues that the step from this tradition to socialism was taken very easily. However, in Germany, where the main religious influence had changed from Catholicism to Protestantism, another version arose, paving the way for an altogether different form of philosophical thought (Chapter 3). Looking at Islam, Armando Salvatore observes its potential for transforming notions and practices of solidarity in Europe, due to the increasing presence in Europe of citizens and residents with an Islamic religious or cultural background. Salvatore argues that the difficulty with which their discourse is received originates in the secular models of cohesion and solidarity of contemporary European societies, which he characterizes as post-Christian. Drawing on the same historical era, he establishes a parallel between today's Islamic intellectuals and the 19th and 20th century's European Jewish intellectuals (Chapter 4).

Once the proper political space for solidarity alongside freedom has been created, and once its religious roots and present have been acknowledged, however, the concept's exact relation to society or the social still needs to be investigated. William Outhwaite's contribution takes a closer look at the place of solidarity in the discourses of the European welfare state and considers it a fundamental resource of the socialist tradition down to the present day, especially in Jürgen Habermas's social theory. Asking whether solidarity is 'what holds society together', which is then to be equated with the very constitution of the social (or, in other versions, 'community'), or whether it is a feeling or a sentiment projected towards others who may or may not belong with us, Outhwaite maps the overlapping and conflicting usages of the concept. Ultimately, he argues, acknowledging the variable geometry of the concept is necessary in order to maintain it (Chapter 5). However, even if we keep a single notion of solidarity, the commonality assumed by solidarity is becoming increasingly problematic: how can a commitment to solidarity be upheld and, at the same time, the exclusions to which it has given rise, in earlier times but also nowadays in Europe, be avoided and rejected? Deconstructing the fixed and uncontroversial social identities presumed by solidarity makes clear that they are both elusive (because of the ultimate impossibility of closing signification around a 'substance') and generative of social antagonisms (because of the boundaries such hegemonic attempts erect). Nonetheless, Mihnea Panu argues for the possibility of a normative definition of solidarity that allows for both the impossibility of fixation and the possibility of politics that transcend the particular to address a 'distant other'(Chapter 6).

The second part of the book picks up the historical and theoretical threads of Part 1 and deploys them along the lines of the crucial issues that contemporary European solidarity faces. Providing a transition from the first part of the book, Claus Offe (Chapter 7) begins with the observation that, from the viewpoint of solidary actions, the 'obligations' of solidarity cannot be neatly opposed to the costs of solidarity. Assuming the European framework of legal guarantees and the rule of law, where the state has a central role to play in defining solidary actions, Offe distinguishes four types of solidarity: liberal, republican, social-democratic and supranational. In all of those, Offe argues, the 'obligations' of solidarity are willingly taken up by actors. The European Union can be regarded as the most striking example of supranationalization that brings about new forms of solidarity. Against the background of competing models of a European society, such as the neo-liberal model and the idea of European regulated capitalism, Steffen Mau shows that the European Union has adopted unique features of solidarity, such as the cohesion policy and European citizenship. Placing particular emphasis on the tension between European enlargement and the development of solidarity, the author points out that if the scheme of the national welfare state is now widely problematized, it is not unproblematic to assert that the EU institutions can replace it (Chapter 8).

The following chapters explore three of the many boundaries that delimit

European solidarity: Eastern Europe, Islam and 'the rest of the world'. Following one of the previous chapter's main concerns, the boundary of Eastern Europe is investigated in more detail. Based on a case study of Romania, Raluca Parvu's contribution draws a broad picture of the collapse of solidarity in Eastern Europe. Against the background of several strong but ambiguous forms of social solidarity under communism, the chapter investigates how the turn towards Western European capitalism has been accompanied by the dissolution of certain identities and, thus, solidarities. Having left Romanians with an acute sense of social disorientation, the fall of Communism has allowed an a posteriori negative reading of the previously existing solidarity and an increased individualism (Chapter 9). By contrast, Herwig Reiter's chapter on Lithuania observes persistently egalitarian values in Eastern Europe. However, these coincide with low levels of involvement in solidary activities. This paradox may be explained by the missing grid for reading social situations: focusing on the issue of unemployment and its relation to solidarity, Reiter points out that 'the unemployed' are not yet recognizable, but are emerging as a group. Thus, the lack of solidaristic action may be due to the fact that social actors do not know with whom to be solidaristic (Chapter 10).

Just as there are many ways of thinking about European solidarity, so there are many ways of thinking about Muslim solidarity, Schirin Amir-Moazami argues, echoing more practical considerations raised by Salvatore's paper. The partly contradictory and conflicting developments of Muslim solidarities in Europe are more complex than had been anticipated. Thus, Amir-Moazami maps out three, distinct Muslim conceptualizations of the relationship between Islam and Europe: Euro-Islam, Islam in Europe and Islamist Europe, showing that the wide-ranging variety of self-understandings of European Muslims is at least partly to be understood as an effect of the different (national) contexts from which Muslim scholars come (Chapter 11). Finally, Chapter 12 brings together the internal and external boundaries of contemporary and historical Europe by counterposing the EU institutional discourse on internal European solidarity and the 'social model' with the discourse on the solidarity of Europe with 'the rest of the world'. These two directions of solidarity have often been constructed as a dilemma, or a zero-sum game, in both institutional and theoretical discourse. Disentangling the various aspects of the concept of solidarity that are involved can help us to resist the idea that if Europe is to become more integrated, it has to cease aid programmes to economically weaker regions of the world.

References

Arendt, H. (1990 [1960]), 'The social question' in H. Arendt, *On Revolution*, London, Penguin.

Brunkhorst, H. (2005), *Solidarity: From Civic Friendship to a Global Legal Community* (transl. J. Flynn), Cambridge, MA., MIT Press.

Donzelot, J. (1984), *L'invention du social: Essai sur le declin des passions politiques*, Paris, Fayard.

Durkheim, E. (1973 [1893]), *De la division du travail social*, Paris, PUF.

Fraser, N. (2006), 'Democratic justice in a globalizing age: thematizing the problem of the frame' in N. Karagiannis and P. Wagner (eds), *Varieties of World-Making: Beyond Globalization*, Liverpool, Liverpool University Press.

Fraser, N. and Honneth, A. (2003), *Redistribution or Recognition? A Political-Philosophical Exchange* (transl. J. Golb, J. Ingram and C. Wilke), London, Verso.

Habermas, J. and Derrida, J. (2003), 'February 15, or what binds Europeans together? A plea for a common foreign policy, beginning in the core of Europe', *Constellations*, 10, 3.

Karagiannis, N. (2005), 'From solitude to solidarity: the third man', paper presented at a conference on 'Solidarity In and Beyond Europe', EUI, Florence.

Karagiannis, N. (2006), 'Multiple solidarities: autonomy and resistance' in N. Karagiannis and P. Wagner (eds), *Varieties of World-Making: Beyond Globalization*, Liverpool, Liverpool University Press.

Komter, A. E. (2005), *Social Solidarity and the Gift*, Cambridge, Cambridge University Press.

Lockwood, D. (1992), *Solidarity and Schism: 'The Problem of Disorder' in Durkheimian and Marxist Sociology*, Oxford, Clarendon Press.

Ludwig, P. W. (2002), *Eros and Polis: Desire and Community in Greek Political Theory*, Cambridge, Cambridge University Press.

Michalski, K. (ed.) (2006), *Conditions of European Solidarity, Volume II: Religion in the New Europe*, Budapest, Central European University.

Papaioannou, K. (1998 [1972]), *Techne ke Politismos stin Arhaia Ellada*, Athens, Enallaktikes Ekdosis.

Santos, B. de Sousa (1995), *Toward a New Common Sense: Law, Science and Politics in the Paradigmatic Transition*, New York, Routledge.

Sewell, W. (1980), *Work and Revolution in France: The Language of Labour from the Old Regime to 1848*, Cambridge, Cambridge University Press.

Simmel, G. (1955), *Conflict and the Web of Group Affiliations*, New York, The Free Press.

Simmel, G. (1971), *On Individuality and Social Forms*, Chicago, University of Chicago Press.

Starobinski, J. (1997), *Largesse*, Chicago, University of Chicago Press.

Stjernø, S. (2004), *Solidarity in Europe: The History of an Idea*, Cambridge, Cambridge University Press.

Part I

Theory of European Solidarity

1   Freedom and Solidarity: Retrieving the European Political Tradition of Non-individualist Liberalism

Peter Wagner

Roughly in the middle of his famous lecture on 'Two concepts of liberty', Isaiah Berlin discussed the danger of 'confounding liberty with her sisters, equality and fraternity', which would lead to 'illiberal conclusions' (Berlin, 1971 [1958], 154).[1] He then subsumes those two sisters of liberty under the notion of the 'search for status and recognition', and appears to come to a clear verdict:

> It is not with individual liberty ... that this desire for status and recognition can easily be identified. It is something no less profoundly needed and passionately fought for by human beings – it is something akin to, but not itself, freedom ... it is more closely related to solidarity (158).[2]

Later, he suggests that goals such as equality and fraternity 'appear wholly, or in part, incompatible with the greatest degree of individual liberty' (161). Four decades later, the European Union chose to ignore this insight by one of the great liberal thinkers of the post-Second World War period when it committed itself to freedom and solidarity as principles of equal rank in its Charter of Fundamental Rights.

With his essay, Berlin contributed to a long tradition of concern in political thought about the proper separation of concepts and commitments. Berlin

---

1   Unless otherwise noted, further references to Berlin are to this text, and the same practice will be adopted with regard to John Stuart Mill's *On Liberty* later.
2   The passage continues, with further conceptual associations, to add another note of distinction from freedom: '...fraternity, mutual understanding, need for association on equal terms, all of which are sometimes – but misleadingly – called social freedom'. He contradicts himself, though, later (160 – see below).

indeed seems to have seen this lecture as an exercise in the liberal 'art of separation', as Michael Walzer (1984) would put it a quarter of a century later. 'Everything is what it is', Berlin claimed:

> liberty is liberty, not equality or fairness or justice or culture, or human happiness or a quiet conscience... It is a confusion of values to say that although my 'liberal', individual freedom may go by the board, some other kind of freedom – 'social' or 'economic' – is increased (125–126).[3]

Berlin cautiously avoids concluding his reasoning bluntly in favour of individual liberty, in terms of what he called 'negative liberty', understood as 'non-interference' or 'liberty from' (126–127). Instead, he emphasizes pluralism of value commitments (171). Nevertheless, his assessment of the relation between individual liberty and other goals is asymmetric, and as such characteristic of much of the liberal tradition of thought.[4] Among those other goals that are discussed as legitimate, but ultimately relegated to a secondary rank, is solidarity.

The objective of this chapter is to demonstrate that such a conceptual separation, and subsequent hierarchization, of freedom and solidarity is ill-founded in a two-fold way. First, the liberalism that proceeds in such a way –referred to hereafter as 'individualist' liberalism – does not achieve its purpose, namely to provide a general and unequivocal grounding for the safeguarding of individual liberty. In the unsuccessful pursuit of this end, though, second, it unnecessarily delegitimizes other political values and commitments, among which, significantly, is the commitment to solidarity. Importantly, individualist liberalism is unable to consider the possibility that commitment to some of these values may be necessary to safeguard liberty.

This chapter is organised in three sections. First, the argumentative strategy on which the priority of individual liberty is based will be reconstructed, to see how far a consistent and sufficient position is developed. This will be done, with all due brevity, by recourse to one key author and text from each of the two past centuries of liberal thought: John Stuart Mill's *On Liberty* and Isaiah

---

3 Some later critics of Berlin, such as Quentin Skinner and Philip Pettit, have tried to avoid references to the social and the economic by suggesting that different concepts of liberty exist, notably a third one beyond Berlin's distinction of two opposed concepts of liberty. Without necessarily disagreeing with those critics, this chapter suggests that a different conceptual strategy might prove more fruitful: rather than redefining liberty, conceptual efforts should concentrate on placing liberty within a comprehensive political philosophy that is articulate about the relations between the political and the social, instead of separating the former from the latter. For further reflections on the relation between the social and the political, see Karagiannis and Wagner, 2005, and Wagner, 2006.

4 See Freeden, 1996 for a reconstruction of political ideologies around key concepts.

Berlin's 'Two concepts of liberty'. Second, it will be shown that both of these authors are aware of alternative arguments that share the concern with liberty but reject the conceptual priority of individual liberty. Suspending the two philosophers' worries about 'illiberal conclusions' for a moment, I will aim to identify the core arguments of the alternatives, which for the sake of clarity may be referred to as varieties of 'non-individualist' liberalism. Without unduly forcing the argument, it will become recognizable that this core can be characterized by commitments to democracy and solidarity in addition to liberty. The third section is devoted to making the full contours of this alternative liberal tradition visible, and this will be done by reference – much more briefly – to one key author for each of the past two centuries, in this case Alexis de Tocqueville and Claude Lefort.

The priority of individual liberty

John Stuart Mill's treatise *On Liberty* – in fact co-authored with his wife, Harriet Taylor, whose name appears as a partial author in the dedication – is rightly recognized as a key statement of the liberal credo. It lends itself to the purposes of this chapter not least because of the precision of its definitions of concepts and problems. Mill offers the following definition of freedom in the sense in which he wants to discuss it: 'The only freedom that deserves the name is that of pursuing our own good in our own way, so long as we do not attempt to deprive others of theirs or impede their efforts to obtain it' (Mill, 1956 [1859], 16–17). Let us note in passing the use of the first person plural – an issue to which I shall return soon. The basic idea is very clear: true freedom does not need to be discussed with others, and should not be interfered with by others, except in the case that others are interfered with by the use of one's freedom. The meaning of freedom is unequivocal, and there is only one problem that derives from the commitment to it: the possibility that one person's freedom constrains another person's freedom.

This latter possibility requires the introduction of means to limit the use of freedom at the point at which it would interfere with others. This problem is accordingly the issue to which the entire treatise is devoted: 'The object of this essay is to assert one very simple principle, as entitled to govern absolutely the dealings of society with the individual in the way of compulsion and control' (13). The search for such a principle, in the view of the author, is successful: 'That principle is that the sole end for which mankind are warranted, individually or collectively, in interfering with the liberty of action of any of their number is self-protection' (13). Mill's treatise has been widely discussed ever since its publication, and its inconsistencies are well

17

known.[5] As plausibly as the question appears to be posed, there is just no way to generally legitimize constraining the freedom of a member of society by theoretical fiat alone. For present purposes, it is rather the structure of the argument that Mill uses for legitimizing constraint that is important.

Mill's reasoning apparently knows only two core elements, and the connection between them determines the argument. One is 'power ... rightfully to be exercised', and the other is conduct that may 'produce evil to someone else' (13). The latter provides for the only case in which power may be exercised over the individual. Implicitly, this entails that solidarity concerns are not legitimate reasons for any society to exercise power over any of its members. However, Mill cannot state his case without reference to something else that remains undiscussed. When he refers to 'self-protection', for instance, the self that is to be protected appears to be mankind, syntactically at least, not any individual's freedom. If this were indeed the meaning, Mill would need a concept of humanity and its relations to the individuals of which it is composed, a concept that, if it existed, would spell out how the 'self-protection' of humanity protects at the same time the liberty of the individuals. None of this, though, can be found in the treatise.

Similarly, Mill's notion of 'society' is intriguing, and this relates to the 'we' that he probably unreflectedly but revealingly uses. From a Millian perspective, the agent that interferes in a constraining manner when one individual violates the liberty of another clearly cannot be just a third freedom-seeking individual. To surely fulfil its task, the agent of the protection of individual liberty must in some way stand above the exercise of liberty. Contextually, nineteenth-century liberals mostly had no problems in identifying these agents in the existing states. However, here the argument comes full circle. Mill aims to determine the limits of 'our' (society's, the state's) interference with individual liberty, but he does not offer any consideration of the nature of this 'we' that would plausibly allow the conclusion that the collective agent would indeed be bound by such reasoning.

Almost exactly one hundred years later, Isaiah Berlin re-stated the question in similar terms when he defined 'negative liberty' as the answer to the question: 'What is the area within which the subject – a person or group of persons – is or should be left to do or be what he is able to do or be?' (Berlin, 1971, 121–122). Unlike Mill, to whom he refers as the key source for such a

---

5   The failure to state this principle becomes evident not least in Mill's use of examples, which often appear much less unequivocal, and much more open to historical change, than he thought. Among recent authors, Berlin (in the text used here, 128–130) and, more recently, Gray (1989) have extensively discussed Mill's failure to accomplish his objectives. Gray's reasoning extends to a general indictment of the theoretical programme of individualist liberalism.

concept of freedom, Berlin is not exclusively orientated towards the objective of enhancing individual liberty. In a note of caution towards the end of his lecture, he states explicitly that he does 'not wish to say that individual freedom is, even in the most liberal societies, the sole, or even the dominant, criterion of social action' (169). This note is needed, though, precisely because he had used formulations earlier that are reminiscent of Mill's way of reasoning: 'If I wish to preserve my liberty ... I must establish a society in which there must be some frontiers of freedom which nobody should be permitted to cross' (164).[6] Liberty is here described by means of a spatial metaphor: as a territory around which a fence is erected so that trespassing cannot occur.

Contextually, it is clear that Berlin's guarded defence of 'negative liberty' is informed by his historical experience of the widespread and radical suppression of liberties during the decades preceding his writing, an experience that Mill did not share in that form. Something else separates Berlin from Mill: the experience of collective mobilizations against the impact of the 'liberty principle' during the nineteenth century. Many of these could be seen as mobilizations for solidarity: both solidarity among the concerned (most importantly, workers' solidarity) and organized solidarity within the frame of a polity (the welfare state). One could say that views about what kinds of action could cause harm to others in a liberal market society changed considerably between 1858, when Mill wrote,[7] and 1958, when Isaiah Berlin's worries about spaces of freedom could not simply mirror those voiced by Mill, but had to take those concerns about solidarity explicitly into account. Surveying roughly those hundred years in his treatise on the rise and fall of market society, Karl Polanyi (1985 [1944]), for instance, talked in almost Millian terms, but contra Mill, about society's historical need for self-defence against a certain form of individual liberty. Intending to show that 'negative liberty' remains a central concern even after those experiences, Berlin, in turn, spends a considerable portion of his lecture rejecting a notion of 'positive liberty' and, as mentioned at the outset, aiming to demonstrate that other values, such as the ones related to the 'search for status', have little or nothing to do with liberty.

---

6 Reminiscent of Mill is also the neglect of the question how 'I', the individual thinking subject, could 'establish a society'. Despite his later critique of reason, this formulation betrays an overly rationalist approach to political theory in this essay.

7 Solidarity had become a key concept in political debate during the first half of the 19th century (see, for instance, Sewell, 1980), but by that time liberals could still pretend that the benefits of a free society would sooner or later accrue to all members of that society.

Continental deviance and the insufficiency of 'negative liberty'

The authors of both texts – though Berlin much more so than Mill – were aware of the fact that their cases were not as compelling as they might have wished, and that they could not fully ignore the existence of alternatives to their ways of conceptualizing the issues. Their modes of presenting these alternatives, accordingly, become significant for understanding the limits of the individualist liberal project.

Mill notes the existence of two particular strands of European liberalism, namely 'the last generation' and 'the Continental section', whose positions deviate in one important respect from what, by implication, he considered the British liberalism of his time. According to Mill, proponents of those strands held that 'too much importance had been attached to the limitation of the power itself' (Mill, 1956, 5) in liberalism, and that this concern had become much less pressing with the increasing diffusion of the idea of collective self-government (democracy). It is worth quoting Mill here in full:

> Men ceased to think it a necessity of nature that their governors should be an independent power opposed in interest to themselves. It appeared to them so much better that the various magistrates of the state should be their tenants or delegates, revocable at their pleasure. In that way alone, it seemed, could they have complete security that the powers of government would never be used to their disadvantage. (5)

This reasoning refers to a major politico-historical transformation – the advent of the idea of popular self-government – and translates it into politico-conceptual concerns. Conceptually, the watershed reads as follows: Individual liberties had to be fought for as long as political power came from elsewhere. As soon as political power is based in the people, this struggle is no longer necessary, or at least much less important.

This reasoning sounds broadly plausible, even to our ears. A major reason why Mill nevertheless rejects it is the experience of democracy itself:

> In political and philosophical theories as well as in persons, success discloses faults and infirmities which failure might have concealed from observation. The notion that the people have no need to limit their power over themselves might seem axiomatic, when popular government was a thing only dreamed about, or read of as having existed at some distant period of the past. (6)

With the rise, in particular, of democracy in the United States of America, however, those apparent axioms were shown not to hold water. Drawing heavily on Alexis de Tocqueville (see also Mill, 1994), Mill discussed the dangers of democratic rule and concluded: 'The limitation, therefore, of the power of government over individuals loses none of its importance when the holders of power are regularly accountable to the community' (6). He added that this was an insight by then well accepted, with the exception of 'the Continental section' of European liberalism.

Continental thinkers – such as Spinoza, Rousseau, Herder, Hegel, Fichte and Marx – also loom large in Berlin's discussions of erroneous approaches to liberty, occasionally accompanied by 'British Idealists' (Berlin, 1971, 148) and 'neo-Conservatives in English-speaking countries' (170). He discusses their conceptualizations at much more length than Mill, though, because he knows, a hundred years later, that their views will not simply wither away in the course of 'the progress of human affairs' (Mill, 1956, 4).

Mill, as we have seen, seemed to think that a convincing statement of the principle of liberty was the most important task that political theory had to accomplish. The political form of the society in which individual liberties were to flourish seemed to matter little to him.[8] Berlin went beyond this view: he recognized that human beings could legitimately hold other political values to be of similar importance, and on those grounds he committed himself to a pluralist understanding of the polity – within which he, though, would always emphasize 'negative liberty'. This is an understandable stand, but it, too, refrains from addressing in detail the larger political setting of liberty and plurality, as a comprehensive political philosophy would need to do.

Like Mill, Berlin was aware of the fact that the argument for collective self-determination could interfere with the argument for individual self-determination and limit the commitment to the latter. He, too, though, preferred not to tackle the question of democracy in its own right at all, but only in so far as commitments to it were seen either as commitments to freedom, or as risk factors for infringements on individual freedom. As shall be shown, the peculiar place of solidarity in his reasoning can only be understood by tracing his understanding of self-government in its relation to individual liberty.

Claiming that 'there is no necessary connection between individual liberty and democratic rule', Berlin (1971, 130) separates the former from the latter

---

8 Discussing Mill's position, Berlin underlines that the individualist liberal concept of freedom is compatible with autocracy and enlightened despotism, provided that the despot 'leaves his subjects a wide area of liberty' (129). He would not have gone as far as redefining the concept of democracy with a view to justifying such an autocracy, as current advocates of 'regulatory government' (Majone, 1996) or government legitimated by efficiency (Scharpf, 1999) do.

in two respects: logically and historically. 'The answer to the question "Who governs me?" is logically distinct from the question "How far does government interfere with me?"' (130). Furthermore, he suggests, in agreement with Mill, that there are substantive tensions that do not fail to materialize historically: 'The connection between democracy and individual liberty is a good deal more tenuous than it seemed to many advocates of both' (130–131). Moving from those general assertions to a diagnosis of his time, he concludes that these commitments are so different 'as to have led in the end to the great clash of ideologies that dominates our world' (131).[9] While one might consider Berlin's starting observations a useful reminder that 'co-originality' of the commitments to liberty and democracy cannot easily be claimed,[10] his latter move leads Berlin to erroneously equate a highly ideologized concept (and practice) of 'popular democracy' with the general concept of collective autonomy, and can only be understood in the context of the time. Any more thorough investigation of the latter is, as a consequence, so much postponed in the lecture that it hardly takes place.

The following four sections of Berlin's lecture are devoted to characterizing in more detail and with great nuance the positive concept of liberty, but they are dominated by the idea that the concept ultimately needs to be understood as a 'doctrine of liberation by reason' (144). While it is true that varieties of rationalism have been a problem in the history of political thought, and maybe they are to some extent still today,[11] the concentration on this topic leads Berlin to lose sight of the question of democracy almost completely.[12] Rather than criticizing (rightly) the alleged rational underpinnings of democracy, he might have dealt in more detail with the argument about the social underpinnings of political forms. To these, though, he turns only rather indirectly when

---

9 It is maybe not too surprising that Berlin saw communism as committed to positive freedom and to democracy; after all, many of the polities governed by Communist parties were called 'democratic republics'. In contrast, one wonders whether one should find it shocking or telling that Berlin refuses to associate Western polities with the commitment to democracy at all. Could he possibly have agreed with Cornelius Castoriadis (1999, 154), who referred to those polities as 'liberal oligarchies', and – in contrast to Castoriadis – be normatively satisfied with that diagnosis?

10 Even though his case may not be so far from the one made here, Habermas's argument about the 'co-originality' of democracy and the state of law is, at the very least, terminologically misleading, since as a historical argument it clearly does not hold. In theoretical terms, the reference to political modernity being built on a commitment to autonomy, and the latter being inevitably interpretable as both individual and collective, would state the argument much more clearly and convincingly.

11 Once common a priori assumptions about rationality that entailed some idea about 'general' (i.e., collective) validity and were, thus, of concern to Berlin may today have given way to the combination of individuality and rationality in economic and rational choice theory. These latter would need to be criticized by different means than those employed by Berlin.

12 For his concluding statement on the liberals' view of government and participation, see 165.

22

discussing the 'search for status' (section VI, 154–162) as a political commitment. In this section of the lecture, which our introductory remarks used as a starting point for relating freedom to solidarity, Berlin gets completely entangled in the web of meanings he had himself spun. Demonstrating the difficulties an advocate of negative liberty can have with solidarity, his reasoning can also be read against the grain to show how solidarity is connected liberty.

In line with the professed art of separation, Berlin first continues to evoke 'the danger of calling any improvement in his social situation favoured by a human being an increase of his liberty', and asks whether this will 'not render this term so vague and distended as to make it virtually useless' (159). Readers who have followed him up to this point are almost obliged to agree. Liberty 'in this sense' – a formula repeated many times in the lecture – is certainly something different from recognition, solidarity, social status, mutual understanding (Berlin uses a large number of terms to characterize this other social commitment). However, being somewhat at a loss in his reasoning, Berlin now acknowledges that an excessive practice of the art of conceptual separation may not be fruitful: 'Social and political terms are necessarily vague. The attempt to make the vocabulary of politics too precise may render it useless' (158). This is in preparation for an admission:

> And yet we cannot simply dismiss this case [calling an improvement in social situation an increase in liberty] as a mere confusion of the notion of freedom with that of status, or solidarity, or fraternity, or equality, or some combination of these... We may refuse this goal the title of liberty; yet it would be a shallow view that assumed that analogies between individuals and groups, or organic metaphors, are mere fallacies ... or simple semantic confusion. (159)

In this world of necessarily vague concepts, Berlin makes use of terms with sociological meanings, such as 'group','organic metaphor', 'status' and 'recognition'. The attempt at identifying what those analogies and metaphors truly are does not lead to any conclusion within this terminology, but requires him to make a significant (re-)connection to a question of political philosophy: namely, 'Who is to govern us?' Since the answers to this question 'are logically, and at times also politically and socially, independent of what extent of "negative" liberty I demand for my own or my group's activities' (160), one needs those other concepts to provide answers. At first sight, Berlin here seems only to be re-stating that negative liberty is something different from anything else discussed. However, at the same time he asserts that these other commitments – 'status, or solidarity, or fraternity, or equality, or some

23

combination of these' – are highly significant and that they cannot be addressed from within a political theory of individualist (negative) liberalism.

At this point, Berlin significantly suggests that whenever such an answer can be seen as

> 'my own', as something which belongs to me, or to whom I belong, I can, by using words which convey fraternity or solidarity, as well as some part of the connotation of the 'positive' sense of the word freedom ... describe it as a hybrid form of freedom. (160)

In other words, the question 'Who governs us?' cannot be answered by exclusive resort to negative liberty, because it is an 'independent' question. At the same time, it tends to be answered by resorting to 'social' bonds between human beings, or to solidarity, broadly understood. If such social bonds can be referred to as 'one's own' and are evoked to answer the question 'Who governs us?', then we have a mode of self-government that can be described as a form of freedom.

We have done nothing here but reworded Berlin's statement. In the light of his early declaration to talk about everything as that which it is, and 'liberty is liberty', this must be considered as a total failure of his intentions. For the purposes of our argument, in contrast, we see him arriving at an important insight: solidarity is, or at least can be, a form of freedom, and it can be so via the idea of collective autonomy, or democracy.[13]

Alternative liberal views

Textually, this observation is incontrovertible. However, it is equally certain that the link between freedom and solidarity was not the author's main intention in this lecture; one might even doubt whether he would have considered establishing such a link.[14] To further understand the nature of the linkage, he and other liberals who emphasize individual liberty are therefore not useful sources. What we said at the outset remains valid: individualist liberals relegate solidarity to a secondary rank, and it is only in the writings of the most sophisticated of them that one finds the acknowledgement of greater complexity.

Both Mill and Berlin refer, explicitly or implicitly, to other authors from the liberal tradition for support. Prominent among these figures are Benjamin

---

13 To be clear: this chapter thus deals with solidarity only in the form in which it exists under conditions of political modernity – that is, in circumstances in which a commitment to autonomy is significant for human beings.

14 See his response to critics in the introduction to *Four Essays on Liberty* (Berlin, 1971).

Constant and Alexis de Tocqueville. The former's *De la liberté des modernes comparée avec la liberté des anciens* (Constant, 1988 [1797]) may have a justified place in this tradition, as he draws a distinction that corresponds rather well with the one Berlin makes between negative and positive liberty, and he emphasizes individual liberty in a way that is very close to Mill. The case of Tocqueville, though, is different. Rather than fitting within this tradition, his *De la Démocratie en Amérique* (1990 [1835/1840]), flanked by the later *L'Ancien régime et la Révolution* (1952–1953 [1856]), provides a possible starting point for reconstructing an alternative, rather neglected, liberal tradition.

Tocqueville's key concern in both these volumes was the historical transformation in the nature of the polity that was brought about by the American Revolution and the founding of the United States, on the one hand, and the overthrowing of the *ancien régime* in the course of the French Revolution, on the other. Even though the latter did not bring democracy about, it, too, was such a profound change that it established a society basically committed to egalitarianism, and thus made democracy the inevitable reference point for an entirely 'new political science' that de Tocqueville saw as urgently needed.

Tocqueville wrote at length about individualism, and certainly was concerned about individual freedom, which was threatened in particular by the possible 'tyranny of the majority' under conditions of democracy. This was demonstrated in the United States in the form of a societal tendency towards conformism, rather than in the form of political oppression (two issues of whose equal importance Mill was also very well aware). Nevertheless, it was not individual liberty that provided the starting point of his reasoning, but democracy as a novel 'form of political society'. Furthermore, he believed that this form of political society instituted the individual (Lefort, 1986a, 208), rather than the other way around, as social contract theory (and individualist liberalism) would have it.

Without space for a deeper analysis, Tocqueville will here be considered briefly in the light of the preceding interpretation of individualist liberalism, focusing on four observations of basic agreement and difference. The two points of agreement are important, but they are easily stated. First, Tocqueville agreed with Mill that the question of individual liberty did not find an automatic and self-evident answer after the advent of democracy; rather, in his view, it needed to be posed with urgency and in a new way. Second, he valued personal liberty as highly as Berlin, and would not want to have seen the commitment towards it replaced with concern for other values.

However, Tocqueville did not conclude from these two assumptions that

25

political theory should start out by posing the question of individual liberty. Rather, he saw democracy as a political form in which the individual is posited as 'unit citizen' – as Stein Rokkan would later say – and thus asked for a 'new political science' to analyse the fate of freedom under these conditions. For Tocqueville, this novel form of political society created both the individuals and their spaces of freedom, and the infringements on those freedoms brought about by general opinion or by majority legislation. Where Mill – and later also Berlin – saw 'society' dualistically, as either a threat to liberty or as the hypothetical agent that could protect the liberty of the individuals (and in each case as exogenous to the individuals and their strivings), Tocqueville saw the political form of society as constitutive of individuals, and thus 'sociologizes' – as we might want to say, without falling into sociological determinism – the analysis of political life. From this angle, he could not consider a defence of individual liberty a plausible or even compelling starting point for political analysis, as it would have led to rather empty normative claims dissociated from the mode of social life.

After having embarked on his strategy of analysis, rather a novel question emerges, and this leads to my fourth and final observation, one that is crucial to the link between freedom and solidarity. The question is: what kind of 'social' life makes democracy a sustainable political form and, in particular, maintains and creates conditions for individual liberty under conditions of democracy? To answer this question, Tocqueville investigated the specific relations of 'association' within American and French society to determine whether they enhanced or constrained liberty. The concept of associative relations comprises everything – and more – that Berlin characterized as status, recognition, mutual understanding and solidarity. Berlin discusses these as being distinct from liberty – as we have seen, rather incoherently. Tocqueville opens up another perspective by seeing them as underlying such freedom-endangering or freedom-enlarging features of democratic society as general opinion and majority will.

As Berlin's example shows, associative relations are not easily introduced into any formal reasoning of political theory. Most versions of individualist liberalism prefer to make them invisible by means of a veil of ignorance, with a view to arriving at generalizable propositions about the political. In other words, most political theorizing prefers to ignore 'the social' by introducing a sharp divide between things political and things social, and then practising a well-intended but ill-conceived 'art of separation'. However, as Tocqueville showed in the case of American democracy, social relations are 'political' in the double sense of being constitutive of political forms (as prior conditions for the forming of political society), and being, in principle, alterable by political intervention. Self-government, given that it cannot rely on external sources for its legitimacy, includes the search for a common understanding of the way of living together. Rather than limiting government from the beginning in the face of possible abuse, as individualist liberals try to argue, the challenge of democracy, as a situation in which human beings give themselves their own law, is to address all issues of the life in common in a comprehensive way.

How, though, does Tocqueville's notion of associative life relate to the concept of solidarity? Applying a Tocquevillean perspective to the individualist liberals' concern for liberty provides an answer to this question: solidarity is a specific form of associative relation, and it is the one that permits the combination of personal liberty and democracy – individual self-determination and collective self-determination.

A comparison between two alternative modes of thinking about the political under conditions of democracy will make the significance of this statement clear. On the one hand, individualist rationalist thinkers, many of whom embrace individualist liberalism, arrive at decisions about the common by an aggregation of preferences. They have no view of social relations between individuals, except those revealed by statistics. There is no safeguard at all against the tyranny of the majority in this conception, and thus individual liberty is at great risk.[15] On the other hand, collectivist interpretativist thinkers, now mostly known as communitarians, stipulate that freedom is exercised within interpretative frameworks, and that it is therefore best secured by establishing polities around common frameworks. Such frameworks can be thought of as structures of social relations that are internally congruent and demarcated from the outside. As a cultural linguistic theory of the polity, such a view was most forcefully expressed in the liberal nationalism of the 19th century. Its social ontology contains valid assumptions, but as a political philosophy it is subject to the liberal criticism voiced by, among others, Isaiah Berlin.

The idea of opening up the question of associative relations to empirical observation allows the overcoming of the dichotomy of individualist aggregation or interpretative commonality. It draws on 18th-century ways of thinking about the social bond. Then, the two dominant ways of thinking about associative relations focused on communication and commerce

---

15 The suggestion that a polity should be composed of individuals with similar preferences only appears to offer a way out. Even if one assumed in a contractarian way that a polity is an association for mutual benefit, political communities differ from all kinds of 'clubs' in automatically accepting the children of their members as new members. This means that they have no control over the preferences of their members. My thanks to Bob Goodin for provoking this reflection.

respectively; in each version, one can find authors who hold that communication or commerce support domestic peace and wellbeing in liberty, and those who see them as destructive. In Mill's words, this was the thought of 'the last generation' before the advent of democracy, and the assumptions about the effects of association were rather speculative. The experience of democracy transforms the question by making the consequences of association, and its absence, in various modes observable, at least in principle.

The conceptual issue has also been sharpened. If political modernity is expressed in the double commitment to individual and to collective self-determination, to personal liberty and democracy, then the analysis of the associative relations between the members of a polity would search to identify the ways in which the former can be combined with the latter, beyond assumptions about aggregation or prior commonality. Human beings in democracy inevitably have the power 'de se declarer leur humanité dans leur existence d'individus, et leur humanité dans leur mode de co-existence, leur manière d'être ensemble dans la cité' (Lefort, 1986b, 54). 'Relations of solidarity' would mean relations between the members of a polity who recognize others as members of the same, self-governed polity, and as free, singular human beings. The relations between individual liberty, democracy and 'status and recognition', that is, solidarity, may be 'tenuous', as Berlin held. They are tenuous precisely because a democracy of free citizens is a fragile entity, and it is only if the questions of freedom and of solidarity are addressed that it can be sustained.[16]

Two concepts of liberalism

There might be one, two, three or even 'more than two hundred senses' (Berlin, 1971, 121) of the term liberty. This debate will go on, but whether it will have significant results seems doubtful. In contrast, it seems necessary to more clearly delineate two basic understandings of liberalism.

The past two centuries of theorizing about political modernity have shown a strong tendency towards two distinct modes of thinking. On the one hand, individualist liberalism persistently – and across historical experiences of the suppression of liberty – argues for the liberty of the individual, but does so by renouncing the elaboration of any comprehensive political theory that addresses the nature of the modern polity. On the other hand, approaches that situate the 'liberty of the moderns' in the socio-political contexts of its

16 For a related argument about the necessary link between democracy, trust and solidarity, unfortunately confined to the political form of the nation state, see Offe, 1998.

emergence, reaching from the religious wars to the democratic revolutions and emerging class struggle, recognize the need for a comprehensive political philosophy, including a 'particular social and economic theory' (an insight shared but not followed up by Berlin, from whom this quote stems: 1971, 123), to sustain any concept of liberty, and thus start their reasoning from an understanding of the society and polity in which human beings can be free, rather than from those individuals themselves.[17]

Some approaches within this latter strand have tended to treat the question of individual liberty too lightly, and that is why the concern of authors such as Berlin arose. By now, however, we should be able to recognize two problematic asymmetries in the politico-intellectual constellation that has resulted. First, not least as a conclusion drawn from historical experiences, the worry about 'illiberal conclusions' is, in theory, so pronounced that any alternative to such liberalism appears unsustainable from the start, and this despite the fact that the insufficiencies of individualist liberalism are widely recognized.[18] Second, more specifically, the emphasis on individual liberty as the alleged primary commitment of political modernity has entailed the neglect of solidarity and democracy, even though these commitments cannot fail to be evoked in any comprehensive political philosophy of the modern polity, as the analysis of Mill and Berlin has shown. As one step towards finding a remedy to these asymmetries, the political tradition of non-individualist liberalism needs to be given proper status in the history of European political thought.[19] It is to this end that the preceding reasoning

---

17 In the introduction to *Four Essays on Liberty*, Berlin acknowledges the need to analyse the 'conditions for liberty', but insists that it would be erroneous to identify 'freedom with its conditions' (1971, lviii). This text also acknowledges 'the ideal of social solidarity', but again as a value distinct from freedom.

18 The insert 'in theory' is meant to suggest that 'in practice', things might be different. On the one hand, the dogmatic insistence on individual liberty as a basic principle in the West encourages the emergence of radical alternatives, such as collectivist fundamentalisms that have illiberal leanings. On the other hand, the belief that Western political modernity already embodies the principle of liberty makes violations of liberties seem justified, such as in the current 'war on terrorism' in the United States of America and the United Kingdom.

19 'Proper status' would be signalled not least by a proper denomination, not just a negative term like 'non-individualism'. As such a term does not exist, it may be worth underlining that terms such as 'social liberalism' or 'national liberalism' refer to known historical traditions that may at times overlap with the one in mind here, but not in terms of key characteristics. 'Republicanism' may be a better candidate, not least because of a recent revival in interest in its intellectual history and political philosophy. Before this term can be adopted, though, the idea (made prominent by Quentin Skinner) that republicanism subsided after the democratic revolutions and gave way to (individualist) liberalism needs to be rethought and revised, since the concern addressed by non-individualist liberalism was important during the period during which republicanism allegedly did not exist. (For sceptical reflections on the coherence of revived republican political theory, see Goodin, 2003.)

aimed to contribute, and the brief observations on Tocqueville and Lefort were meant to serve as illustrations of the existence of such a tradition.

Individualist liberalism clings to a tradition of thinking that aimed to defend frontiers beyond which authorities should not interfere with the lives of human beings. It is based on a highly significant normative commitment, and even though the concern emerged in periods of unjustified external rule, there is no reason to assume that its relevance will ever decrease. Confusion in political theory, however, was created when such liberalism started – justifiably – to address the dangers to individual liberty that could emanate from forms of collective self-government. From this moment onwards, the defence of individual liberty became a conceptual battle against anything in society, anything 'social', from which political commitments could emerge. This move has, at best, limited the capacity of political theory to address important issues of the life in common. At worst, it has contributed to weakening ways of being together that rely on solidarity.

In contrast, what I have called non-individualist liberalism takes collective self-government as its starting point. Under conditions of political modernity, collective self-determination is the only source of legitimacy, with all the risks that this may entail. There may be good reasons to conclude from historical experience that any democracy should commit itself to extended spaces of individual liberty, as Berlin and other individualist liberals argue. Unlike other forms of non-individualist political thought, non-individualist liberalism takes this commitment to be of a specific kind, and not subsumable under any prior notion of reason or substantive collective commitment. However, according to this type of liberalism, there are equally important reasons, no less strongly suggested by historical experience, to make solidarity with others a basic commitment of the polity as well.

Following Mill and Berlin, many contemporary political theorists hold that any such equivalence of solidarity and liberty has potentially dangerous political implications. They see the former as a substantive commitment that no pluralist polity can embrace without endangering freedom. Here, in contrast, some continuity within the 'continental section' of European liberalism was defended, in which political philosophy always aimed to address questions of the life in common in a comprehensive way, including its 'social' features. The constitution of a polity, in this view, should not be limited to a bill of rights plus an institutional architecture, a conception many individualist liberals would find satisfactory. It should commit the polity to freedom and solidarity at the same time – as does the EU Charter of Fundamental Rights, rightly defying the wisdom of much of contemporary political theory.

References

Berlin, I. (1971), 'Two concepts of liberty' in *Four Essays on Liberty*, Oxford, Oxford University Press.

Castoriadis, C. (1999), 'Quelle démocratie?' in *Figures du pensable: Les carrefours du labyrinthe VI*, Paris, Seuil.

Constant, B. (1988 [1797]), 'The liberty of the ancients compared with that of the moderns' in *Political Writings*, Cambridge, Cambridge University Press.

Freeden, M. (1996), *Ideology and Political Theory: A Conceptual Approach*, Oxford, Clarendon.

Goodin, R. A. (2003), 'Folie républicaine', *Annual Review of Political Science*, **6**.

Gray, J. (1989), *Liberalism: Essays in Political Philosophy*, London, Routledge.

Habermas, J. (1999), 'Über den internen Zusammenhang von Rechtsstaat und Demokratie' in *Die Einbeziehung des Anderen*, Frankfurt, M. Suhrkamp.

Karagiannis, N. and Wagner, P. (2005), 'Towards a theory of synagonism', *Journal of Political Philosophy*, **13**.

Lefort, C. (1986a), 'Réversibilité: liberté politique et liberté de l'individu' in *Essais sur le politique xixe–xxe siècles*, Paris, Seuil.

Lefort, C. (1986b), 'Les droits de l'homme et l'État-providence' in *Essais sur le politique xixe–xxe siècles*, Paris, Seuil.

Lefort, C. (1986c), 'De l'égalité à la liberté' in *Essais sur le politique xixe–xxe siècles*, Paris, Seuil.

Lefort, C. (1992), 'Tocqueville: démocratie et art d'écrire' in *Écrire à l'épreuve du politique*, Paris, Calmann-Lévy.

Majone, G. (1996), *Regulating Europe*, London, Routledge.

Mill, J. S. (1956 [1859]), *On Liberty*, Indianapolis, Bobbs-Merrill.

Mill, J. S. (1994 [1840]), *Essais sur Tocqueville et la société américaine*, Paris, Vrin.

Offe, C. (1998), 'Demokratie und Wohlfahrtsstaat: Eine europäische Regimeform unter dem Streß der europäischen Integration' in W. Streeck (ed.), *Internationale Wirtschaft, nationale Demokratie*, Frankfurt, M. Campus, 99–136.

Polanyi, K. (1985 [1944]), *The Great Transformation*, Boston, Beacon.

Scharpf, F. W. (1999), *Governing in Europe: Effective and Democratic?*, Oxford, Oxford University Press.

Sewell, W. B. (1980), *Work and Revolution in Nineteenth-century France: The Language of Labour from the Old Regime to 1848*, Cambridge, Cambridge University Press.

Tocqueville, A. de (1990 [1835/1840]), *De la démocratie en Amérique*, Paris, Vrin.

Tocqueville, A. de (1952–1953 [1856]), *L'Ancien régime et la Révolution*, Paris, Gallimard.

Wagner, P. (2006), 'Social theory and political philosophy' in G. Delanty (ed.), *Handbook of Contemporary European Social Theory*, London, Routledge.

Walzer, M. (1984), 'Liberalism and the art of separation', *Political Theory*, **12**, 315–30.

2 Goli Otok:
The Formation of the New Man

Senadin Musabegović

In this chapter, I ask the following questions: to what extent can solidarity be constructed by repressive methods, and in which ways does solidarity legitimate torture? The broad framework in which these questions can be situated is the exploration of the inclusion or exclusion of community members, through mechanisms of organized violence, in the former-Yugoslav ideological projects of Communism and nationalism. The specific case that I will be looking at is Goli Otok, a Yugoslav prison camp.

There are two different modes of exclusion in the historical memory of our inherited cultural models that are connected to the idea of solidarity. One, as Bauman (2000) points out, is based on the cannibalistic swallowing of the enemy, i.e. their internalization, or the annihilation of their difference within one's own cultural determination. The other model is based on the 'regurgitation' of the consumed enemy, i.e. their expulsion and eradication. In the former case, it is a matter of 'digesting' the enemy or foreigner so that s/he melts within the boundaries of one's own cultural or ideological identity; in the latter case it is a matter of regurgitating the digested body of the enemy and spitting him or her out onto the other side of the border enclosing 'our' identity. To reformulate my questions along these lines: in which way, while creating awareness of a universal belonging to the proletarian struggle, was the international Communist project – and, more specifically, the torture techniques employed in Goli Otok – marked by the processes of internalization, inclusion or devouring?

Through punitive rituals, the Communist project strove to correct and rectify the prisoners' 'perverted' thoughts. The thinking was that the prisoners had been manipulated or seduced, and the goal was to internalize them, re-educate them and revive their awareness. By contrast, the nationalist project strove to cleanse the 'biological waste' – intruders, foreigners – so as to cleanse itself and be revitalised and purified. Although I have separated them into two different processes of exclusion and inclusion, nationalism and Communism both contain elements of internalization and elements of expulsion. We can, therefore, say that the first form of Communist organized violence, though it strives to classify each individual being punished or tortured within its law of universal revolution, contains elements of expulsion and regurgitation. Similarly, every national project that strives to mummify itself within its own national boundaries contains conscious or unconscious elements of interiorizing foreigners, those on the other side of its boundaries. The specificity of the totalitarian project, however, lies in an ambiguity: on the one hand, it is created as a messianic dream of unification, where all conflicts and differences are to be united and bridged by collective will; on the other hand, when it comes to power, the totalitarian system creates atomizing and isolation within its collectivism, where the only legitimate solidarity is that with the Party, and where everyone becomes the potential enemy of everyone else.[1]

Internalization of conflict and internalization of punitive violence

The political prisoners who were interned at Goli Otok supported the Informbiro Resolution of 1948. This means that they agreed with Stalin's criticism of the Yugoslav state authorities, so their imprisonment was a consequence of the historical split between the Soviet Union Communist Party and the Yugoslav Communist Party. It is important to point out that their acceptance of Stalin's decisions did not arise out of a premeditated political programme, or a conflict within the Yugoslav Communist Party. Before the Resolution there had been no official conflict with the Soviet government; on the contrary, it was believed that the construction of Communism would be realized through international cooperation between the Yugoslav Communist Party and the Soviet Communist Party.

Yes these fellow Party members working towards the construction of Communism became political enemies. Overnight, they became traitors whose attitudes were to be revised, corrected, brought back onto the right track. They were not traitors according to the classical Marxist definition of 'class enemy'; they were members of the Communist Party, and shared its ideas about the construction of a new society, the new man and a new social justice. It was just that some chose loyalty to another state, represented by Stalin, while others chose to rely on 'their own resources', represented by Tito.

---

1 Let me point out that this refers to Bolshevik totalitarianism, not Yugoslav totalitarianism. However, Yugoslav totalitarianism encompassed the potential for this thought process.

The motives for these choices remain obscure, as they were never based on any fixed cultural, racial or fractional criteria, but were made through individual declarations of political loyalty. This set the scene for arbitrary denunciations, where false attestations were used to charge many Yugoslav citizens with conspiring to cooperate with Stalin, although sufficient evidence of such activities was lacking. The consequent obligation to declare loyalty points at some of the main paradoxes of revolutionary Marxist ideology. Marxism insists on creating a revolutionary system that will lead to a new society and a new consciousness through a single idea. Here, with a political decision, the class subject determines himself in the logic of history and time and also overcomes his cultural and biological determinism.

In this context, organised violence was used to alter the opinions of comrades who had made a 'mistaken' political choice. It was to have the educational function of raising awareness, of pointing out mistakes and fallacies. Its function was not to exclude certain Party members, but to create a new consciousness of their role in the construction of the Yugoslav Communist system through mechanisms of educational torture. By punishing them, tacitly and invisibly, the Party also punished itself. Through their re-investigation it was meant to revise its own previous views, and to correct them. It was supposed to fundamentally revise its own fallacy, its own delusion.

Consequently, in terms of totalitarian ideology, prison was not only a place where people's actions were monitored, prisoners penetrated, and control perfected to a utopian degree. For Yugoslav Communists – before they came to power in the former Yugoslavia – the experience of prison also meant the possibility of organization and education. Ugo Vlaisavljević's book *Lepoglava and the University* (2003) shows the parallel between the experience of imprisonment and the idea of education in capitalist Yugoslavia. Indeed, many former Communists were educated in Lepoglava, the famous prison of the Yugoslav monarchy where Tito, among other Communists and revolutionaries, was interned. Thus, the experience of prison was a preparation for revolutionary activities; it served the purpose of organization. It was in prisons that the plan for seizing power, realized during the German occupation of 1941–1945, was prepared. Against this background, the prison logic at Goli Otok was intended to be the opposite of that at Lepoglava, where solidarity between prisoners had been maintained despite persecution. All solidarity between prisoners at Goli Otok was to be eradicated so that prisoners would be forced to identify solely with the Yugoslav Communist Party, and not with their fellow prisoners, who were being tortured and persecuted.

Utopia

The prisoners did not have legal trials; they were exiled to Goli Otok.[2] Its name implies isolation, a barren place where convicts were reduced to a bare existence, as described by Giorgio Agamben (1995). Vlaisavljević (2003) speaks of Goli Otok as a utopia, and draws a parallel between the utopian pre-mythological island that preceded civilization, and the Communist dream to embody a utopian reality on Earth. The word 'utopia' means a non-place, an absence in time and space, and Goli Otok was a non-place where non-people – monsters and beasts, as this author describes it – were sent.

Reinhard Koselleck (2002) has noted that, in modernity, there is a rift between historical experience and the utopian perspective. The starting point is the observation that every religious mythological image of the world includes in its prophesizing vision the relationship between apocalypse and heaven. Religious paradigm requires, in order for this world to be externalized in its divine essence, the experience of the apocalypse: disintegration must occur in order to reinvent divine unity and harmony. Taking the place of the relationship between apocalypse and heaven in the modern age is the relationship between crisis and progress (utopia). This relationship is not based on a static prophetic determination, as with the relationship between apocalypse and heaven, but on an 'open horizon of expectations' in which there is a rift between historical experience and the expected utopian perspective of the future. Taking our cue from this analysis, we could argue that the experience of displacement (such as exile to an island) is a step towards utopian reality. Thus, if crisis is the link to utopia, then that crisis must be maintained in order to maintain control over the utopia. In the same line of thought, imprisonment can be conceptualized as enabling the utopian vision as an 'expected perspective' to be maintained. The experience of prison strives to capture the utopian dream before it evaporates in order to conserve its expectations within prison cells. Thus, Goli Otok was, first of all, constructed as an expression of the totalitarian utopian tendency to control the human body. It was the manifestation of the totalitarian utopian dream of absolute control over society.

We can outline three relationships between Goli Otok and utopia. The first is connected to the idea of the past: Goli Otok was a non-place from a time before civilization, so it belonged to the archaic form of exile, as pointed out by Vlaisavljević:

---

2 Literally, 'desert island'.

> As in the biblical myth of exile from Eden turned into a caricature where the enlightened represent theological dogma, those who have committed the gravest sins have fallen to the level of animals; they have returned to nature. Goli Otok is Eden, a paradise island as envisioned by Communists for those who have the wrong view of a heavenly society. (2003, 76)

This author's interpretation of utopia is connected to a mythical cyclic time, in which temporal structure is marked by the idea of returning to the pre-mythical centre, where the paradise oasis coincides with a descent into animalistic, pre-civilization forms of life.

The second relationship between Goli Otok and utopia is connected to the future, and the idea that there is a link between crisis and progress. The current crisis is a type of tempering, a step towards the utopia that will be made manifest in the future. This relationship is based on a more modern, linear concept of time, in which society progresses and moves towards utopia through a series of conflicts. Finally, the third relationship is connected to the present, because Goli Otok is a reflection of totalitarian aspirations to control the human body by eliminating the division between private and public, destroying all privacy. Here time is suspended, so nothing can be expected: utopia is reduced to the here and now, because within it control is absolute.

It should be pointed out that all three concepts are founded on the impossibility of their realization. It is impossible to 'return' the exiled prisoners to a pre-mythic time; it is impossible to reach utopia via crisis; it is impossible to completely control the human body and society in the here and now. For the very reason of its own impossibility, the utopian vision cannot be realised through war, or imprisonment connected to war. That is why Vlaisavljević notices the parallel between the logic of war (where the enemy must be radically negated on both the symbolic and the corporal level) and the logic of Goli Otok (where people became non-beings, objects, beasts). For Vlaisavljević, the manner of punishment at Goli Otok was based on a concept of the enemy created and resolved in stories about the Second World War. In such stories, enemies were represented without physiognomy or faces. Accordingly, every act of the prisoners was proof that they had nothing human in them.

Vlaisavljević's remark about the connection between the violence of war during the People's Liberation Struggle and the police violence when it came to the internment of Informbiro sympathisers is challenging. He notes that the treatment of the enemy as beasts, monsters and non-humans was continued at Goli Otok. For him, Goli Otok was a pre-modern form of exclusion, a hole in the modernization system where non-people disappeared.

Goli Otok 'was not an institution, nor could it be a punitive institution in the real sense of the word' (2003, 74).

However, it should be pointed out that this negated man, who had been reduced to a non-being and was supposed to have lost all the social norms that guarantee moral dignity, was at the same time supposed to become a new man through torture: he was supposed to be modernized. The methods of punishment were also meant to re-educate and enlighten the prisoners so that they may become new people. In that way, the archaic form of exile to a desert island where the values of civilization have not yet been developed becomes also a method of civilizing, of education. Exclusion was used to wipe people clean and to inscribe them with new values of civilization. Thus, the process of education went hand-in-hand with the process of evolution. However, I believe that despite the pre-modern treatment of prisoners as animals, Goli Otok was also a modern, efficient mechanism for the bureaucratic supervision of traitors, counter-revolutionaries and enemies. Borislav Kosier, author of the novel *Bezbožnici (The Godless)* (1991), was interned at Goli Otok. He described it as 'a place designated by the prison term of "socially useful" labour' (10), and has pointed out that the strategy of the internment camp was re-education and a final reversal of the prisoners' attitudes. The methods of education, as outrageous as their primitive violence was, and their grotesque theatrical set design belonged to the arsenal of modern brainwashing techniques. At Goli Otok, no prisoners had been officially sentenced to death, as in concentration camps and the Gulag, but it was necessary to reduce fellow Communists to mechanical biological functions. They had to be exiled to pre-civilization so that, through organized violence, the values of Communism could be re-inscribed into them – the same values that they had fought for.[3] Yet the values of Communism are implicit in the ritual tortures of this 'education'.

---

3   As stated in *Bezbožnici*, Informbiro supporters were bad Communists as far as public policy was concerned. They were seen as 'malingerers in their essence', so the Informbiro Resolution was an opportune moment for expressing their treacherous predetermination. There were methods to re-educate malingerers with a view to allowing them to participate in everyday life. None of the prisoners could expect a career within the Yugoslav Communist Party, but they were meant to be incorporated into the system once they left prison, at least as second-rate citizens. 'This course, then, did not lead to re-education through dialectic re-examinations of the historical conflict between YCP and VKP, but straight to the IMPLOSION OF A MAN INTO HIMSELF, and the price of that process was: BEING FREED and the possibility of a quiet, unnoticed life as a second-rate citizen... which the great majority of Goli Otok inmates accepted. What else could they do?' (Kosier, 1991, 10).

War: the myth of creating a new man

In my doctoral thesis (Musabegović, 2004), I pointed out that certain ideological values of the Yugoslav Communist Party were created through the symbolic presentation of war – that is, the 'People's Liberation Struggle'. Constant remembrance of war creates an unconscious projection that the state political unity was created thanks to the war. In that sense, the connection between internment camps and the military strategy of enemy elimination is logical. By contrast, Goli Otok was not a process of spontaneous maturation that created a consciousness of solidarity through a division into 'us' and 'them': rather the opposite. The prisoners who had built the war morality, and who were partisans of the Communist idea, were imprisoned by their own project. They were put in prison by former comrades, and there were instances of prisoners being recognized by guards with whom they had once shared all the perils of war. In some cases they might have saved each others' lives. Now those same comrades were deciding the fate of their fellow fighters.

What are the precise connections between war and internment, and the role of internment in the formation of Communist affiliation? Torture is akin to military control, but instead of the enemy being on the other side of a border or physically opposed to the subject, the enemy is within oneself –in the very heart of the partisans of the Communist idea. The values of the new man, the new collective, the new workers' proletarian solidarity are not built through spontaneous collective will forged through war. On the contrary, an oppressive system based on military strategies that penetrate the bodies of the prisoners with methods of everyday surveillance, military drills and discipline strives to create a new morality, a new consciousness of the collective, a new consciousness of solidarity, by demanding that the enemy be sought among the prisoners. The prisoners begin condemning one another as enemies, and must be merciless towards those with whom they share the experience of internment.

In *Democracy and Totalitarianism*, Raymond Aron (1997) mentions three forms of terror in the history of the Bolshevik Party: one was conducted as a result of the struggle between opposing political interpretations of Marxism, i.e. the conflict between the Mensheviks and the Bolsheviks; the second was a retribution against the kulaks, or landowners; and the third was the Moscow trials, in which many members of Communist parties were proclaimed publicly guilty by participating in the 'fabrication of their own case'. They admitted to their fictitious guilt and legitimated their own elimination.

The latter phase coincided with a process of modernization and bureaucratization, when revolutionary passion was brought under control and the idea of permanent revolution abandoned. In such a period, terror is used to eliminate all potential enemies, and to create a stable state apparatus whose purpose is not to radically change the social order, but to preserve the existing order that gradually takes on more and more elements of counter-revolutionary government. There is a certain parallel between Goli Otok and Stalin's purges, although it cannot be said that they are identical. People were not condemned to death at Goli Otok, and the political situation was not identical, because Stalin's purges were based on a danger that he perceived in every segment in society, while UDBA's[4] internments were based on a real danger – a Soviet invasion of Yugoslavia – that Tito courageously defied. The smallest armed upsurge by Stalin's sympathisers in Yugoslavia would have warranted his intervention. One similarity, however, was the modus operandi of the Yugoslav secret police, which was borrowed from the Soviet Union. Another was the abandonment of the idea of revolutionary violence as a trigger for the creation of a new consciousness in favour of a principle of control that strives to stabilize the status quo. The intention of Goli Otok was to preserve the peace, stability and sovereignty of a country, and not to start a revolutionary movement.

Rituals of violence in prison

Regarding the creation of an invisible collectivist party body (Lefort, 2000) that is able to recognize enemies within itself and to reconcile the condemned with that party, it can be useful to note some of the analyses of knowledge and power offered by Michael Foucault (1977). Foucault analysed discursive practice, the technology of telling the truth about oneself. In his analysis of power, he did not rely on repressive power that negates or blocks. In his view, power incites: it is provocative, it produces. In the same way, the strategy of a confessional discourse is not based on a reprimanding logic meant to negate and block the subject, or, so to speak, castrate him internally. For him, power is dispersed: it does not originate in a single centre, authority or institution. For example, the confession ritual is not only a matter of an individual submitting to control (represented by the authoritative power of the church). Foucault did away with the distinction between the external and the internal, so that power passes through the subject who confesses in a certain way: through the free will of his own confession, the subject constitutes and controls himself. Foucault may be criticized for the radical changes in his thinking, but what his acute analysis shows is that through certain punitive practices and

4   The State Security Directorate.

sexual control arising from a multitude of historical relations, power is not only a repressive mechanism negating human nature, or blocking freedom; on the contrary, it becomes productive; it constitutes the subject.

In the same way, all members of the Communist Party strove to create their political selves by participating in Party meetings. There was no rift, no separation of private and Party decisions, since all disagreement could be done away with during discussions and constructive criticism, but final Party decisions formed the opinions of the individual – that is, they auto-determined him or her. Many Party comrades truly believed that they should subjugate themselves to the mission of Communism, even by sacrificing their lives, but the question remains as to how much of their faith was structured by external relations on a conscious or unconscious plane. In the ritual Party meetings, where the individual formulated the truth about society, him/herself, history and his/her own freedom, it is questionable whether there were some invisible oppressive mechanisms of control that were conceived as freedom but were structured out of what Nietzsche (1994) termed '*ressentiment*' and 'desire for revenge' over the uncertainty of life.

All of these are open questions, but we can claim with certainty that the rituals at Goli Otok arose as an expression of repression, as a clear example of negating freedom. The Party was prepared to turn its members against each other, to create a constant potential war within them, which resulted in the only possible solidarity being with the Party itself.[5] Thus the Party, which was supposed to represent humaneness and to possess a messianic role of putting every person at his or her true measure, demanded that an individual thwart his or her own courage in its name, that he or she should not express solidarity with another person through concrete corporal suffering, but instead that he or she should denounce him/herself and those with whom s/he shared the experience of suffering in the name of the idea of solidarity. The Party could, therefore, become the only thing with which everyone identified.

I would now like to analyse a series of ritual forms of torture, preceded by

---

5 At Goli Otok, one of the best examples of an individual negating themselves by negating another was the theatrical representation of conspiratorial activities. This ritual was described two by two female prisoners, and is presented by the famous writer Danilo Kiš. Both prisoners of Jewish origin, and both were innocent. They described a violent theatre game in which woman A and woman B swapped identities. Woman A took on the identity of woman B, called herself by the other's first and last names, and confessed to her conspiratorial activities against comrade Tito, the Communist Party, and the constitutional order of Yugoslavia. (Of course, in most cases, these confessions were fictitious and extorted.) Woman B denounced her as a traitor, and her duty was to re-educate woman A through beatings and insults. So, on a symbolic level, by persecuting woman A, woman B was actually persecuting herself. She was proving that she had renounced her opinions, and that she had become a new person with new beliefs.

a reflection on forced labour, in order to highlight the relation between torture and an ideological value such as solidarity.

Forced labour

Communist ideology was epitomized by the figure of the warrior-worker. Thus, the myth of the partisan warrior was transformed into the myth of the worker constructing a new society. The myth of the warrior developed during the People's Liberation Struggle, in which the partisans strove to construct a new society and a new man by fighting the enemy. The myth of the hero-worker was grafted onto it; the hero-worker strove to create the new society and new consciousness with his or her muscles. War and labour became identical social practices that determined historical processes. These social practices reflected true virtue, as manifested in the strong and monumental body of the warrior-worker. The worker's muscles represented the will to which all contradictory historical processes would be subjugated. Labour became part of the education at Goli Otok, as prisoners were made to carry rocks from one place to another and to split them daily. The work was repetitive and exhausting, blunting any spontaneous will capable of constructing a new society.

Vasiljević's frequently-used metaphor comparing Goli Otok with a utopian island will be useful in elaborating on the relationship between labour and utopia. In the dictatorship of the proletariat, the individual ascends through labour, and is enlightened by the emergence of a utopian reality – communism. In this utopian reality, everything is supposed to be harmonious and balanced, like some collective body in which every organ moves in a magnum opus of labour. Although Marxism evolved as a criticism of capitalist labour marked by an alienation from the means of production and the final product, the experience of alienation presents a possibility for the class subject to understand him/herself historically, to be enlightened and to take part in the final utopian reality of communism, which is marked by harmonious labour that makes the rational/mechanical coincide with the corporal/organic.

Labour played an important role in both Stalinist and Nazi camps. One feature of totalitarianism was that it colonized the human body, which became material for biological experiments or a medium for the will of the Party and its values. As well as being used as a symbol – the healthy, strong body of the worker in harmony with him/herself – labour was also used to apply totalitarian values in society, so that they became internalized. Labour was used to unify contradictions, to subjugate everyone to a common project, to have them constantly mobilized, and thus to close down opportunities for conspiratorial counter-revolutionary organizations. Labour became the

41

mechanism of military and party control and mobilization both inside and outside the camps.

However, as opposed to the Holocaust, Bolshevik terror allowed for the normative possibility for everyone to change, because the process of Communism involved all people individually. In Stalin's purges, it was very important that those indicted should confess their guilt before being sent to their deaths. It was through confession that they recognized the will of the party and were thus incorporated into the construction of Communism. So, in a paradoxical way, the death sentence was an educational act and a product of labour in the construction of Communism.[6]

Goli Otok did not entail the same amount of violence as concentration camps and the Gulags did. However, there were methods of torture connected to work, and one of the instruments of torture was called 'the hauler'.

The hauler

As described in *The Godless*, the hauler was a tool made up of four handles and wooden planks used to carry stones or sand. The prisoners constantly carried the hauler on their chests across the craggy terrain of Goli Otok, regardless of weather conditions. There was no rational purpose for carrying the stones such as the construction of a building. It was used for 're-education', to exhaust the prisoners and keep them constantly moving without allowing breaks or other activities to distract them. Those carrying the hauler were not differentiated according to professional function; they were all the same, equal under the weight of the hauler pressing upon them. Carrying the hauler was a daily duty that inserted them into the monotony of a numbed body, cut off from their families and from the whole outside world. Carrying the hauler was particularly dangerous because if another person let go of a handle this would make the load of stones tumble onto those supporting the other end on their

---

6 Jovica Aćin's book *Gatanje po pepelu* (*Reading from Ashes*), which is about the experience of a prison camp, points out the logic of work and death in concentration camps. 'At the main gates of the women's camp in Kolima, there was a sign saying: "Arduous work will make you part of the great family of labourers," and "Work liberates" was the motto on the gates of Nazi camps. However, work in the camps exceeded the limits of human strength or, and sometimes simultaneously, nullified itself by its futility. This "liberating" labour that makes camp prisoners part of the "great family of labourers" cannot be compared with either exploitation or classical slave labour. If the purpose of work is creating values and reproducing life, then work in camps remains something completely opposed to this: it terminated values, and life was renewed through live death. The purpose of work in the camps is self-termination of work and termination by work. The work sabotaged itself, and the victim of that sabotage was not the camp system, but the prisoner. Work and death became equivalents. Instead of a way of survival, work becomes a form of death. "Forced labour! What a blessing!"' (Aćin, 2003, 134)

chests. The possibility of slipping and hurting the one with whom you share the fate of forced labour was something that simultaneously bound those concerned to their comrades in suffering and also produced a constant feeling of guilt that mistakes would result in bodily harm. In a nutshell, it was a matter of prisoners overseeing each other's bodies in 'collectivist isolation'. It was very important for collective labour to exist, but it was meant to take place mechanically, without zeal or enthusiasm; it was meant to be imposed repetitively, as a model of functioning in which everyone oversaw everyone else.

The ironic character of the 'hauler' was that it looked like the stretcher used by partisans to carry the wounded during the People's Liberation Struggle. Only, instead of people, it was used for rocks that were to be transferred from one place to another in the manner of Sisyphus. The symbolic figure of the exhausted stretcher-bearer is represented in many pictures and films. The symbolic representation always accentuates the readiness of partisans to sacrifice themselves for a wounded comrade, not to leave him or her behind, despite their physical exhaustion. So, the partisans carrying their wounded comrades had to go through the same suffering; but that suffering was also an initiation process through which the collective was united and through which closeness between people and nationalities was created, precluding the possibility of feeling rejected or isolated in one's own suffering. However, in the case of the hauler, everyone felt isolated and rejected, but at the same time connected through surveillance and control in a collective mobilization. The suffering of warriors constructing the new society through their own will was turned into suffering during which the new man was forged out of collective isolation. Organized violence was charged with the role of re-creating and re-uniting. Goli Otok embodied one of the most complex totalitarian processes: the relation discussed by Hannah Arendt (1973) between atomizing, fragmenting and uniting.

The revolutionary Communist movement in Yugoslavia arose from a desire to liberate and unify the occupied and divided country, to forge brotherhood and unity through the bloody suffering of war. This new unity between the Yugoslav peoples was not to be based on national unification, but on social unification. The aim at Goli Otok was to intensify atomization through collective participation in forced labour, the difference being that it was not marked by liberal isolation, but created isolation through collective mobilization. The idea of change turned against the camp prisoners, and they became its captives. The carrying of the hauler formed, through isolation and labour, new relationships between the prisoners, authority, the state, legality and the idea of communism.

Warm rabbit

The 'warm rabbit' was a prison ritual described in Antonije Isaković's *Moment II* (1982), where one prisoner had to run the length of a hallway lined on both sides with his fellow prisoners, whose job it was to hit him as he ran by. The marked man – or the boycotted man, as he was called – had to run as fast as possible. Whoever hit him most softly, or missed, would be the next to be boycotted. Those who managed to run through would be 'rewarded' by the prison authorities, by being permitted to hit and re-educate in the next ritual.[7] The ritual was clearly intended to break the prisoners' morale: the socialist realist imagery of brave partisans sacrificing themselves for their Party or their comrades was being mocked. The heroism that the Communists believed in was being shattered. In addition, everyone had to participate in the mistreatment of others, so it could be said that this was an expression of solidarity: everyone was a victim of the warm rabbit, and everyone participated in it. The collective embrace, in which everyone is connected in a collective body, is one of the main symbolic representations of socialist realism. The idea of regeneration or cyclic revolution is also represented, in that anyone might be a victim; anyone might be sacrificed. It was also very important that this was a way to show loyalty towards a Party that no longer demanded heroic sacrifice, but rather wanted the prisoners to simply subjugate themselves, to become loyal subjects blindly following orders to hit and be hit, to sacrifice themselves and to sacrifice others.

A prisoner could also prove his correctness by re-educating another prisoner through beatings and verbal insults. It was possible to become a new man by re-educating and overcoming oneself through the negation of another, both physical and verbal, all the while seeing oneself reflected in that person: 'Hell is other people! For they are a reflection of me!' Through the narcissistic animal – the warm rabbit made up of prisoners whose task it is to renew themselves through their own wounds – the new man is created, along with a new political identity, a new solidarity with the Yugoslav Communist Party.

7 In the book, the ritual of the 'warm rabbit' was presented through literary expressionism: 'You go into a tunnel made up of human bodies; bent over and already sweaty, they pant, the stench of rams is deadly; they have closed off all views from you and every trace of sky; you are in an intestine, wriggling like excrement" (59). In a scene involving a prisoner and his interrogator, the interrogator explains that unlike in a capitalist prison, where such a ritual would be imposed from above, the warm rabbit was the product of the prisoners' own initiative, an attempt to re-educate each other. I believe there is no need to comment on the reliability of this fact, but it is true that through constant criticism of others and self-criticism, which included elements of mutual torture and persecution, the prisoners tried to prove that their opinions had been revoked and corrected. The proof of one's renouncement laid in the acceptance of beatings, and in the beating of others, on a daily basis, as an animal would revel in its own and another's blood. This was the way to prove that one had been re-educated, ideologically cleansed and renewed.

Criticism and self-criticism

One ritual (termed by Isaković 'the process of criticism and self-criticism') to prove that the prisoners had changed and accepted the new values of Communism involved prisoners interrogating each other. The prisoner had to disclose everything, including the reason for his or her internment at Goli Otok, all the while being interrupted by forceful accusations from other prisoners that would cause internal confusion. For Communism, humans are beings of practice, created through physical and intellectual labour, so punitive violence was marked not only by techniques of labour and physical violence, as in the hauler and the warm rabbit, but also by intellectual drills of self-negation: the brainwashing practised in the ritual of criticism and self-criticism. The prisoner had to accuse him/herself, and admit to all the things s/he was accused of by others, in order to prove that s/he had re-educated him/herself and could leave Goli Otok. In Kosier's *The Godless* (1991), this process of critical verification was described as being particularly pronounced when new prisoners arrived. Older prisoners would get the opportunity to perfect their critical attacks, proving that they had 'taken the right path' by insulting the newly arrived prisoners and constructing antagonistic and treacherous activities for them. Through discursive practice, the prisoner was supposed to produce the truth about him/herself, to speak out about his or her treason, to become 'the animal that admits'.

Conclusion

Can a political system construct solidarity by repressive methods? Is solidarity possible when built on a foundation of repressive methods? For Yugoslav Communists during the war, the idea of solidarity was authentic: it arouse out of a common struggle against the enemy, and it included beliefs about the construction of a new society, and about the future of socialism being built through joint action. One might criticize that belief because it was based on war logic, and derived some of its elements from a mythology of blood and violence. However, I believe that the construction of Yugoslav Communism was something that was authentically believed, and that Tito's conduct of policy, which developed certain social issues, was efficient and stable. Was Goli Otok an anti-system, a mistake? The answer is that this island spoke about socialism in Yugoslavia, because it uncovered one of the faces of totalitarianism, one of the potential mechanisms constituting Tito's socialism. No system functions according to a monolithic logic, a single principle, even though the totalitarian system strives to view all social contradictions and processes in a monolithic manner (i.e., as a single mechanism leading to utopia). Goli Otok illuminated one of the mechanisms always present in totalitarianism, which could easily have spread across Yugoslavia. I must emphasize, however, that this did not happen.

One cannot assume that the convicts believed in the idea of Yugoslav Communism after suffering so much violence. However, for a number of understandable reasons, they consented to participate in certain mechanisms of self-control and violence. One had to negate others in order to save oneself; one could feel relieved for being beaten, because one could also beat another; when a prisoner was charged, s/he could charge another; when a prisoner criticized and insulted another out of spite, s/he knew that s/he was abolishing him/herself, devouring his/her own dignity. Of course, many did not take sadomasochistic pleasure in insulting and torturing other prisoners, but they were forced to undertake the rituals anyway. Therefore, even though this system was not paradigmatic of the wider reality of Yugoslavia, it was one of the potential scenarios, and would probably have been more widely realized if Stalin had gone through an occupation of Yugoslavia. A system of control in which people had to spy on and denounce others in order to prove their loyalty to the Party, even though they knew that they could be the next victim, could have grown up in Yugoslavia. That is how things were in the USSR, and the reason it did not happen in Yugoslavia was not culturally determined, but simply to do with the dynamics of the constellation of power. In fact, if Yugoslavia had had a different dictator, like Enver Hoxa in Albania, it would probably have been a mental and political bunker.

Apparently, the methods of education at Goli Otok comprised of disciplining prisoners to behave the way Stalin's system would have demanded of them: to be obedient, to allow the will of the Party to spread throughout the prison society. What were people expressing solidarity with when they denounced others, or were themselves being denounced? With what did they feel solidarity when they named potential enemies of society and were, at the same time, victims of that society? Was the power of the Party so strong that its logic was unquestionable?

I would like to propose a few answers. First, it could be said that in the criminal act of denunciation, everyone was an accomplice: the crime was not limited to an elite, but was shared by the most insignificant party officer, so that anyone and everyone could feel like the free creator of the criminal structure and its political power. In fact, everyone could feel some small satisfaction as their own selves became identical with the will of the party. Second, the bureaucratic political myth is based on the constant production of enemies, even if that means that the people themselves become the enemy. It is important that the myth about the enemy never dies, because if it disappears, the system will have to look at itself, at its own flaws. Third, there is the logic that runs: we are all the same; like brothers, we are all opposed to one another and are intoxicated by the mutual conspiracy that unites us. I am doing what another would do, because I spy on him knowing that he spies on me. It is the 'other' that wants it to be so. Fourth, in a state where everyone is a potential enemy and everyone reports on everyone else, I purify myself: I create a temporary illusion in which I am clean, the only one who is innocent. Fifth, the arbitrary nature of a society in which everyone can be guilty at a given moment constructs a power that becomes omnipresent and manifest in everything. Sixth, the human sadomasochistic impulse emerges in certain situations of collective paranoia, where everyone is suspect, recognisable and local. Finally, when the idea of military solidarity is accepted as the main driving force of society, it becomes necessary for it to be maintained, even when the Party 'eats its own children'.

References

Aćin, J. (2003), *Gatanje po pepelu*, Beograd, Stubovi Kulture.

Agamben, G. (1995), *Homo sacer: il potere sovrano e la nuda vita*, Turin, Einaudi.

Arendt, H. (1973), *The Origins of Totalitarianism*, New York, Harcourt Brace Jovanovich.

Aron, R. (1997), *Demokratija i totalitarizam*, Novi Sad, Izdavačka knjižarnica Zorana Stojanovića Sremski Karlovci.

Bauman, Z. (2000), *Liquid Modernity*, Cambridge, Polity Press.

Foucault, M. (1997), *Microfisica del Potere: Interventi Politici*, Turin, Einaudi.

Isaković, A. (1982), *Tren II [Moment II]*, Beograd, Prosveta.

Koselleck, R. (2002), *The Practice of Conceptual History : Timing History, Spacing Concepts*, Stanford, CA, Stanford University Press.

Kosier, B. (1991), *Bezbožnici [The Godless]*, Sarajevo, Svjetlost.

Lefort, C. (2000), *Prijepor o komunizmu*, Zagreb, Politička kultura.

Musabegović, S. (2004), 'War: the construction of the totalitarian body' (unpublished PhD thesis), Florence, European University Institute.

Nietzsche, F. (1994), *On the Genealogy of Morality*, New York, Cambridge University Press.

Vlaisavljević, U. (2003), *Lepoglava i univerzitet, Ogledi iz političke epistemologije, Sarajevo*, Sarajevo, Univerziteta u Sarajevu.

3 *Solidarité* and *Solidarität*: The Concept of Solidarity in France and Germany in the Nineteenth Century

Thomas Fiegle

Many social scientists consider 'solidarity' to be a fundamental concept of political and social thought. However, they also mention its complex and ambiguous nature. In fact, the concept of 'solidarity' can be used in various contexts, ranging from a political catchphrase to a key concept of modern sociology. Setting out a unique and strict definition is certainly beyond our means. Nevertheless, it seems possible to retrace the concept's history and to propose a typology of its various meanings.[1]

It is important to note that the conceptual history of solidarity is not restricted to the history of the word, since it is not mainly interested in its linguistic use but in its meaning. Furthermore, conceptual history is also to be distinguished from the traditional history of ideas. Instead of treating its object as an almost static and eternal essence, conceptual history insists on its historical nature, its multiple changes and transformations in time and space. Conceptual history can thus be seen as a hermeneutical method, which allows for the reconstruction in particular of the philosophical and theological horizon of meaning of a word.[2]

In current studies of the conceptual history of solidarity, this hermeneutical dimension is almost absent. Most authors focus exclusively on the social aspects of the concept's history. I will argue in this article that the reconstruction of the concept's history requires both its philosophical and its theological backgrounds. Neither the French nor the German history of the

1 This article is based on my book on the history of the concept's transfer from France to Germany in the 19th century (Fiegle, 2003).
2 For the methodology of conceptual history, see especially Koselleck, 1995.

concept of solidarity can be understood accurately without considering counter-revolutionary Catholic thought at the beginning of the 19th century and the complex subsequent process of secularization. As far as the German perspective on *Solidarität* is concerned, the argument presented emphasizes the importance of Kant's and Hegel's writings as well as their religious, mainly Protestant, underpinnings in order to reach an understanding of the change from *solidarité* to *Solidarität* in the mid-19th century.[3]

Solidarité

The French noun *solidarité* is derived from the expression *in solido* in Roman law. It designates collective responsibility among two or more debtors (*obligatio in solidum*) (Rey, 1992). The Latin noun *solidarietas* was shaped by Roman Catholic social thought at the end of the 19th century (Kerber, 1996). In French dictionaries, the word appears first in the 17th century. The *Code civil* from 1804, finally, defines *solidarité* as follows:

> L'obligation est solidaire entre plusieurs créanciers lorsque le titre donne expressément à chacun d'eux le droit de demander le paiement du total de la créance, et que le paiement fait à l'un d'eux libère le débiteur, encore que le bénéfice de l'obligation soit partageable et divisible entre les divers créanciers. (*Code civil*, 1804, §1197)[4]

Furthermore, the term *solidarité* can be found in various other articles of the *Code civil* (especially Articles 1197–1215), the *Code du commerce* (Articles 20, 22, 24, 28, 140 and 187) and the *Code pénal* (Article 55). In French civil law, this meaning has remained unchanged to the present day (Borgetto, 1993).

As a political and social concept, *solidarité* emerges only at the beginning of the 19th century, very much later than the legal concept. It has often been said that solidarity as a political concept is a legacy of the French Revolution. In reality, however, it was formulated at the time of the counter-revolution. Authors like François-René de Chateaubriand, Joseph de Maistre and Pierre Simon Ballanche seem important for this semantic shift. They all belonged to the ultramontanist intellectual and religious movement. This term refers to the main idea of the movement: to rebuild the unlimited authority of the Pope, who from the French geographical perspective lives 'over the mountains'. In

---

3 For a bibliographical overview of the history of solidarity, see Fiegle, 2003. The excellent dictionary article by Wildt (1996) is also mainly focused on the French and German development of the concept.

4 The official English version of the *Code civil*, translated by Georges Rouhette and Anne Berton, can be found on the French government website: www.lexinter.net/ENGLISH/civil_code.htm (accessed 25 June 2007).

politics, they favoured the realization of a paternalistic and patriarchal state, in which the king would be seen as a father rather than a leader. In their common devotion to the father, the people would recognize themselves as brothers. When they talked about fraternity, they meant this kind of love between brothers, not the egalitarian and pagan brotherhood of the revolutionary masses. At the same time, the 'ultras' were convinced that only a new, even more radical revolution, a Christian counter-revolution, could restore the lost world of the ancient monarchy (Rémond, 1982, 54).

One of the first examples for a political understanding of the concept of solidarity is a statement in Chateaubriand's famous book *Le Génie du christianisme* (1978)[1802]. Chateaubriand believes that the sacrament of the baptism consists in transmitting our faults to our sons, creating thereby a community of sinners: 'que les fautes rejailliront sur nos fils, que nous sommes tous solidaires' (Chateaubriand, 1978 [1802], 488). Baptism, which is for Christians the symbol of hope, takes on the opposite meaning: nobody can escape the original sin of mankind. In fact, the legal meaning of solidarity as a collective debt is here transformed into the metaphysical idea of collective guilt. This conception is part of an apocalyptical vision of human history: only the last fight between good and evil, between Christians and pagans, can relieve humanity of its original sin and open the way to a new era. The Gnostic origins of this conception are even clearer in the writings of Ballanche and de Maistre. Therefore, one of the main sources is the Augustinian doctrine of the two cities. The ultras were fascinated by the eschatological writings of Giaccomo di Fiore, a medieval Italian monk who coined the expression 'the third age', that of the holy spirit, which would come after the reigns of God the father and the son of God. Gnostics believed in a duality, a good and an evil city: on the one hand the city of sinners, which is the evil creation of an imperfect God-like being called the demiurge; and on the other hand the city of the saints, which will come after the apocalypse. From a Christian point of view, Gnostic theology is problematic because it reverses the relation between God and man: it is no longer God (or Jesus Christ) who saves humanity, but humanity who saves God (de Lubac, 1979).

The concept of *solidarité* can, within this theological context, have two opposite meanings, one positive and one negative. In its negative meaning, all men are intrinsically linked by original sin. In this view, solidarity is considered a common destiny of humanity, as Ballanche said in his *Essai sur les institutions sociales* of 1818:

> On ne saurait le redire, l'homme n'est pas fait pour être seul, l'homme n'est rien tout seul, l'homme ne peut pas séparer sa destinée de celle de ses

semblables; et le genre humain tout entier est solidaire.' (Ballanche, 1991[1818], 194)

This type of solidarity can be called 'cosmological solidarity', with the cosmos representing – as in Stoicism – an enormous prison.

In the positive meaning, there is a solidarity among men in the future, in a New Age. In his book *Les soirées de Saint-Pétersbourg*, published in 1821, de Maistre applies this view to French politics. Set during his exile in Russia in the immediate aftermath of the French Revolution, one of the figures of this book imagines a new France, which would be delivered from the twin evils of rationalist philosophy and Protestant criticism. In this new world, de Maistre claims, it would be possible to rediscover a natural and sacred primitive state of mankind, which he calls *solidarité*:

> Il y a une foule d'exemples de ce sentiment naturel, légitimé et consacré par la religion, et qu'on pourrait regarder comme des traces presque effacés d'un état primitif. En suivant cette route, coyez-vous [...] qu'il fût absolument impossible de se former une certaine idée de cette solidarité qui existe entre les hommes (vous me permettez bien ce terme de jurisprudence), d'où résulte la réversibilité des mérites qui explique tout?' (de Maistre, 1821, 208)

This second, positive type of solidarity can be called 'eschatological solidarity', as the 'good' is restored at the moment of greatest loss – in this case, when the French aristocrats were into exile.

It is perplexing to see that it is just a small step from this extremely conservative conception to early socialism. Pierre Leroux, a former Saint-Simonist, in his book *De l'Humanité, de son principe et de son avenir* (1840), was notable in writing about a philosophical concept of solidarity. The book's subtitle announced the author's critical position towards Christianity and religion in general: 'où se trouve exposée la vraie définition de la religion et où l'on explique le sens, la suite et l'enchaînement du mosaïsme et du christianisme'. For Leroux it was humanity, as opposed to God, which constituted the highest point of philosophy. Humanity is the true religion. This was clearly expressed in the title of the central chapter: 'Ce qu'il faut entendre aujourd'hui par charité, c'est la solidarité mutuelle des hommes' (Leroux, 1840, livre IV, chapter 1).

Leroux blamed the Christian tradition for misinterpreting the genuine meaning of the command of love, in the sense of 'love God'. He criticized Christian theology for overemphasizing the love of God, while love among humans, despite the commandment 'Love thy neighbour', was denigrated.

Consequently, he suggested the following definition of solidarity:

> Aimez Dieu en vous et dans les autres
> Ce qui revient à
> Aimez-vous par Dieu dans les autres;
> Ou à;
> Aimez les autres par Dieu en vous. (Leroux, 1840, 209)

In fact, Leroux simply radicalized the consequences of the Gnostic understanding of the concept. The tendency to secularization that is implicit in Gnosticism was thereby strengthened. Although the concept of solidarity changed, its dualist structure remained intact: a cosmological solidarity, identified with liberal and industrial society; and, opposed to it, an eschatological solidarity, that is, social relations in a future socialist society. Heinrich Heine, who lived in Paris and was in contact with the most important figures of early French socialism, ironically describes Leroux's theoretical position thus:

> Leroux ist ein Pontifex Maximus: er will eine kolossale Brücke bauen, die, aus einem Bogen bestehend, auf zwei Pfeilern ruhen soll, wovon der eine aus dem materialistischen Granit des vorigen Jahrhunderts, der andere aus dem geträumten Mondschein der Zukunft verfertigt worden. (Heine, 1994 [1843], 558)[5]

Although Leroux has not been accurately remembered by his successors, perhaps because his position remained too close to theology, his conception of solidarity underpinned its use throughout the greater part of the 19th century in France. This was also true for Auguste Comte, another former Saint-Simonist, who tied the concept to the idea of the division of labour. For him, the division of labour was necessary in human society ('la condition la plus essentielle de notre vie sociale'), but the society of his time was characterized in terms of negative solidarity, because of social disintegration and its tendency to over-specialize (Comte, 1969 [1839], 478; see also Cingolani, 1992, 46ff.). While Comte wanted to introduce a new religion, his famous 'religion de l'Humanité', to counterbalance this development, other authors who shared his analysis – like the solidarists of the Third Republic – preferred a more practical solution, such as the establishment of social insurance (Bourgeois, 1913; Bouglé, 1924; see also Ewald, 1986). The dualist concept of solidarity in the solidaristic thought remained unchanged, but was

---

5 'Leroux is a Pontifex Maximus: he wants to build a colossal bridge, which shall stand on two piles. The first one is built by the materialist granite of last century, but the second one is constructed by the dreamed moonshine of the future.'

further secularized. This was also the case for Durkheim's well-known distinction between two sorts of social solidarity: 'mechanical' and 'organic'. The first corresponded to negative solidarity, the second one to positive. Nevertheless, if Durkheim's concept of solidarity, which he elaborated in his 1893 work *La division du travail social*, was clearly rooted in the French tradition of social philosophy, the issues it covered already responded to a new intellectual configuration (Durkheim, 1994 [1893]). This configuration was the 'science allemande', the philosophy of France's worst enemy at the time.

Solidarität

In Germany, the concept of solidarity can be found first – as in France – in the context of civil law. The noun *Solidarität* – derived from the French *solidarité* – was used by lawyers in the 18th and 19th century. In 1900 it was replaced in the German civil law code (the Bürgerliches Gesetzbuch) by the term *gesamtschuldnerische Haftung* (collective responsibility for debts). This explains why, in German, the legal sense of *Solidarität* has practically disappeared today (Wildt, 1996; see also Grimm, 1973). The concept was probably first used in a political and social sense by German emigrants and fellow travellers in France in the 1840s. One of the early German leaders of the workers' movement, Wilhelm Weitling, had a conversation in 1846 with Karl Marx about the idea of justice, solidarity and brotherly love ('Idee der Gerechtigkeit, der Solidarität und brüderlichen Liebe'; Wildt, 1996). Stephan Born, another workers' movement leader, founding father of the Arbeiter-verbrüderung, wrote in 1848: '"Freie Konkurrenz! Jeder für sich!" wird hier gegenübergestellt dem Prinzip der Solidarität, der "Verbrüderung! Jeder für Alle!" ('Instead of "Free market! Every man for himself!" we propose the principle of solidarity: "Fraternization! Every man for all!"'; Wildt, 1996). This formulation prefigured the later motto of the workers' movement: 'Einer für alle! Alle für einen!' ('One for all! All for one!'). Not only socialists, but also authors like the liberal Hermann Schulze-Delitzsch, used the concept during this period (Wildt, 1996). It was characteristic in this early period of the concept's history in Germany that – in contrast to France – *Solidarität* was seen as almost identical to *Brüderlichkeit* (brotherhood). Furthermore, the concept's use was very restricted: only very few references can be found, especially compared to the loose use of the term *Brüderlichkeit* around the time of the 1848 revolution. Real acceptance of the concept in Germany occured only after 1848; it was taken up mainly by philosophers and social thinkers from the Young Hegelian movement, in particular Lorenz von Stein, Moses

Hess, Karl Grün and, of course, Karl Marx.[6] However, the meaning of the concept changed again: it was no longer simply *Brüderlichkeit*, as in the first half of the 19th century, nor did it represent cosmological and eschatological solidarity, as in France.

In order to understand this meaning, it is necessary to consider briefly the development of German idealism in the 19th century. In attempting to reach an understanding of such a schematic reconstruction, we shall distinguish between several things: first, Kant's idea of morality; second, the problem of the historical realization of that idea from Kant to Hegel; and, third, the critique of Hegel's speculative solution of this problem by the Young Hegelians.[7]

How can we explain the difference in development of the concept between the French and the German? The different religious and theological backgrounds of the two countries have to be taken into account. As argued above, the French concept of solidarity was forged by a metaphor: collective debt in a legal sense was transformed into collective guilt in the Gnostic sense. Original sin was seen as the original bond of humankind. However, one might ask: is original sin a 'sin'? Is the sin I inherited from my forefathers a 'sin'? Isn't a sin something personal, something *I* am responsible for, responsible for only to God? This was, at least, Martin Luther's theological opinion, and probably that of most of his Protestant and even non-Protestant compatriots. *Solidarität* was shaped by this new understanding of guilt and the resulting philosophical conception of personality.

Indeed, the conception of strictly personal guilt implies a philosophical question: which act or volition is, in the final analysis, likely to be considered a sin? Apparently, only strictly autonomous acts and volitions can attain such a status. However, what exactly does 'autonomous' mean? This is precisely the central question of Kant's moral philosophy: What is 'autonomy'? In fact, there is only one statement that fits the bill: one of pure volition, i. e., volition without an object. Of course, there is no such thing as pure will in reality. Nevertheless, the idea of pure will can serve, as Kant says, as a regulative idea. It can motivate a process of 'autonomization': a process in which the subject tries to sublimate his or her physical and psychological needs. In fine, the problem of the 'autonomy of the will' is resolved by its temporalization: 'autonomy' is transformed into a task for the individual's moral development.

Thus Kant's idea of autonomy not only enables us to conceptualize the

---

6 The most important publications during that period were: von Stein, 1842, 1921 [1850]; Grün, 1845; Hess, 1961. Karl Marx used the concept only after the Paris Commune of 1871.
7 For a more detailed presentation, see Fiegle, 2003, 171–233.

process of individuation, but also that of socialization. Since autonomy consists in submitting every volition to a test of universalization – the only way to ensure that no heteronomous need or tendency in reality commands the will – this process is implicitly an intersubjective one. Sharing the common horizon of universalization (called 'the kingdom of ends' in Kantian terminology), the different subjects are able to recognize themselves and each other in their reciprocal attempts at becoming autonomous. In the Kantian perspective, the social bond does not result from substantial resemblance, but, on the contrary, from the subject's effort to overcome his or her substantial identity. In short, empirical subjects recognize themselves and each other in their reciprocal efforts to become moral subjects (Kant, 1974a).

From a theological perspective this represents an interesting inversion of the Augustinian conception that original sin would bind men to each other. In the German context, it appears, men were no tied to one another by the fact that they were sinners, i.e. their *Sündhaftigkeit,* but by their desire to be worth a sin, their *Sündwürdigkeit.*[8]

This takes our argument a step further: since the conception of a community based upon reciprocal recognition was, for Kant, just a regulative idea, how could this idea be realized? How could the 'categorical imperative' and the imperative of the phenomenal world, the famous 'struggle for life', be reconciled? Kant tried to respond to this question by introducing the argument of the 'trick of nature'. He developed this point in the 'Critique of the faculty of judgement' (§83): human selfishness was here identified as the engine of a dialectical movement that lead to civilization and the creation of a republican order (Kant, 1974b, 387–393). Obviously, the scheme underlying this argument was Adam Smith's 'invisible hand'. It was this 'liberal' idea of the *development* of an intersubjectively founded community, more than the idea in itself – at least at the beginning of what would later be called 'German idealism' – which provoked criticism from Kant's followers. This was especially true for Hegel. The young Hegel shared Kant's idea of a community of mutual recognition, but – on the level of the historical realization of that idea – he wanted to overcome the Kantian conception.

In 1803 Hegel wrote *System der Sittlichkeit,* in which he exposed this conception (Hegel, 1967 [1803]). He distinguished three levels in a process of socialization, reaching from the single subject to the realization of a community of mutual recognition. The first level is 'love', the second 'law' and the third 'state' or 'community' (in the sense of the Greek word *polis*).

---

8 The distinction between *Sündhaftigkeit* and *Sündwürdigkeit* refers to the Kantian one between *Glückseligkeit* and *Glückwürdigkeit.* See Cassirer, 1961.

The engine of this process was no longer 'nature' – as it was for Kant – but the *Geist* ('spirit' or 'mind') of a people. In this politically republican period, Hegel considered the *Geist* as a symbolical form for art, religion and science. The constitution of the *Geist* was therefore essentially communication. This communicative conception of the *Geist* in his early writings led Hegel to locate the progressive force in history not in a struggle conceived in naturalistic terms, but in the so-called 'struggle for recognition'. Having abandoned this conception in his later works, Hegel conceived history not as the communicative process of the constitution of a community based on mutual recognition, but as a dialectical process of the self-alienation and self-reconciliation of the original *Volksgeist*.[9]

Therefore it was not Hegel himself who prepared the new understanding of the concept of solidarity in Germany. It was only after a period of criticism of their master's work that some of his scholars looked back to the early social philosophy of the young Hegel, which was based on Kant. One of the young philosophers – and I limit my analysis here to this author, as he was certainly the most influential theorist of the German 'welfare state' – who tried to conceive social theory as a process of a 'struggle for recognition' was Lorenz von Stein. In 1850, von Stein published his book *Geschichte der sozialen Bewegung in Frankreich von 1789 bis auf unsere Tage*, an analysis of the social movement since the French Revolution (Stein, 1921 [1850]). In the introduction, Stein developed a social theory based on the observation of the laws of political economy, long before a similar attempt by Marx in *Das Kapital*. For him, history mainly consisted of a struggle between social classes (Stein, 1921, 14ff.). The young-Hegelian conception of a struggle for recognition was now mediated by the products of human work. As far as these products were seen as attempts at the realization of the self, the fact that there was a social class that could not realize itself through work but was restricted to its biological reproduction was equivalent to its non-recognition. At the level of liberal society, this contradiction led to a kind of modern apocalypse: the social revolution (Stein, 1921, 137ff.). If this conception again seems to be very close to that of the young Marx, Stein did not just link this analysis to concrete historical studies: he also broke with the Hegelian and Marxian idea that it is possible to know history in its totality. For Stein, history was an open process. Thus Stein – unlike Marx – did not believe that the social revolution would resolve anything. The antagonism between labour and capital would stay the same, with only their historical representatives changing.

9 On the Hegelian concept of a 'struggle for recognition', see the works of Taylor and Honneth, especially Taylor, 1979 and Honneth, 1994.

Consequently, one social revolution would follow the next. Nevertheless, for Stein there was an important point about this negative spiral of social revolutions. It consisted of social reform. Since all members of society must fear such a negative spiral, he argued, they all have a common interest in avoiding such a development. In other words, capital's fear of a social revolution constituted the motivational basis for social reform. Thus the negative spiral of revolutions could be replaced by a positive spiral of social reform. It was this common interest that Stein called *Solidarität*: 'If society is asked to work at its own reform, this reform must lie in its own interest' (Stein, 1921, 137). This solidarity was certainly not identical to the idea of mutual recognition, but it could be regarded as a first step in the attempt to realize the ethical idea of a community based on mutual respect.

In conclusion, Stein's reformist conception of solidarity contrasted considerably with the French one. Insofar as Stein depicted an apocalyptical vision, a never-ending circle of social revolutions, Gnostic theology was also the hermeneutical horizon of the concept of solidarity. However, the crux of Stein's conception of solidarity was not to use it to bind subjects. Depicting the perspective of the social apocalypse, Stein by contrast tried to give a motivational basis to the ethical claim for recognition of those excluded from economical and political power by the dominant class. As such, it may be seen as one of the theoretical foundations not only for the German welfare state, but also for various other enterprises rooted in solidarity.

References

Ballanche, P. (1991 [1818]), *Essai sur les institutions sociales*, Paris, Fayard.

Borgetto, M. (1993), *La notion de fraternité en droit public français. Le passé, le présent et l'avenir de la solidarité*, Paris, Librairie générale de droit et de jurisprudence.

Bouglé, C. (1924), *Le solidarisme*, Paris, Marcel Giard.

Bourgeois, L. (1913), *Solidarité*, Paris, Armand Colin.

Cassirer, E. (1961), *Zur Logik der Kulturwissenschaften. Fünf Studien*, Darmstadt, Wissenschaftliche Buchgesellschaft.

Cassirer, E. (1971), *Das Erkenntnisproblem in der Philosophie und Wissenschaft der neueren Zeit*, Volume 3, Hildesheim, G. Olms.

Chateaubriand, F. de (1978 [1802]), *Essai sur les révolutions: Génie du christianisme*, ed. M. Regard, Paris, Gallimard.

Cingolani, P. (1992), 'L'idée d'humanité chez Auguste Comte: solidarité et continuité' in J. Chevallier and P. Ansart (eds), *La solidarité: un sentiment républicain?*, Paris, Presses universitaires de France.

Code civil des Français. Edition originale et seule officielle (1804), Paris, Imprimerie de la République.

Comte, A. (1969 [1839]), *Cours de philosophie positive*, Volume 4, Paris, Anthropos.

Durkheim, E. (1994 [1893]), *De la division du travail social*, Paris, Presses universitaires de France.

Ewald, F. (1986), *L'Etat providence*, Paris, Grasset & Fasquelle.

Fiegle, T. (2003), *Von der Solidarité zur Solidarität – Ein französisch-deutscher Begriffstransfer*, Münster, Lit-Verlag.

Grimm, D. (1973), *Solidarität als Rechtsprinzip. Die Rechts- und Staatslehre Léon Duguits in ihrer Zeit*, Frankfurt, Athenäum.

Grün, K. (1845), *Die soziale Bewegung in Frankreich und Belgien. Briefe und Studien*, Darmstadt, Leske.

Hegel, G. W. F. (1967 [1803]), *System der Sittlichkeit* (ed. G. Lasson), Hamburg, Meiner.

Heine, H. (1994 [1843]), 'Kommunismus, Philosophie und Klerisei' in *Werke in vier Bänden*, Volume 3, Frankfurt, Insel.

Hess, M. (1961), *Philosophische und sozialistische Schriften (1827–1850)* (ed. A. Cornu and W. Mönke), Berlin, Akademie-Verlag.

Honneth, A. (1994), *Kampf um Anerkennung. Zur moralischen Grammatik sozialer Konflikte*, Frankfurt, Suhrkamp.

Kant, I. (1974a), 'Kritik der praktischen Vernunft' in *Werke* (ed. W. Weischedel), Volume VIII, Frankfurt, Suhrkamp.

Kant, I. (1974b) 'Kritik der praktischen Vernunft' in *Werke* (ed. W. Weischedel), Volume X, Frankfurt, Suhrkamp.

Kerber, W. (1996), 'Solidaritätsprinzip' in J. Ritter and K. Gründer (eds), *Historisches Wörterbuch der Philosophie*, Volume 9, Darmstadt, Wissenschaftliche Buchgesellschaft.

Koselleck, R. (1995), *Vergangene Zukunft. Zur Semantik geschichtlicher Zeiten*, Frankfurt, Suhrkamp.

Leroux, P. (1840), *De l'Humanité, de son principe et de son avenir*, Paris, Perrotin.

Lubac, H. de (1979), *La postérité de Joachim de Flore*, Volume 1, Paris, Lethielleux.

Maistre, J. de (1821), *Les Soirées de Saint-Pétersbourg*, Paris, Librairie grecque, latine et française.

Rémond, R. (1982), *Les droites en France*, Paris, Aubier.

Rey, A. (ed.) (1992), *Dictionnaire historique de la langue française*, Volume 2, Paris, Bordas.

Stein, L. von (1842), *Der Socialismus und Kommunismus im heutigen Frankreich. Ein Beitrag zur Zeitgeschichte*, Leipzig, Wiegand.

Stein, L. von (1921 [1850]), *Geschichte der sozialen Bewegung in Frankreich von 1789 bis auf unsere Tage*, Volume 1, Munich, Drei Masken Verlag.

Taylor, C. (1979), *Hegel and Modern Society*, Cambridge, Cambridge University Press.

Wildt, A. (1996), 'Solidarität' in J. Ritter and K. Gründer (eds), *Historisches Wörterbuch der Philosophie*, Volume 9, Darmstadt, Wissenschaftliche Buchgesellschaft.

4 Organic Solidarity Versus Connective Justice? Islam's Critical Presence in Europe

Armando Salvatore

Introduction: the critical potential of Euro-Islamic views of solidarity

In this chapter I will discuss how Islam's insertion in European socio-political life, marked by the increasing presence in the old continent of citizens and residents with an Islamic religious or cultural background, has the potential to reconfigure notions and practices of solidarity. This potential is partly rooted in the way Islam articulates some leitmotifs of Abrahamic religions. Yet the most immediate vehicle of this potential contribution to opening up norms of solidarity is the role of Muslim intellectuals, scholars and activists who redefine the vocabulary of republican citizenship and commitment to the common good by straddling the border between conventional notions of tradition and modernity, of communitarian closure and universalistic openness, of inclusion and exclusion. The specific positioning of European Muslim public personalities as both internal and external to the European political and philosophical traditions is here a critical asset.

For the observer and the scholar this requires moving beyond sterile typologies based on the interpretative syndrome of 'political Islam', and in particular on the dichotomy between a radical/fundamentalist/communitarian Islam and a moderate/modernist/liberal Islam. One needs to look at the differential capacity of Muslim actors to penetrate a wider political process directly related to the deep transformations of the nation state, and to the complex remaking of Europe within new global scenarios. These changes also cut across timid and contradictory attempts by the old continent to effect a post-colonial disengagement, whose fragility is evidenced both by the effects of the Iraq war and by the crisis of the so-called Euro-Mediterranean partnership.

The basic work hypothesis here is that Islamic intellectuals can play an innovative role in today's Europe, as much as Jewish intellectuals did in the formative phase of sociology and anthropology. In other words, the double heritage, Islamic and European, of the emerging Islamic intelligentsia – presently led by the Swiss-born scholar and public activist Tariq Ramadan – allows a privileged angle in objectifying the strengths and weaknesses of the social frameworks and political constitutions of contemporary European societies, which are based on largely secular yet post-Christian models of cohesion and solidarity. This helpful double perspective also applied to Jewish intellectuals in the 19th century and for a large part of the 20th century (prior to the almost complete annihilation of mainland European Jewry by the Nazis and their allies, including Vichy France).

It has been observed that two of the most influential theoreticians of solidarity – Emile Durkheim and Marcel Mauss, both French Jews – had a different, albeit implicit, relationship to their Jewish heritage, and that this divergence might also account for their different approaches to the nature of the social bond and therefore to the notion of solidarity. Mauss insisted on a continual reading of social facts that could not be reduced to a central symbolic meaning, which for Durkheim resided in the basic identity of God and society. In this sense, Mauss addressed, coherently with the Jewish-rabbinic tradition, the 'letter' of facts in order to perpetually reconstruct their meanings. Durkheim, instead, saw religion as the basic constitutive force of society, much as Christians see the sense of the Old Testament in Christ and his mystical body, the Church. Therefore, he made a rigorous distinction between 'letter' and 'spirit,' the surfaces of facts and their deep, authentic meanings (Tarot, 1999, 353–358). In this difference of approach is prefigured a diverging conception of the social bond and of the nature of solidarity: mainly organic in the case of Durkheim (based on a one-to-one correspondence between collective symbol and social reality), and mainly connective in the case of Mauss (based on a continual reconstruction of dyadic, triadic and collective relations).

This chapter will argue that Islamic intellectuals today have redeveloped a specific critical potential that transcends the limits of any immanent critique of modern society. Such limits are due to the fact that the immanence of the critique is based on the same postulates of the essential, yet post-Christian, dimension of modern social cohesion that inheres in organic notions of solidarity. It is important to lay stress on the fact that 'solidarity' is here employed as a keyword in the classic sociological sense, without paying attention to the nuances and paradoxes that led to its adoption in the 19th century (see Chapter 3, this volume). For the same reasons, referring to this concept with regard to epochs preceding its adoption as a crucial sociological keyword (and indeed prior to the rise of sociology as an academic discipline) has an ineliminable anachronistic component. Yet we can discount this anachronism by invoking a second, somewhat larger meaning of solidarity if referring to prior periods: something like 'solidarity at large' or, more precisely, the ensemble of notions, practices and institutions that in a given historical and cultural context constituted the relevant genealogical antecedents to the modern sociological notion of solidarity.

The origin of connective justice as a relational form of solidarity

Jan Assmann has asserted that a pristine conception of solidarity is inherent in the political theology underlying larger notions of order, embracing not only the socio-political dimension of order but a larger cosmological level. His focus is mainly on the genesis of the Mosaic opposition to the Pharaonic state in ancient Egypt. This process marked the beginning of what Assmann calls the 'Mosaic distinction', the condition of all the future attitudes of both Judaism and Islam (the Mosaic narration has a prominent place in the Qur'an) towards the state's ultimate guarantee of social cohesion and more encompassing notions of order. To translate this concept of order into sociological parlance, it is the idea that solidarity can't be organically provided by a structured division of labour and attending concepts of sacredness bestowed upon the key-symbols of the groups and the institutional forms of their cohesion (the 'state' and its antecedents). A similar argument has been made by Michael Walzer, and extended well into the new problems Jewish communities faced in the European diaspora (Walzer, 1996). To refer, again, somewhat generously, to inherited sociological typologies of solidarity, this type of solidarity without the state, based not on ignoring the state but rather on constructing a higher, transcendent instance of guarantee of the social bond, would be tantamount to an upgrading of the 'mechanical solidarity' of Durkheim through a sort of connective justice. This is the idea that through the mediation of a common fellowship in God, ego and alter are fair to each other, and thus build the cell of a larger socio-political body. The exact limits and the precise shape of this larger body are nonetheless kept normatively unclear (Salvatore, 2007).

The perception that Islam could figure in this context as the continuation of Judaism by other (more powerfully universalistic) means was not missed by sociologists and social theorists. In particular, Robert Bellah saw in the paradigm of the emergence of Islam a capacity to reduce the social bond to its unmediated kernel, and so to de-sacralize every form of power (Bellah, 1970). One could add that Islam displayed a sort of self-sociology from the beginning, i.e. from Muhammad's preaching. This is particularly evident in the function of the month of Ramadan, which is holy to the extent that it institutes a fasting obligation on the members of the community, solidifying its solidarity through the common thinking of the poor. The poor here are not just symbols, but the key concretization of 'the other', which recalls God's presence in the social bond as the ultimate guarantor of solidarity.

Yet Jan Assmann reminds us that the injunction to see God in the weakest, and so to fear divine justice, was instituted in ancient Egypt before the Mosaic distinction came to maturation, and also as a significant antecedent to it (Assmann, 2000). This was evident in the obligations of solidarity with orphans and widows, which became a leitmotif in both Judaism and Islam: God provides for those who are not provided for, but this can only occur through the solidarity-oriented behaviour of the pious and faithful. Here the common ground is the focus on connectivity. Assmann points out that this idea of connective justice as the original fundament of solidarity corresponds to an idea of politics that is different from the Greek concept and practice. The root of the notion that develops from Egypt to Israel is in a tension between a vertical hierarchy (Egypt) and a regulated anarchy (Israel). These systems shared the imperative of 'withness' and connectivity, not the concept of an encompassing *nomos* as 'structure' (Assmann, 2000, 199–204).

This type of connective justice is vectored by notions of transcendence that are only problematically present in, though not completely extraneous to, Greek concepts of politics and of the organization of the social bond. In Judaism and Islam, the fundament of solidarity is in the triad ego-alter-Alter/God. Doing good to another is not only a test for God's judgement, but is the only practically effective way to relate to God, by connecting to the absolute Alter through the concrete alter found in everyday interactions. On the other hand it is only possible to relate to the alter, and so to construct solidarity, through trust in the Alter. In this vein, Martin Buber has proposed that connectivity means relational openness, even dialogue (Buber, 1992). There is no Christ that predetermines or symbolically pre-condenses the meaning and the outcome of the relation. Assmann has stressed the similarity of the ancient notion of *maat* (meaning basically 'justice') not only with the Jewish *sedeq*, but also with the Chinese *tao*. These are all concepts denoting connective justice and relational solidarity, or rather their fundamental principle, as being indissolubly social and metaphysical, mundane and religious (Assmann, 2000, 202). Christian *caritas* is, in this sense, a reformulation and specification of the same conceptual cluster, albeit in terms of imitating Christ through being Christian. We will see what kind of difference this makes in terms of imagining and instituting organic notions of solidarity.

It is thus not surprising that Jewish scholars have often manifested a mixture of fear and admiration towards Islam, as a remaking of Judaism that tames messianism, accommodates Jews and Christians and overcomes primordialism. One can detect this attitude in a wide array of thinkers of the 20th century, from Martin Buber to Shmuel N. Eisenstadt, who unambiguously wrote:

> the emphasis on the construction of a political–religious collectivity was connected in Islam with the development of a principled ideological negation of any primordial element or component within this sacred political–religious identity. Indeed, of all the Axial Age civilizations in general, and the monotheistic ones in particular, Islam was, on the ideological level, the most extreme in its denial of the legitimacy of such primordial dimensions in the structure of the Islamic community... In this it stood in opposition to Judaism, with which it shared such characteristics as an emphasis on the direct, unmediated access of all members of the community to the sacred (Eisenstadt, 2002, 148–149).

While the primordiality of sacrifice in Christianity was sublimated in the self-sacrifice of the God-man, in Islam sacrifice, and with it sacredness, are tuned down through a sort of ritualized sociology, re-enacting the substituting gesture of Abraham in the most important festivity (along with the end of Ramadan): the feast of sacrifice in the month of the pilgrimage to Mecca. Ritual and memory are metabolized into a post-primordial accommodation of the chain of Semitic prophets. This approach requires a reasoned rejection of the Christ, based on the fear of a manipulation, through an over-symbolization, of the God–man relationship, a manipulation made possible by sheer human interest. The christological disputes denounced in the Qur'an reflect the fear of arbitrary priestly power, and so of a manipulation of the triadic link between ego, alter and Alter/God. It might seem paradoxical, but is an historical fact that the Qur'an, which according to Islamic dogma is the definitive word of God overcoming human manipulation of scripture, authorized biblical criticism. This was best reflected in the work of the medieval scholar from al-Andalus, Ibn Hazm, which should be considered a key antecedent to the biblical criticism of Spinoza, whose roots are also in the Jewish mysticism and Islamic philosophy of the Iberian peninsula (Salvatore, 2005).

Organic solidarity and the recuperation of connectivity in a republican context

Organic views of solidarity are instead distinctly post-Christian, to the extent that they are a sort of perfecting and thus overcoming (or, better, *Aufhebung* in Hegelian parlance) of Christianity. In such views, the *telos* is now immanent to society, which is its own messiah, and the state is its church. Society is its own god, and solidarity is the immanent *telos* of society, more than the concrete infrastructure of society materializing through the following of discrete injunctions, as in the prophetic calls to protect the weak (first incarnate in widows and orphans) and help the poor. In European modern post-Christian history, the state and the church are engaged in a fierce competition, but their genealogy unfolds through a mimetic process. The best examples of this mimesis were the taumaturgical powers of French kings, which reached a climax in the High Middle Ages, when the uniqueness and independence of what would become the French nation and its state were shaped.

In Durkheim's idea of organic solidarity, the organic dimension no longer resides in the mechanical and cellular character of the social bond where ego faces alter, but in a qualitative growth of the symbolic power of humans: from simply human to social, and from metonymical to metaphorical. The secularity of the organic stage of solidarity reveals teleologically the authentic social function of religion. The secular is the *Aufhebung* of unreflected, totemic religion. It spells out solidarity as the *telos* of society (Tarot, 1999).

The socio-ontological dualism between individual and society is synthetically solved by organic solidarity. This type of solidarity dissolves the discursive, parabolic dualism of the prophets, also recognized by Spinoza, and which crystallized in the envisioning of a double order, immanent and transcendent. Though Durkheim's conception was also Mauss's platform of departure, the latter ended up taking an anti-essentialist and connectivist stance, stressing the relational dimension of solidarity, in its traditional dimension, as a permanent glue to the social bond. Essentialism is a post-Christian and, in many ways, neo-Gnostic syndrome, deliberately missing the nuances and ambivalence of the social bond and opposing an ideally perfect order to the imperfect order of the world. Durkheim was essentialist to the extent that he tried hard to envision an immanent order of society that was invisible to its outer mechanisms. This can be interpreted as a sign of assimilation for an intellectual with a Jewish background.

For Durkheim, religion was as intensely entrenched in the social bond as its secular republican successor, while religion was inherently diffuse for Mauss, and thus not a crucial issue in the theorization of the social bond. Durkheim was post-Christian in this respect, since society and the state replaced the church, while Mauss kept a link with Jewish traditions, and so relativized the centrality, not only of the state, but also of society. The

Durkheimian 'social fact' was, for Mauss, 'total' because it was diffuse and fragmented, and coherence within society was recreated in a piecemeal and visible (not organic and invisible) fashion. Like Bourdieu later, Durkheim jumped from the anthropologically delimited realm of community to modern society, and so bypassed the prophetic stage in the trajectory of constitution of order. Mauss depicted a different story, and underlined the connective dimension of prophetic speech without betraying the secular republican commitment of Durkheim, but in fact by deepening it.

While the Durkheimian model makes the messiah organic to society, the connectivity model can dispense with an accomplished messianism and constructs an altogether different model of secularity. In the connectivity model, the practice of solidarity is always localized, as a lowly institutionalized infrastructure attending to the micro-processes of constituting and reproducing the social bond. It does not need a messianic projection into the future. It is possible that this model does not really attain the level of solidarity intended in a fully modern sense, i.e., as intimately linked to the regulatory mechanisms of the modern state and to the promissory notes of citizenship. If this is the case, Durkheimian sociology is right in pointing out that solidarity, when not mechanic, can only be organic, while connective justice (as an expression of relational, not of organic solidarity) can only be a transitional stage in its development.

Indeed, as highlighted by Talal Asad, as far as the nature of the European state is concerned, Durkheim was right (Asad, 2003). Both Judaism and Islam project connectivity on a universalistic screen and are therefore more than the enemy within: they present global challenges. It is wishful thinking to believe that a secular form of solidarity commensurate with the modern state can be injected into European Islam, such as 'Islam de France'. This kind of secularity (of a Durkheimian type) has yet to be achieved, and will only be attained if Christian notions of the person and the community penetrate Islam, so effecting its de-Islamization. The Wars of Religion and their aftermath have changed these concepts, which means, they have given them other, stronger forms, best reflected in the current human rights discourse. European modernity is, however, still at a post-Christian stage, and isn't yet able to acknowledge cultural diversity and a plurality of traditions.

In this context, the difficult presence of Islam in Europe is not just another problem in dealing with religion in the old continent, but sometimes plays a strategic role in questioning post-Christian notions of secularity and the related notions of solidarity centred on the nation state. This presence has the potential to promote concepts and practices that are not aligned with the post-Christian bias and are thus, at least potentially, more truly universal. This singular misfit of Islam's critical presence in Europe is exemplified by the mistrust with which an iconic representative of Euro-Islam, Tariq Ramadan, is met by many officials and intellectuals in various countries. Euro-Islam is an element that can expose the inherent contradictions and weaknesses of the European secular models that were the product of the Wars of Religion, and the secular arrangements between churches and states going back to the 19th and 20th centuries. Religion becomes a sharply delimited field, a crude essence, only in this historical-political scenario: it becomes the representation of belief via symbols that sometimes compete with and sometimes accommodate the state and its symbols. This constitution of religion as a field is an alternative to one which sees a connectivity of social practices rooted in visions of the world and the hereafter, and in the ideas of justice relating them.

The main Muslim public intellectual in today's Europe is Tariq Ramadan (see Chapter 11 in this volume). He advocates the civic engagement of Muslims in Europe, linking the local, national and transnational levels. The national level of citizenship and solidarity is important, yet part of a wider connection linking the local to the global. This is not uncommon for new social movements. Indeed, Ramadan is also a major, though controversial, leader of the European Social Forum (ESF), the umbrella organization of European groups fighting against neo-liberal globalization (also known as the alter-globalization movement), and the European branch of the World Social Forum, a socio-political movement associated with the slogan 'another world is possible', born out of the Seattle World Trade Organization protests of 1999. It is symptomatic that the episode most closely associated with a distrust of Ramadan was when he tried to claim the same critical public function that he sees now being eroded among European Jewish intellectuals. Amid the escalation of tensions in the Middle East that followed the Anglo-American occupation of Iraq in 2003, Ramadan spoke out in favour of Palestinian rights and against the war in Iraq. In an article provocatively titled 'Critique des (nouveaux) intellectuels communautaires' (Ramadan, 2003), he accused some French thinkers – whom he identified as being of Jewish background (in one case erroneously), and who had vocally supported the Iraq war – of hypocritically endorsing values of justice and freedom in some international crises, while justifying military occupations in other cases (in particular in Palestine and Iraq).

While the discussion of the Islamic veil issue, which was current at the same time, was not part of Ramadan's argument, some of the intellectuals that he criticized, like Alain Finkielkraut and André Glucksmann, had played leading roles in the campaign against the headscarf since its first eruption into public consciousness in 1989, and were generally not known to be enthusiastically

Islamophile (see Amir-Moazami, 2001). The main conceptual arrow in Ramadan's offensive was that these thinkers were trapped in a communitarian logic, and therefore betrayed the key secular republican values of justice and solidarity, especially when these values acquired transnational and global dimensions. A counter-offensive followed from many sides. It ranged from denouncing Ramadan as a member of the Muslim Brotherhood and an al-Qa'ida supporter, to depicting him as an anti-Semite who propagates conspiracy theories in the style of the 'Protocols of the Elders of Zion'.

The main scandal, especially in a country like France, lay in identifying intellectuals by their communitarian belonging, aggravated by the fact that this community was Jewish. This move by Ramadan reflects a sharp competition for European, universalistic and republican credentials, in which he seemed to play the role of an aggressive *parvenu*. Jews and Muslims are certainly competing at the level of secularizing their commitment to the common good – and therefore of modern solidarities – at a European and also at a global level. That the conflicts in the Middle East, and especially the unsolved Palestinian question, exacerbate this competition is obvious to all. Yet there are deeper layers to the story. Euro-Islam is not simply a problem of integration, but an opportunity to reframe older issues and to address deeper contradictions in the European secular model that accommodated Jews only after their almost complete annihilation. Talal Asad, commenting on Joan Wolf's book on the symbolic significance of the Holocaust in France, has observed that post-war France's political rehabilitation crucially depended on a public recognition of Jewish suffering. The result, however, was to minimize Vichy's anti-Semitism and to focus on Islamism, or even Islam, as its substitute (Asad, 2005). If this is true, the problem is with the symbolic pinpointing of the organic–national conceptions of solidarity, usually dependent on a symbolic over-commitment (Tarot, 1999), and not with the mixed forms of critical Euro-Islam. Ramadan intended to break through this blockage and restore Islam's republican credentials, but his move has backfired to a large extent.

The Islamic critical re-articulation of connective justice as relational solidarity in today's Europe

Ramadan's project, which is far from dead but rather still at its fragile beginnings, is to show that Islam in today's Europe re-actualizes Judaism's role as an internal challenge to European Latin-Christian identities, yet possesses a more universalistic orientation. The fact that Muslims in Europe are positioned in a way that is comparable to the Jews between the two world wars emphasizes the potential and dangers of the present situation (Khan, 1994). More generally, from Spinoza's *Tractatus Theologico-Politicus* to Jan Assmann, the Mosaic example has served as a prototype of the construction of a model of solidarity alternative not only to the Greek invention of politics, but also to that problematic synthesis of Jewish and Greek mythologems that is the body of Christ. Assmann was sanguine in judging the notion of salvation brought up by a sequence of Egyptian and Jewish narratives as a primordial vehicle for socialism. Further up the historical trajectory of the Euro-Mediterranean civilization, it is widely acknowledged that Jewish thinking, from the First to the Third International and Zionist socialism to the kibbutzim movement, has been very important to building notions of solidarity. This move from orthodoxy to socialism was justified by pointing out a primordial deficit of Judaism. Yet, as Eisenstadt reminded us in the quotation given before, Islam has no such deficit. The *umma* has, by definition, no ethnic closure. Another difference with Judaism is that while Jewish thinkers had to face Christianity head-on and explicitly (because of the messiah issue), Islam never had such a need. What is disturbing for many observers is that Tariq Ramadan jumps from an Islamic view of connective justice as relational solidarity rooted at a local level, to a post-Islamic view of solidarity that seems to appropriate all of the key attributes of European post-Christian organic solidarity: republican, universalistic, socialist and even secular (almost appearing as a neo-Dreyfusard).

The 'leap', however, is only a leap from the viewpoint of post-Christian European secular republicanism. It is quite in line with modern Islamic reform discourse in the age of colonialism and imperialism. The lesson that Islamic reform wanted to teach was that Islam could recover, and be fully Islamic, if it became European enough (in the sense of making explicit, rediscovering and developing its alleged commitment to rationality, universalism and solidarity). The Muslim discovery of Europe as a frontier of rationality is reflected in the literature of Muslim travellers, most of them scholars, from the 18th century and especially the 19th century, from the Maghreb and the Ottoman Empire. This Islamic discovery of Europe is nowadays echoed, multiplied and magnified by many Muslim leaders living, and often born, in Europe. The admiration of the continuous development of the machine of solidarity of the modern state was one of the main elements of the Muslim experience of Europe in colonial times. Solidarity was even more a key idea than the more problematic development of democracy. In other words, it was understood as socialism. The Arab nationalist idea of Islam as a pristine form of socialism and Muhammad as a social reformer stems from this historic experience. It was not a mere ideological construction of the post-colonial era for the sake of legitimizing new elites. Assmann himself, when talking about the traditional notion of connective justice, uses the word socialism explicitly and provocatively, and stresses its genealogical affiliation to ancient Egypt and biblical Israel, and not to Athens and the philosophical tradition.

Yet the link between Islam and the nation state was highly problematic from the very beginning of the Islamic reform discourse, unlike the situation in Europe, where it was an heterodox crystallization of the notion of the body of Christ (Voegelin, 1999; Gauchet, 1997 [1985]). Muslim reformers showed elements of weakness and strength as they coped with the modernity of nation states. The weakness was due to a defective sociology, residing in the lack of an endogenous concept of the organic character of the social bond (see, however, Farag, 2001). The strength was rooted in their capacity to imagine a broader form of solidarity, and so to maintain a critical perspective towards the negative aspects of solidarity in the nation state form, especially and concretely in a colonial setting.

In today's Europe, the episode of Tariq Ramadan's argument with the Jewish thinkers is indicative of a problem with the grammar of solidarity which is particularly acute in the French context, but not exclusive to it: good solidarity is associated with republican citizenship, while bad solidarity is situated outside of citizenship and suspected of a 'communitarian' closure. An ingrained diffidence towards the Islamic model evidences a problem with European sociology in general and the sociology of religion in particular (Salvatore, 2007). Solidarity became the crucial notion of the social with Durkheim, and through it religion was reconceived in a reductionist way as the primordial engine of solidarity. If we remember the model of connective justice of Assmann, which is also a Spinozian model to a large extent, the difference with Durkheim and the mainstream European sociology is in the elimination of the connective third element, and so the immanentization of justice and solidarity into an organic social being called either 'state' (Hobbes's *Leviathan*) or 'society', or indeed embodied in the state–society nexus. Here, organicity contradicts and even negates connectivity. You can have either one or the other.

The main dilemma for Tariq Ramadan is how to legitimize his critical Euro-Islamic project by buying into the organicity parlance of European republican citizenship, yet starting from a connectivity model: in doing so he raises the suspicion of promoting a communitarian approach. Another problem is how to fully invest into the high connectivity of an Islamic *umma* whose structures of solidarity are strongly imaginative and lowly institutionalized, and thus opaque to the mechanisms of surveillance of modern states and transnational agencies.

69

Misunderstandings of, and diffidence towards, Ramadan are therefore the symptoms of a more general problem with Islam in Europe. The main problem can be identified with the fact that his approach, variously indebted to modern currents of Islamic reform, is still strongly permeated with connectivity. When organicity surfaces in his discourse, it is played out rhetorically, maybe even not very consciously and aptly, thus creating the suspicion of 'double talk', of paying lip-service to European secular republican values. Interestingly, the leap from connectivity to organicity (as from a micro-model to a macro-model of solidarity) was successful for many Jewish thinkers in the modern era, since they did not have a global *umma* but a scattered diaspora to refer to. Spinoza, himself a second generation migrant, in order to qualify as a truly European thinker and shed the suspicion of 'communitarianism', promoted a *res publica* based on the power of the multitudes. This was not a blank cheque to the rising state, and, therefore, configured a project still indebted to a connectivity model.

It would be ungenerous to reproach Ramadan for not being a new Spinoza. Yet instead of invoking the tradition of Islamic reform and appropriating – no doubt, in my view, with conviction – the vocabulary of republican citizenship, he could enlarge his own bounds of reference to include a political philosophy of connectivity that is larger and stronger, in Europe itself, than Islamic reform. This would not require abandoning a commitment to the Islamic *umma*, which fits well into the connectivity model. This would also be a better way to preserve the autonomy of the individual sphere and immunize his project against the totalitarianism of modern, sectarian, political religions.

For sure, in the exchange of accusations between Tariq Ramadan and the French Jewish thinkers there were several layers of tensions involved in invoking configurations of solidarity in Europe situated between religious and secular, connective and organic models. Ramadan felt confident in displaying his republican credentials and exposing the communitarianism of his antagonists, as traitors to their claimed intellectual cause. Yet Judaism has been – at the price of the Holocaust – well integrated in the European solidarity consensus, whereas Islam hasn't yet, and the task is even harder for Islam due to its stronger universalistic projection that configures a feared global challenge. This challenge is even greater, to the extent it will be able to show a democratic and even socialist vocation: in other words, to the extent that it can become an attractive alternative at the global level.

However, the condition for valuing the contribution of Ramadan and other Euro-Islamic intellectuals is that the legitimacy of their critique should not be pre-emptively neutralized by accusations of split loyalty and double-talk. The fragile emergence of a Euro-Islamic public sphere reflects a perspective that is internal to the European quandaries of secularity, yet allows for a duplication of angles. The older immanent critique of secular modernity has intrinsic limits, for it is built on the same postulates of the essential, yet post-Christian, secularity of modern power.

A certain duplication of perspectives was also the strength of the Jewish-European critical sociological approach, and so is useful and even necessary nowadays in order to avoid a pre-emptive culturalization of the meaning of secularity. It gives attention not just to the power relations between state authorities and religious groups, but to the metamorphosed notion of power that secularity incorporates. Without such packaged dichotomies as between secularity and religion, or between the privateness of religion and the publicness of religious neutrality, the argument of the critics of Tariq Ramadan falters. This type of argument cannot capture the viewpoint of a reform tradition in Islam whose trajectory since the 19th century has included serious attempts to develop an original commitment to republican universalism, while it also consistently resisted a one-sided definition of secularity.

As in the works of the French commission that at the end of 2003 recommended a ban on all 'ostentatious' religious symbols in state schools (the main target being the Islamic veil), this definition of secularity is a theoretically informed (and theoretically conservative) response to a crisis of republican authority dictated by a state of emergency. The collateral damage effected by this response is visible in a demonization of all social and civic activism inspired by an Islamic commitment. It is interesting that the best critique of such a procedure, as voiced by the Spinozian French philosopher Etienne Balibar, was also stimulated by the conflicting voices of Muslim intellectuals. The pan-European dimension of Tariq Ramadan's discourse exerts a strong appeal on younger Muslim leaders and cadres, but also attracts the hostility of Muslim scholars with post-structuralist leanings (Salih, 2004; Mas, 2004).

Conclusion: Euro-Islam and European sociology

At a theoretical level, it is interesting that the dispute enhances the mobility between internal and external perspectives and facilitates a post-colonial critique of Europe performed in the name of European ideals. The controversy also de-essentializes the functionality of the public sphere itself, and releases it from a one-sided subservience to an uncontested notion of secularity, which covers a one-sided notion of organic solidarity strictly reflecting the interests and procedures of European states. The short-term strictures are further narrowed when an embattled secularity is reaffirmed with sociological blindness by a commission, as in the French case, installed by the state, yet incapable of taking (or unwilling to take) into account the changing modalities of religiously-motivated action. In this situation, Talal Asad's critique is as follows:

if the secularization thesis no longer carries the conviction it once did, this is because the categories of 'politics' and 'religion' turn out to implicate each other more profoundly than we thought. (Asad, 2003, 201)

As also noted by Balibar, the frequent astonishment among observers that 'politics' and 'religion' do not evolve along the institutional lines of the separation of state and church is seldom turned into a reasoned acceptance of the increasing level of complexity and overlapping in their relations. It is more often rigidly applied to a dogmatic re-affirmation of their normative distinction (Balibar, 2004).

Indeed, it is thanks to this post-colonial rigidity that, by way of reaction, a Euro-Islamic discourse on solidarity is now coming into being. Pace all European classics on the sociology of religion, the transformations of religion do not easily fit into an evolutionist trajectory. At best, the movement looks more like a spiral. This shows that far from being mutually functional, secularity and organic solidarity within European modernity can be in a reciprocal tension, and their tense relationship is subject to critique and also to unpredictable transformations.

This predicament encourages several actors and observers to develop a constructively critical attitude to the dominant framing of secularity and to the patterns of solidarity that support it. It is through questioning the unquestioned authority of secularity that a chance for its renewal, which might relaunch the relational dimension of solidarity, is emerging. Increasingly, key Muslim actors in Europe appear ready to tackle such nodes. These attempts presently face the daunting task of striking a balance between the needed reconstruction and democratization of tradition, on the one hand, and the necessity to tune the arguments into the institutional concerns of a European republican framework placed under increasing strain, not least at a global level, on the other.

The provisional conclusion that we can draw is that the potential universalism of Islam has generated a current of proactive socio-political criticism, the asserted goal of which is to reconstruct forms of secular republicanism and solidarity in institutionally compatible ways with the heuristic help of non-totalizing Islamic norms. This process is stimulating and sometimes channelling the critical capacity and civic engagement of new

Muslim subjects. This 'critical Islam' might have a better capacity than critical ideas of Europe to bypass national allegiances, and so to earn the distrust of committed national republicans, while becoming attractive to pan-European institutions. Whatever the conflicts in politics and the conceptual deficits in sociology, Euro-Islamic notions of solidarity have carved a niche and shown a potential to frame in convincing ways the dilemmas of Islam's integration within European societies.

References

Amir-Moazami, S. (2001), 'Hybridity and anti-hybridity: the Islamic headscarf and its opponents in the French public sphere', in A. Salvatore (ed.), *Muslim Traditions and Modern Techniques of Power*, Hamburg, Lit.

Asad, T. (2003), *Formations of the Secular: Christianity, Islam, Modernity*, Stanford, CT, Stanford University Press.

Asad, T. (2005), 'Reflections on laïcité and the public sphere', *Social Science Research Council: Items and Issues*, 5.

Assmann, J. (2000), *Herrschaft und Heil. Politische Theologie in Altägypten, Israel und Europa*, Frankfurt, Fischer.

Balibar, E. (2004), 'Dissonanzen in der Laizität' (transl. N. Tietze and M. Bauer), eurozine.com, June 16.

Bellah, R. N. (1970), *Beyond Belief: Essays on Religion in a Post-traditional World*, New York, Harper & Row.

Buber, M. (1992), *On Intersubjectivity and Cultural Creativity* (ed. and with an introduction by S. N. Eisenstadt), Chicago, University of Chicago Press.

Eisenstadt, S. N. (2002), 'Concluding remarks: public sphere, civil society, and political dynamics in Islamic societies', in M. Hoexter, S. N. Eisenstadt and N. Levtzion (eds), *The Public Sphere in Muslim Societies*, Albany, NY, SUNY Press, 139–161.

Farag, I. (2001), 'Private lives, public affairs: the uses of *adab*', in A. Salvatore (ed.), *Muslim Traditions and Modern Techniques of Power. Yearbook of the Sociology of Islam*, Hamburg, Lit, 95–122.

Gauchet, M. (1997 [1985]), *The Disenchantment of the World: A Political History of Religion* (transl. O. Burge), Princeton, NJ, Princeton University Press.

Khan, M. R. (1994), 'From Hegel to genocide in Bosnia: some moral and philosophical concerns', *Journal of the Institute of Muslim Minority Affairs*, 15, 1–2.

Mas, R. (2004), 'Love as difference: the politics of love in the thought of Malek Chebel', *European Review of History/Revue Europeénne d'Histoire*, 11, 2.

Ramadan, T. (2003), 'Critique des (nouveaux) intellectuels communautaires', oumma.com, October 8.

Salih, R. (2004), 'The backward and the new: national, transnational and post-national Islam in Europe', *Journal of Ethnic and Migration Studies*, 30, 5.

Salvatore, A. (2005), 'The Euro-Islamic roots of secularity: a difficult equation', *Asian Journal of Social Science*, 33, 3.

Salvatore, A. (2007), *The Public Sphere: Liberal Modernity, Catholicism, Islam*, New York, Palgrave Macmillan.

Tarot, C. (1999), *De Durkheim à Mauss: l'invention du symbolique*, Paris, La Découverte.

Voegelin, E. (1999), 'The history of political ideas, volume VII: the new order and last orientation', in J. Gebhardt and T. A. Hollweck (eds), *The Collected Works of Eric Voegelin*, Volume 25, Columbia, MO, University of Missouri Press.

Walzer, M. (1996), 'Politik und Religion in der jüdischen Tradition', in O. Kallscheuer (ed.), *Das Europa der Religionen. Ein Kontinent zwischen Säkularisierung und Fundamentalismus*, Frankfurt, Fischer, 121–140.

5 Who Needs Solidarity?

William Outhwaite

It is not difficult to identify what should be the core values of a party that belongs to the family of modern European social democracy. Top of anyone's list must come solidarity – the principle that the strength of a society is measured by the extent that its rich members support vulnerable fellow citizens. Next comes the commitment to humanitarian rather than commercial priorities, and its corollary that the market should be managed to meet people's needs rather than the people harnessed to serve the market. (Robin Cook, *Guardian*, February 4 2005)

[European integration] ... is not world peace, not disarmament and not enervation, but it is conflict reduction, economy of effort and solidaristic civilisation. (Walther Rathenau, cited in Beck, 1997)

'Solidarity', like 'society', is one of those terms that some social thinkers make central to their analysis, while others barely use it.[1] In the case of solidarity, these differences are particularly striking in the discourses around social welfare with which this chapter is principally concerned. I shall also examine the use of the term in the socialist tradition and, in particular, in the social philosophy of Jürgen Habermas. I shall suggest that, like 'society', 'solidarity' is a valuable conceptual resource for social and political theory and practice.

The term solidarity is a central element of the Marxist and, more broadly, socialist tradition. Eduard Bernstein, for example, gave solidarity a particularly prominent place, making it a precondition for the socialist pursuit

---

1 For a critical overview of uses of the term 'society', see Outhwaite, 2006. The present chapter is informed by my earlier work with Larry Ray, in which I learned from him that I had been much too quick to assume the unproblematic centrality of the term 'solidarity' to the discussion of social order and welfare (see Outhwaite and Ray, 2005, Chapter 3). I am grateful to Larry Ray, John Holmwood and Nathalie Karagiannis for their advice on the present chapter. Translations are my own except where otherwise indicated.

of equality and freedom (Münkler, 2004, 15). It was also central to the work of Emile Durkheim, who established its use in the late 19th century as a theoretical category of the emergent discipline of sociology. Writing against the background of a political doctrine known as solidarism,[2] which dominated French political thinking in the second half of the 19th century (Zeldin, 1973, Chapter 21), Durkheim devoted his first major work, *The Division of Labour in Society* (1984 [1893]), to an ambitious contrast between the 'mechanical solidarity' of simple societies, based on their homogeneity, and the organic solidarity of more complex and differentiated societies, based on the mutual dependence of individuals.

Durkheim differed from orthodox economic theory, Herbert Spencer's sociology and Hayek's later notion of catallaxy in arguing that this solidarity was not an automatic product of self-legitimating commercial exchanges. Rather, it was grounded in deeper moral sentiments and ties reaching 'far beyond the short moments during which exchange is made' (Durkheim, 1984 [1893], 227; Ray, 1999, 97; Crow, 2002,12ff.). Durkheim's main interest was to develop this view against utilitarian and contract theories (such as Spencer's) on the one hand, and Marxist materialism on the other. Solidarism was connected in complicated ways to the politics of mutual aid, friendly societies and what became the welfare state (Flora, 1981, 363).

There is, then, a broad concept of social solidarity, which makes it equivalent to an answer to the question: 'How is society or social order possible?'. The Durkheimian tradition, influenced by late-19th century solidarism, claims that it is central, while an economistic tradition says it is not. In his lectures on social solidarity at Bordeaux in 1887, Durkheim described the problem of sociology as being: 'What are the bonds that unite men to one another, that so to speak determine the formation of social aggregates?'[3] Sociologists have subsequently learned from David Lockwood's path-breaking article of 1964 to conceptualize this issue in terms of social-versus-system integration. In Lockwood's *Solidarity and Schism* (1992), which is concerned with the problem of social order in the work of Durkheim and Marx, solidarity represents the limit case 'where there is widespread conformity with, and internalization of, the normative expectations attaching to the roles making up institutions' (Lockwood, 1992, 12).[4]

---

2 Solidarism advocated state intervention, social legislation and voluntary associations to create a middle way between laissez-faire liberalism and revolutionary socialism. Durkheim shared the desire for social solidarity, but believed in more thorough social reconstruction than voluntary associations (Lukes, 1973, 350–354).

3 'Introduction à la sociologie de la famille', quoted by Howard Andrews, 1993, 116.

4 He later cites de Grazia (1948, 4), for whom '*solidarité* … [is] … the expression Durkheim used

Claus Offe (2000), at the beginning of a rather pessimistic analysis of the state of contemporary post-communst societies, provides a similarly broad account of solidarity as a global feature of well-functioning societies:

> The 'horizontal' phenomena of trust and solidarity (linking citizens to each other) are preconditions for the 'vertical' phenomenon of the establishment and continued existence of state authority, manifested in effectively ensuring the performance of civic duties. In simple terms, this means that before citizens can recognize the authority of the state, they must first mutually recognize each other as being motivated by – and hence reciprocally worthy of – trust and solidarity. It is precisely when this abstract but resilient trust in 'everyone else' as the collective co-author of the obligating norms is undermined, or when citizens' active interest in each other's wellbeing is successfully discredited, that liberal notions about curtailing the scope of the state's authority flourish. Trust in one's fellow citizens provides the cognitive and moral foundations for *democracy*, the risks of which no one would reasonably accept otherwise. The solidarity citizens feel toward one another, or to which they allow themselves to be obligated through their representative institutions, is the moral basis of the *welfare state*. Thus, both democracy and the welfare state are dependent upon the prior existence of binding motives, which in turn are tied to the form of political integration found in the nation state.[5]

Some commentators, like Offe, would see solidarity as the source and animating spirit of the European welfare state or, more broadly, social model. For Hartmut Kaelble, in Kaelble and Schmid (2004, 40–41):

to designate the perfect integration of a society with clear-cut values that define the status of each member of the community'(Lockwood, 1992, 66n.). Lockwood suggests, following Parsons, that Durkheim's conception of organic solidarity is '... unacceptable, because the fact of the interdependence of functions, from which the moral rules regulating this interdependence are supposed spontaneously to arise, is in itself just as likely to eventuate in conflict as in solidarity'. In particular, it may give rise, à la Marx, to conflict between opposed classes solidaristic only within themselves.

5 See also Chapter 7 in this volume, in which Offe presents a more cautious analysis of solidaristic thought and action and of its embodiment in national and transnational institutions. Offe's pessimistic assessment, formulated at the beginning of the 1990s – but which many, including perhaps its author, would still advance – sees a situation characterized by the weakness of social democratic political forces on the one hand, and on the other an 'associational wilderness which ... must today be described as a pluralist-syndicalist-populist hybrid that is a far cry from Western European patterns.' Such conditions, Offe (1996, 240–241) points out, form 'the worst possible structural background for the emergence of social policies and social policy institutions'. In a somewhat less negative vein, Graham Crow (2002), whose book on social solidarities includes a useful discussion of Solidarność in Poland, looks comparatively at the problems of social solidarity in what he calls 'unsettled societies', including those in post-Communist Europe.

Through the development of the modern welfare state the European national state acquired a new source of legitimation. There arose new duties for citizens, contributions (*Solidarbeiträge*) for social insurance, as well as new citizen rights to the services provided by the welfare state. In this way a national solidarity was established between the economically active and the old, between the well and the sick, between those at work and the unemployed... The welfare state stabilized the then discredited national states in the second half of the 20th century, in a way which could hardly have been imagined half a century ago.

Tony Judt (2005, 360) gives a similar account:

The 1960s saw the apogee of the European state. The relation of the citizen to the state in Western Europe in the course of the previous century had been a shifting compromise between military needs and political claims: the modern rights of newly enfranchised citizens offset by older obligations to defend the realm. But since 1945 that relationship had come increasingly to be characterized by a dense tissue of social benefits and economic strategies in which it was the state that served its subjects, rather than the other way around.

Joe Weiler (2002, 569–570) is one of many commentators who glosses this development in terms of solidarity: 'Europe prides itself on a tradition of social solidarity which found political and legal expression in the post-war welfare state.'[6]

Others, however, would see state-supported welfare policy as a *substitute* for solidarity, as much as it is a substitute for uncoordinated acts of private charity. More technical and policy-oriented discussions of the welfare state tend to avoid the term solidarity, while a third group of more reflective commentators often use it as a way of marking out certain forms of welfare state from others. The historian Peter Baldwin (1990), discussed in more detail below, differentiates between 'solidaristic' welfare systems, by which he means redistributive, and more limited welfare systems, while Walter Streeck (1999) conceptualizes the European Union's developing social model as 'productivist-competitive solidarity'.[7]

Behind these discussions, then, there is a broader question about how far

---

6 He goes on to say that 'the consensus around the classical welfare state is no longer as solid as before'.

7 In a rather different vein, Bo Rothstein (2001, 223, 226) uses the term 'solidaristic' to describe the behaviour of those who contribute to or use benefits; here it means something like refraining from free-riding (in the former case) or from fraud (in the latter). See also Bayertz, 1998, 44.

welfare is seen to be the result of market relations,[8] state intervention or more informal and solidaristic practices at the societal level (Wolfe, 1989). As Jürgen Habermas (2004, 227) puts it in a recent informal contribution, 'the changing form of societal solidarity since the late 18th century is a concomitant to the extension of the markets of territorial states and the increasing density of the organizational operations of the bureaucratic state'.

The European welfare state, from its beginnings in the late 19th century, had been in large part an oblique answer to 'the social question', responding to political demands for democracy and/or socialism with the consolation prize of welfare regimes. Bismarck's social legislation of the 1880s was initiated in the middle of a twenty-year period during which the socialist party was banned. In democratic France, in the aftermath of the 1848 revolutions, conflicts such as that over the 'right to work' pointed up potential challenges to the state. Tocqueville pointed out that this would mean, if taken seriously, that the state either itself should become an employer or that it should impose rigid controls on independent entrepreneurs (Donzelot, 1984, 44). The question, then, for France, was how to give rights to those whose social conditions did not match their political status, 'without these rights giving them rights against the state' (Donzelot, 1984, 71). As Jacques Donzelot argues, it was the rise of the social sector, with social legislation, an ideology of solidarity and an institutionalized practice of negotiation, which answered these dilemmas. Similarly in Britain, the more protracted development of social policy legislation, from the restriction of night work for children in 1802 to the fully-fledged post-Second World War welfare state, was in part a response to the challenge of radical democrats inspired by the French Revolution or, later, socialist voters radicalized by the two world wars. 'Initially, the policy of integration was directed exclusively at the working class, whose militancy against the system was to be restrained and channelled...' (Flora, 1981, 343). In France, in particular, 'solidarity' has been the organizing slogan for social policy, and to some extent for state ideology as a whole, from the late 19th century to the present[9].

The French political scientist Pierre Rosenvallon, whose book on the crisis of the welfare state was a fundamental contribution to discussion in the 1980s, continues to frame the issues in terms of solidarity. Foreshadowed by Leibniz at the end of the 17th century, the principle of social insurance, 'acting as a

---

8   Johannes Berger (2004) is a recent advocate of the primacy of markets, suggesting that excessive solidarity may be a source of instability. See below.

9   This is marked, for example, in the current title of the 'Ministère des affaires sociales, du travail et de la solidarité'. The term is also invoked in the constitutions of, for example, several states in Eastern Germany since 1990 (Thumfart, 2002, 104).

sort of invisible hand of solidarity', becomes in the late 18th and 19th centuries another way of conceptualizing the 'social bond', along with contract and the market (Rosenvallon, 1995, 19). Over time, the notion of insurance is superseded by more explicitly solidaristic forms of welfare provision (Rosenvallon, 1995, 45, 49), culminating in recent attempts in Europe to act directly on the social relations of individuals through programmes encouraging self-reliance, healthy living, 'family preservation' and so on. Here, the solidarity represented by the state complements, incorporates and acts through 'local and family solidarities' (Rosenvallon, 1995, 215–216). For Rosenvallon (1995, 223), this demands a rethinking of politics: 'Only a deeper vision of democracy and a clear redefinition of the reforming idea can give birth to a renewed practice of solidarity'.

In Rosenvallon's analysis, then, a political conception of the welfare state goes alongside a more technical or institutional one.

> ... there are two possible histories of the welfare state. The first is an institutional history, based on the analysis of the application of insurance techniques to the social policy domain and on their extension. The second is a philosophical history, articulated around the notion of citizenship, establishing a relation between social rights and the debt which the State enters into with individuals. (Rosenvallon, 1995, 49).

While it is fairly clear what Rosenvallon understands by solidarity, it is interesting that the only explicit definition he provides is one formulated in terms of practice rather than sentiment:

> One can define solidarity very schematically as a form of compensation for differences. It is therefore characterized by the positive act of sharing (Rosenvallon, 1995, 56–57).

Fine, one might say, but what is explicitly solidaristic in this process of redistribution, especially if it is, as he assumes, coordinated by the state? Would not utilitarianism and the principle of marginal utility underwrite such a policy – not to mention the sort of concerns for the healthy state of the 'nation' or 'Volk' that tended to motivate social policy innovations in the late 19th and early 20th centuries?

It is considerations of this kind that Peter Baldwin (1990) makes the focus of his detailed comparison of welfare systems in five European countries from 1875 to 1975:

> Not all, in fact very little, social policy has been solidaristic. Welfare states have varied much in this respect. Where their nature was determined by

elites who were still persuaded that self-reliance was feasible, redistribution was restricted. (Baldwin, 1990, 21)

The welfare state raised the possibility of equality in the real terms of risk redistribution, the possibility of solidarity. Only some welfare states have gone significantly beyond the levels of social policy necessitated by economic optimality and basic political legitimacy to achieve a degree of redistribution that speaks as much to the needs of the least fortunate as to the fears of the better-off. How such solidarity was possible is the concern of this book. (Baldwin, 1990, 7)[10]

Solidarity, for Baldwin, is attributed to policies rather than to individual or collective sentiments.

Solidarity – the group's decision to allocate resources by need – is only misleadingly analogous to altruism. An individual sentiment, altruism is generally confined to narrow circles of the like-minded. Solidarity, in those few instances where it has been realized, has been the outcome of a generalized and reciprocal self-interest. Not ethics, but politics explain it. (299)

Whether or not Baldwin is right in his explanation of the historical development of what he calls solidaristic welfare states,[11] his book usefully marks out one of the distinctions that I wish to explore here, between solidarity as a sentiment, which may be grounded in sympathy, a kind of *souffrance à distance* (Boltanski, 1993) and/or in a feeling of commonality or 'we'ness,[12] and solidarity as a label for an institutionalized practice.

Even in Durkheim, it may be possible to demonstrate a tension between his conceptions of solidarity. In the original model of the *Division of Labour*, there was already the contrast between the 'warm' solidarity based on

---

10 Baldwin's answer, in a word, is that solidaristic or seriously redistributive welfare policies emerged in Scandinavia and the UK, and much later in France and Germany, where not just the working class but middle class groups came round to the idea. 'In many cases, solidarity – a more inclusive risk community, a wider and fairer spreading of social costs – was realized only when sufficiently powerful social groups among those who, in other respects, were favoured also saw their interests thus to be safeguarded. By themselves, the needy have rarely won significant advantage. Only when risk, redistributive advantage and political clout coincided was solidarity possible.' (42)

11 There is prima facie something odd about defining altruism as an exclusively individual predicate, whereas one might expect it to be at least susceptible to imitation and contagion, if not a more genuinely collective sentiment.

12 One of the most useful explicit definitions of solidarity is by the anthropologist M. Llewelyn-Davies (1978, 206, quoted in Crow, 2002, 6): 'a commitment to some kind of mutual aid or support, based upon the perception, by those who are solidary, that they share certain characteristics, or that they are equal with respect to some social principle'.

similarity, and the cooler organic solidarity based on interdependence. This is reflected in Durkheim's somewhat vague remarks about the changing states of the 'conscience commune'. In his preface to the second edition, he writes at length about an institutional recommendation: the famous occupational corporations. These are of course at the heart of his lectures, first delivered in the 1890s but posthumously published in English as *Professional Ethics and Civic Morals*, in which the term 'solidarity' does not appear. It may seem that in theorizing about social order, institutions increasingly substitute for sentiments in Durkheim's analysis.[13] On the other hand, in this same work, and in other later works, we find him emphasizing the importance of collective sentiments as a common source of conceptions of charity and justice (Durkheim, 1957, 218ff.).

> To us it does not seem equitable that a man should be better treated as a social being because he was born of parentage that is rich or of high rank. But is it any more equitable that he should be better treated because he was born of a father of higher intelligence or in a more favourable moral milieu? It is here that the domain of charity begins. Charity is the feeling of human sympathy that we see becoming clear even of any special merit in gifts or mental capacity acquired by heredity. This, then, is the very acme of justice. It is society, we find, that is coming to exercise complete dominion over nature, to lay down the law for it and to set this moral equality over physical inequality which in fact is inherent in things. (Durkheim, 1957, 220)

A similar conception can be found in a lecture given early in 1914, quoted by Jean-Claude Filloux (1993, 225):

> We aspire to a higher form of justice... All that matters is to feel beneath the moral coldness which reigns upon the surface of our collective life, the sources of warmth which our societies bear within them.

13 One conjecture would be that Durkheim came to see the notion of solidarity as too specific, and suggesting a psychological basis for a social phenomenon in the way he had forbidden in *The Rules of Sociological Method*. As Ceri (1993, 164) writes, 'We have seen how Durkheim upholds the principle of the irrelevance of the content of beliefs. An analogous principle holds for sentiments, whose specific characteristics ... he does not consider relevant. It is not the specific content or reference of sentiments ... that explains behaviour, but their *intensity,* as an expression of the moral state of the group.' This would, however, contrast with the overall development of Durkheim's thought towards the *Elementary Forms of Religious Life,* where the stress is increasingly on representations. (This is what prompted Parsons (1937, 445) to suggest that he had gone 'clean over into idealism'.) Another interpretation would be simply that he felt he had been insufficiently precise: '... since he bases his argument largely on the antithesis between the individual and society, the vehicles of organic solidarity are not dealt with in detail' (Müller, 1993, 100). As Müller points out (107, n.2) Durkheim remedies this deficiency with his preface referring to occupational groups in the second edition of *Division of Labour.*

It is ideas of this kind that led Mike Gane (1992) to speak of 'the radical sociology of Durkheim and Mauss', expressed, for example, in their conception of socialism and professional corporations.[14] For Durkheim, these corporations must

> be genuinely interdependent in two vital senses: they possess a high degree of relative autonomy and internal moral solidarity, but, crucially, coming together within the limits of a real unity. It is only the intervention of the latter which prevents the internal political form of the corporation from degenerating into despotism and the abnormal forms of the division of labour on the one hand, or being incorporated into the state on the other. (Gane, 1992, 149–150)

Hans Joas (1993, 238–239) offers a somewhat similar Habermasian reading of Durkheim, in which the division of labour results from 'a morality of cooperation':

> If ... only just rules fulfil Durkheim's conception of organic solidarity, his concept of the division of labour is intrinsically bound to his notions of justice... Organic solidarity would then be a type of morality which arises in the participants by means of an act of reflection on the universal conditions of their cooperation.

This is an attractive reading, but one which I think makes Durkheim look too much like a pragmatist, whereas for Durkheim the origin of organic solidarity seems to lie in more structural causes, even if it might be given a functional explanation or a philosophical reconstruction along these lines.

Marcel Mauss' socialism was more explicit, and his conception of solidarity correspondingly closer to an orthodox socialist one: 'the trade union and the socialist cooperative are the foundations of the future society'. The Belgian cooperatives were 'an achievement of worker and popular solidarity'.

> ... we must first of all organize the cooperative into an enormous bloc of consumers. When we have succeeded in creating huge cooperative workshops, models of communist production; when we have succeeded in invading the various branches of production in every way ... when we have succeeded in creating, by means of a whole level of institutions of solidarity, a close union between all the members of the workers' cooperatives; when we have succeeded in establishing our relationship with the various workers' organizations ... then we could contemplate organizing ourselves

14 Armando Salvatore (Chapter 4 in this volume) addresses other interesting points of comparison between Durkheim and Mauss.

completely on an international basis: to join ourselves into a federation for administering together wealth which will have become the wealth of a universal proletariat. (Quoted by Gane, 1992, 140–141)

What remains, more broadly, of solidarity in the socialist tradition? The word remains prominent, as in the quotation from the late Robin Cook at the beginning of this chapter, but Cook's depreciation of the market in this quotation puts him outside the New Labour orthodoxy, in which the market is primary and solidarity appears more as an optional extra, present in a muted form as in Giddens' defence of the 'third way': 'Third way politics … aims to empower people: to help citizens plot their way through the major revolutions of our time: globalization, transformations in personal life and our relationship to nature' (Giddens, 1998, 64). And while 'Third way politics should preserve a core concern with social justice' (65), these issues 'are not about social justice, but about how we should live after the decline of tradition and custom, how to recreate social solidarity and how to react to ecological problems.' (67)[15]

On the difficult but, for many, inescapable terrain located between Marxist socialism and third way realism or opportunism, the work of Jürgen Habermas may provide some guidance. An excellent collection of interviews with Habermas, edited by Peter Dews, has the title *Autonomy and Solidarity* (Habermas, 1986). The autonomy theme is of course self-explanatory in Habermas's thought, which is centrally concerned with the autonomous use of reason, but less attention has been paid to the importance of notions of solidarity in his thinking. In no less than three of the interviews (Habermas, 1986, 139, 242), Habermas refers to Walter Benjamin's concept of anamnetic solidarity. In the first of these, dating from 1977, in a section on the relevance of social theory to more individual existential predicaments, he mentions Marxism in passing as promising the prospect of 'forms of life with greater solidarity' before addressing the more Benjaminian theme:

> How can there be universal solidarity with the victims of merciless historical progress, when past crimes, when the sufferings, the humiliations and the misery of past generations, appear irreversible to the secular gaze, and beyond redress? Benjamin, groping for response to the horror of all this, developed the idea of anamnetic solidarity, which could bring about atonement solely through the power of remembrance.

15 Cf. Anheier and Freise (2004, 123): 'In the Third Way the shaping of politics is no longer the sole responsibility of the state, but is shared with other institutions: the citizenry, voluntary organizations and the interests of the economy.'

Solidarity in this rather speculative sense is clearly an important element of Habermas's thinking, and relates to biographical issues interestingly addressed by Charles Turner (2004). More directly relevant to the concerns of this chapter, a lecture from 1984, reprinted in *Erläuterungen zur Diskursethik* though not in the English version, *Justification and Application*, has the title 'Justice and Solidarity: On the Discussion of <Stage 6>' (Habermas, 1991). This somewhat coded title refers to the psychologist Lawrence Kohlberg's model of moral development, in which individuals advance from conventional to more reflective conceptions. [16] Habermas was attracted by Kohlberg's idea of a complementary relationship between the psychological claim that 'individuals prefer the highest stage of reasoning they comprehend, a claim supported by research' and the 'philosophical claim that a later stage is "objectively" preferable or more adequate by certain moral criteria'; this view of the interrelationship between philosophy and science is one which Habermas himself has advanced at various times. However, he concedes that even if empirical psychology restricts the choice of acceptable moral theories to those which are consistent with the psychological evidence, the choice between competing ethics 'has to be settled with another kind of argument'.

The problem can be avoided, Habermas suggests, by treating the moral reasoning of post-conventional subjects as on a level with the metatheoretical disagreements of moral philosophers: the oppositions between utilitarianism, contract theory, and so on. In relation to Stage 6, Habermas argues that an ethics of justice, criticized, as it has been, for sharing 'the narrow perspective of the civil intercourse of bourgeois subjects of private law' (Habermas, 1991, 62), needs to be augmented not, as Rawls had suggested, with benevolence or other aspects of private morality, but by solidarity, where justice and solidarity are seen not as two complementary moments but as 'two aspects of the same thing' (70).

> From a communication-theoretical perspective there is ... a close connection between concern for the good of one's neighbour and an interest in the common good: the identity of the group reproduces itself

16 Habermas adds a Stage 7 to Kohlberg's six-stage model (Habermas, 1991, 90). Kohlberg's Stage 6 focuses on individual conscience, whereas in Habermas's Stage 7, 'the principle of justification of norms is no longer the monologically applicable principle of generalizability, but the communally followed procedure of redeeming normative validity claims discursively.' Stages 5–6 are post-conventional, but incompletely so, in that they postulate conceptions of utility (Stage 5) and principles and duties (Stage 6), which themselves have to be relativized against one another in Stage 7, where concrete moral dilemmas flow naturally into meta-ethical discourses about conflicting fundamental principles.

by means of intact relations of reciprocal recognition. Thus the complementary perspective to individual equal treatment is not benevolence but solidarity...

Justice refers to the equal freedoms of unrepresentable and self-determining individuals, whereas *solidarity* refers to the good of the consociates (*Genossen*) united in an intersubjectively shared form of life – and therefore to the preservation of the integrity of this form of life itself...

As a component of a universalistic morality, solidarity loses its merely particular meaning, limited to the internal relations of a collective which closes itself off ethnocentrically from other groups... Post-conventionally conceived justice can only converge with solidarity as its other when this is transformed in the light of the idea of a universal collective process of will formation...

It is above all in the reciprocal recognition of accountable subjects, who orient their action to validity claims, that that the ideas of justice and solidarity become actual (*gegenwärtig*). But these normative obligations do not *of themselves* extend beyond the boundaries of a concrete lifeworld of family, tribe, town or nation. These limits can only be broken through in discourses, so far as these are institutionalized in modern societies. (Habermas, 1991, 71)

This passage prefigures much of Habermas's subsequent formal work on morality, law and democracy and their subsequent extension to a cosmopolitan or post-national scale. In his Tanner Lectures on Human Values, delivered in 1986 and entitled 'Law and Morality', he addressed the underlying question of how legal forms of state authority can be legitimate. It is not, he stressed, a matter of just extending morality into law or complementing it with law in order to give it teeth. Rather, law and morality must be treated as two aspects of the same principles, in both sociological and philosophical or logical terms.

The tension between facticity and validity in legal discourse and practice, Habermas (1992, xlii) believes, is ultimately resolved through democracy: the idea 'that in the sign of a fully secularized politics the constitutional state cannot exist or be preserved without radical democracy'. However, this tension continues to be reflected in an ambiguous social context, characterized by the following.

- The eclipse of socialism, both as a concrete political project and (in Habermas's preferred broader formulation) as representing the democratic self-organization of a legally constituted community (*Rechtsgemeinschaft*).

- A triumphalist capitalism, which endangers the social solidarity expressed inter alia in law (Habermas, 1992, 33–34).
- The complexity of modern societies, with the result that models of state and society have become problematic (Habermas, 1992, 1).

Thus modern law, which treats the *addressees* of law as also its *originators*, can be seen in ideal terms as living off and reinforcing 'a solidarity concentrated in the role of the citizen and [which] ultimately derives from communicative action' (Habermas, 1992, 33; translation modified to fit the original).

Habermas recognizes, though perhaps not quite as fully as we might wish, that in offering this analysis he is engaged in a delicate balancing act. More importantly, modern societies are also doing this. On the one hand, there is the expansion of communicative action, human rights discourse and democracy; on the other, there is the degradation of natural environments, welfare states and political debate. This matters particularly to Habermas's analysis, because it relies on the mutual support of law, morality, democracy, public opinion, civil society and so on, without a mechanism for weaknesses in one area being compensated for by strengths in another. All this indicates a further tension between universalistic principles and realms of discourse which, in the case of moral discourse, point towards a community of world citizens, and the sense that these can only be articulated and made real in bounded constitutional states.

In the preface to *The Inclusion of the Other*, Habermas declares his

interest in the question of what conclusions can still be drawn from the universalistic content of republican principles, in particular for pluralistic societies in which multicultural conflicts are becoming more acute, for nation states that are coalescing into supranational units, and for the citizens of a world society who have been drawn unbeknownst to themselves into an involuntary risk society.[17]

Conclusion

We are left, then, with something like the following list of partially overlapping and partially conflicting usages of the term 'solidarity'. The letters denote relations of opposition on the same issue.

1a) Solidarity is a fundamental condition of social order (Durkheim, Offe).

---

17 This development in Habermas's more recent work is discussed elsewhere in this volume by Nathalie Karagiannis.

1b) Solidarity is either unnecessary to, or is a by-product of, self-legitimating market exchanges (Spencer, economic theory, Hayek).

1c) Solidarity is an ideal limit case of social order (Lockwood).

2a) Solidarity is the fundamental source or animating spirit of welfare policies (Kaelble).

2b) Solidarity, like charity, is rendered unnecessary by welfare policies in differentiated modern societies.

2c) Solidarity accompanies or animates some, but not all, social welfare policies (Baldwin).

3a) Solidarity is fundamental to class action (most Marxism, Habermas).

3b) Solidarity is irrelevant to, or a by-product of, class action, which should instead be explained in terms of individual rationality (rational choice Marxism).

4a) Solidarity refers to practices of various kinds.

4b) Solidarity refers to orientations of various kinds.

To this list, one might add a useful distinction introduced by Lindenberg (1998) between strong and weak solidarities, in which primacy is given to collective and individual interests respectively. Weak solidarities have something conditional about them: they operate within limits such as 10 per cent for 'tithing' or 0.7 per cent of gross national product for development aid.

'Solidarity' is, then, poised between a generalized sentiment, something like altruism though more specific, and a set of redistributive or insurance-like practices. These may, however, be linked. The variable geometry of solidarity may in fact be seen as a virtue, in that it can be used to bridge the gap between sentiment and action, specificity and diffuseness. I can feel solidarity with a close friend or colleague, but also with distant earthquake victims, for whom the practical expression of my solidarity is likely to be highly mediated. This flexibility in the concept of solidarity will indeed be particularly advantageous in cases of transnational solidarity, such as that across the boundaries of European states, where the conventional ideological and factual (e.g. fiscal) reinforcements may be lacking. I cannot plausibly demand that support paid for by my taxes go only to residents of my own neighbourhood, but I might join a pressure group against the extension of transfer payments to poorer parts of the EU or against an increase in development aid. The failure of the EU properly to Europeanize social policy is no doubt substantially driven by a fear that large numbers of citizens might indeed resist such initiatives.[18] The

18 There is some worrying, though controversial, evidence that even ethnic, linguistic or cultural diversity within a single state may have a negative impact on levels of welfare spending; see van

replication of even a rather cold, Bismarckian welfare state on a European level seems both essential and unlikely – unless, that is, it achieves the mobilization of bias in the same way that the Common Agricultural Policy, substantially supported by farmers, was grudgingly accepted by urban Europeans. In Fritz Scharpf's view, a Europeanization of social policy is unfeasible, and the best alternative is a legal framework setting minimum standards for member states (Scharpf, 2002).

This is, of course, to assume that solidarity, even if intangible, is important. An alternative view would be that systematically interlinked mechanisms that secure the same outcome are what counts, just as markets may be understood as more or less closely simulating genuinely social production for socially agreed needs via the operation of the individual profit motive. System integration, in other words, matters more than social integration. Many aspects of the development of modern societies may be seen to support this latter view. On the other hand, there are also increasing demands for what Habermas would call communicative justification of societal policies. As Habermas (2004, 228) notes, conflicts of interest over questions such as 'health reform or immigration policy, the Iraq war or military conscription, are debated more in the light of principles of justice than with reference to the fate of the nation'.

Is it, then, useful to think in terms of a single notion of solidarity, stretching from vaguely sympathetic individual sentiment to institutionalized arrangements such as the tax levy (*Solidarbeitrag*) following German reunification? I think it is, and the variable geometry of the concept fits a reality in which the scope and bearers of solidaristic sentiments and practices are increasingly diverse and unpredictable.

Societies need solidarity, though not in quite the form envisaged by Durkheim, by North American normative functionalism, or by nationalism and its racist and religious avatars.[19] Welfare states need solidarity if they are to be effective and to respond to legitimation deficits, especially in a multicultural and transnational context. Even markets may need a degree of lubrication by solidarity, whether or not they contribute to it or substitute for

---

Parijs, 2004. The European Union, like the national states that gave birth to it, started off as, and is still, an elite project marked by a democratic deficit; it remains to be seen whether it can grow the sort of roots that national states were able to stimulate or simulate through banal (Billig, 1995) and not-so-banal nationalism.

19 As Kaufmann (2004, 67) puts it, the fact that national identity has lost its exclusive claim 'is less a loss of solidarity than a proliferation of horizons of solidarity: these raise problems for the conventional conception of the state and enable its inhabitants to refer to different identities and thereby to legitimate different strategies of action.'

it.[20] Most importantly, people need the solidarity provided (in principle) by life in society, for the essentially Aristotelian reason that this is how we are: we are not beasts (or, as we would now say, non-human animals) or gods.

To put this another way, modern societies, having developed relatively disembedded market economies and relatively autonomous bureaucratic national states, are again confronted by the inescapable primacy of sociation as a nexus of social and political relations. As Alan Wolfe (1989, 259) suggests, 'It is only because liberal democrats take society for granted that they can even consider relying on the market or the state to structure rules of moral obligation.' Society, or more specifically civil society,[21] may also be able to address dimensions of social integration where markets and states have reached their limits. A globalized economy cannot make whatever contribution to solidarity might be obtained from more localized or national ones.[22] The same goes for welfare states: they either over-stretch the readiness of populations to contribute to the welfare of others, resulting in backlashes against taxation or 'scroungers' (or, in the vigorous Australian expression, 'dole bludgers'), or they under-stretch, and hence undermine this spontaneous readiness to help others (Münkler, 2004, 24–25).[23] Civil society, despite its lack of institutional clout, has a kind of spontaneity and flexibility that may, in favourable circumstances, become a vital source of solidarity.[24] As Wolfe (1989, 261) puts it, in the final paragraph of his book:

> The message that sociology offers modern liberal democrats is neither complacent nor apocalyptic. It is commonsensical: here is society; you have given it to yourselves as a gift; if you do not take care of it, you should not be surprised when you can no longer find it. That message by itself cannot

20 Some Hayekians, especially in post-Communist Europe (Wainwright, 1994), would argue that markets can become a source of solidaristic networks, even if that is not their prime purpose. On the other hand, Johannes Berger (2004, 247), in an otherwise enthusiastic defence of markets as a source of social integration, stops short of attributing solidarity to them: '... markets do have a specific moral quality, but they are not sources of solidarity.' Social integration can, however, in his view, be secured by markets in such a way as to leave societies needing less solidarity: 'In the course of modernization, the need for solidarity probably diminishes' (Berger, 2004, 257).

21 On the relations between these two notions, see Outhwaite, 2006, especially Chapter 7.

22 More generally, as Münkler (2004, 25) points out: 'Where the market comes into play, solidarity is replaced by insurance.'

23 Something of this kind may be seen in the vacuum left by the universalistic Communist welfare systems; see Outhwaite and Ray, 2005, Chapter 3.

24 Cf. Münkler (2004, 25–26): 'Civil society has become the reserve tank for everything which is no longer secured by the functioning of the market, which can only inadequately be secured by the state and which is however not just socially desirable but in principle unavoidable... The rather unconvincing results which this conception has so far achieved suggest that a decisive element has been overlooked: that of *education* to solidarity in civil society.'

tell people how to satisfy their obligations to intimate and distant others simultaneously, but it at least makes it clear that if people themselves do not continue to try to meet those obligations, no one else will do it for them.

References

Andrews, H. F. (1993), 'Durkheim and social morphology' in S. Turner (ed.), *Emile Durkheim: Sociologist and Moralist*, London, Routledge.

Anheier, H. and Freise, M. (2004), 'Der Dritte Sektor im Diskurs des Dritten Weges' in Beckert et al. (eds), 109–25.

Baldwin, P. (1990), *The Politics of Social Solidarity: Class Bases of the European Welfare State 1875–1975*, Cambridge, Cambridge University Press.

Bayertz, K. (ed.) (1998), *Solidarität: Begriff und Problem*, Frankfurt, Suhrkamp.

Beck, U. (1997), 'Mißverstehen als Fortschritt. Europäische Intellektuelle im Zeitalter der Globalisierung'. *Laudatio* for Pierre Bourdieu (Ernst-Bloch-Preis 1997)', http://www.homme-moderne.org/societe/socio/ubeck/laudaD.html

Beckert, J., J. Eckert, M. Kohli and W. Streeck (eds) (2004), *Transnationale Solidarität: Chancen und Grenzen*, Frankfurt/New York, Campus.

Berger, J. (2004), 'Expandierene Märkte, schrumpfende Solidarität?', in Beckert et al. (eds), 246–261.

Billig, M. (1995), *Banal Nationalism*, London, Sage.

Boltanski, L. (1993), *La souffrance à distance*, Paris, Editions Métailié, 1993.

Brunkhorst, H. (2002), *Solidarität: Von der Bürgerfreundschaft zur globalen Rechtsgenossenschaft*, Frankfurt, Suhrkamp.

Ceri, P. (1993), 'Durkheim on social action' in Stephen P. Turner (ed.), *Emile Durkheim: Sociologist and Moralist*, London, Routledge, 139–68.

Crow, G. (2002), *Social Solidarities*, Buckingham, Open University Press.

de Grazia, S. (1948), *The Political Community: A Study of Anomie*, Chicago, University of Chicago Press.

Donzelot, J. (1984), *L'invention du social*, Paris, Fayard.

Durkheim, E. (1984 [1893]), *The Division of Labor in Society*, New York, Free Press/ London, Macmillan.

Durkheim, E. (1957), *Professional Ethics and Civic Morals* (second edition), London, Routledge.

Filloux, J.-C. (1993), 'Inequalities and social stratification in Durkheim's sociology' in Stephen P. Turner (ed.), *Emile Durkheim: Sociologist and Moralist*, London, Routledge, 211–28.

Flora, P. and Heidenheimer, A. J. (eds) (1981), *The Development of Welfare States in Europe and America*, New Brunswick, Canada, Transaction.

Gane, M. (ed.) (1992), *The Radical Sociology of Durkheim and Mauss*, London, Routledge.

Giddens, A. (1998), *The Third Way: The Renewal of Social Democracy*, Cambridge, Polity Press.

Habermas, J. (1986), *Autonomy and Solidarity: Interviews* (ed. Peter Dews), London, Verso.

Habermas, J. (1991), *Erläuterungen zur Diskursethik*, Frankfurt, Suhrkamp.

Habermas, J. (1992), *Between Facts and Norms*, Cambridge, Polity Press.

Habermas, J. (1998), *The Postnational Constellation*, Cambridge, Polity Press.

Habermas, J. (2004), 'Solidarität jenseits des Nationalstaats: Notizen zu einer Diskussion' in Beckert et al. (eds), 225–35.

Joas, H. (1993), 'Emile Durkheim's intellectual development: the problem of the emergence of new morality and new institutions as a leitmotif in Durkheim's oeuvre' in Stephen P. Turner (ed.), *Emile Durkheim: Sociologist and Moralist*, London, Routledge, 229–45.

Judt, T. (2005), *Postwar*, London, Heinemann.

Kaelble, H. and Schmid. G. (2004), *Das europäische Sozialmodell: Auf dem Weg zum transnationalen Sozialstaat*, Berlin, WZB-Jahrbuch.

Kaufmann, F.-X. (2004), 'Sozialstaatliche Solidarität und Umverteilung im internationalen Wettbewerb' in Beckert et al. (eds), 51–72.

Kohli, M. and Novak, M. (2001), *Will Europe Work? Integration, Employment and the Social Order*, London, Routledge.

Lindenberg, S. (1998), 'Solidarity: its microfoundations and macro-dependence. A framing approach' in P. Doreian and T. J. Fararo (eds), *The Problem of Solidarity: Theories and Models*, Amsterdam, Gordon and Breach, 61–112.

Llewelyn-Davies, M. (1978), 'Two contexts of solidarity among pastoral Maasai women' in P. Caplan and J. Bujra (eds), *Women United, Women Divided: Cross-Cultural Perspectives on Female Solidarity*, London, Tavistock.

Lockwood, D. (1964), 'Social integration and system integration' in G.K. Zollschau and W. Hirsch (eds), *Explorations in Social Change*, London, Routledge.

Lockwood, D. (1992), *Solidarity and Schism: The Problem of Disorder in Durkheimian and Marxist Sociology*, Oxford, Clarendon.

Lukes, S. (1973), *Emile Durkheim: His Life and Work*, London, Allen Lane.

Muller, H.-P. (1993), 'Emile Durkheim's political sociology' in Stephen P. Turner (ed.), *Emile Durkheim: Sociologist and Moralist*, London, Routledge, 95–110.

Münkler, H. (2004), 'Enzyklopädie der Ideen der Zukunft: Solidarität' in Beckert et al. (eds), 15–28.

Offe, C. (1996), *Modernity and The State: East and West*, Cambridge, Polity Press.

Offe, C. (2000), 'The democratic welfare state: a European regime under the strain of European integration', *Reihe Politikwissenschaft*, 68.

Outhwaite, W. (2006), *The Future of Society*, Oxford, Blackwell.

Outhwaite, W. and Ray, L. (2005), *Social Theory and Postcommunism*, Oxford, Blackwell.

Parsons, T. (1937), *The Structure of Social Action*, New York, Free Press.

Prior, P. and Sykes, R. (2001), 'Globalization and the European welfare states: evaluating the theories and evidence' in R. Sykes, B. Palier and P. M. Prior (eds), *Globalization and European Welfare States: Challenges and Change*, Basingstoke, Palgrave.

Ray, L. (1999), *Theorizing Classical Sociology*, Buckingham, Open University Press.

Rosenvallon, P. (1995), *La nouvelle question sociale: Repenser l'État-providence*, Paris, Seuil.

Rothstein, B. (2001), 'The future of the universal welfare state: an institutional approach' in S. Kuhnle (ed.), *Survival of the European Welfare State*, London, Routledge, 217–233.

Scharpf, F. (2002), 'The European social model: coping with the challenges of diversity', *Journal of Common Market Studies*, 40, 4.

Sen, A. (2001), 'Global justice: beyond international equity', *polylog*, 3, http://them.polylog.org/3/fsa-en.htm

Streeck, W. (1999), 'Competitive solidarity: rethinking the "European Social Model"', Max Planck Institute for the Study of Societies Working Paper 99/8, Cologne, MPIfG.

Therborn, G. (1986), 'Neo-Marxist, pluralist, corporatist statist theories and the welfare state' in A. Kazancigil (ed.), *The State in Global Perspective*, Aldershot, Gower, 204–231.

Thumfart, A. (2002), *Die politische Integration Ostdeutschlands*, Frankfurt, Suhrkamp.

Turner, C. (2004), 'Jürgen Habermas: European or German?', *European Journal of Political Theory*, 3, 3, 293–314.

van Parijs, P. (2004), *Cultural Diversity versus Economic Solidarity*, Brussels, Deboeck Université Press. Also available at http://www.etes.ucl.ac.be/Francqui/Livre/Livre.htm

Wainwright, H. (1994), *Arguments for a New Left: Answering the Free-market Right*, Oxford, Blackwell.

Weiler, J. (2002), 'A constitution for Europe? Some hard choices', *Journal of Common Market Studies*, 40, 4.

Wolfe, A. (1989), *Whose Keeper? Social Science and Moral Obligation*, Berkeley, CA, University of California Press.

Zeldin, T. (1973), *France 1848–1945, Volume 1: Ambition, Love and Politics*, Oxford, Clarendon Press.

6 The Politics of 'Us': On the Possibility of Solidarity without Substance

Mihnea Panu

This chapter explores the political horizons opened by an ontology[1] that considers that our conceptualizations of solidarity are directly related to our understandings of the others, and thus to the visibility and relevance the events involving those others have for us. I shall start from a general conceptualization of solidarity as 'concern for the wellbeing of the other' and try to suggest that, although an ontology that abandons any attempt to know the 'real' outside the systems of signification might make a 'metaphysics of solidarity' impossible, it doesn't also exclude a normative-ontological justification for solidarity. That is, an ontology where all identities result from agonistic practices of signification and therefore lack any immanent 'anchoring point' can still answer affirmatively the question: 'Is there a possible justification for solidarity, a possible community without commonality?' Moreover, somewhat paradoxically, contesting the 'substance' of social identities makes solidarity itself more 'substantive', if by that we mean closer to our concerns and more difficult to circumvent, hence more 'real'.

I elaborate this idea of solidarity with a specific subject in mind: the Western, and specifically European, citizen. When I refer to a 'Western

---

1 For the purposes of this chapter, I shall use the term 'ontology' to mean 'the processes of formation of knowledge about the nature of objects'. Such an understanding of ontology is evidently unorthodox, since it subsumes it to the processes of truth-formation; I use it in an attempt to suggest that thinking about the nature of being is a process that actively participates in the creation of that being, rather than a discovery of hidden essences. Since identity-formation is itself understood in this chapter as a process of formation of knowledge about oneself, then ontological thinking does not just reveal what an identity 'is', but also takes part in the formation of that 'is'. My main intention was not to blur the differences between truth and being (this debate exceeds the scope of such a chapter), but rather to emphasize that thinking about the nature of things is always a political endeavour.

subject' I do not imply any homogeneity of those subjects, but rather name an understanding of oneself and the other formed within the relationship between an identity posited as 'Western' and one posited as 'non-Western'. The particular interest in this subject is prompted by the role it plays in the contemporary political landscape: firstly, being formed within the relation with the 'West' and its ontological categories – which are posited as both particularly European and universal – is inescapable for most contemporary identities. Secondly, the Western subject still possesses a disproportionate ability to influence the lives of 'non-Westerners' if compared to the influence those 'non-Westerners' can have on the Western subject. An analysis of identity and solidarity must therefore consider both the inclusions/exclusions practised when constructing identities as 'Western' or 'non-Western', and the political implications of a Western subject who thinks of the world in terms of an individualistic 'I', and the self in terms of a singular and fully bounded 'interior'. It is in order to respond to those imaginings of the self that I assess solidarity from the perspective of the 'I'(for a critique of the conceptualizations of freedom based on such ideas of the individual that also illustrates the prominence of such conceptualizations in the Western thought, see Chapter 1 by Peter Wagner in this volume). I shall therefore argue that, once closely scrutinized, the immanentist 'I' of the Western subject reveals itself as the 'abstract result of a decomposition' (Nancy, 1991, 3): that is, of an ontological process of erasure of its constitutive relations and hence of the presence of many 'others' in the 'self'. It follows that a political focus on the individual, once understood as the permanent contestation of 'what we are', must always remain open to the other, and therefore not only avoids solipsism but also injects a normative dimension into solidarity.

Truth without 'substance'

The ontological starting point of this inquiry is the relational nature of truth and social identities, an assumption that contends that knowledge is not the result of the object yielding its immanent characteristics within a transparent process of interaction (observation, perception) with the subject, but rather that any object becomes intelligible through its integration into a relational system of meaning, which includes that of inquiry itself.[2] To the extent that

2 The ontology advocated here considers as crucial the notion that epistemological individualism is untenable. Hence the views of the agents, e.g. the practices regulating the nature of evidence, cannot be isolated 'starting points', but are always created in relation to other aspects of an exclusively 'in common' epistemology, (see, for example, Nelson, 1993, 121–124). Even more explicitly, when observing an object our perceptions and their transformation into knowledge are always already structured by a system of meaning that places the object in a system of relations

the systems of differential positions that cause objects to emerge are named 'discourses', reality is fully discursive, since any attempt to understand the world from somewhere outside of the grids of intelligibility that make both the world and a specific modality of inquiry about it possible is illusory. Once any social object is considered to emerge at the intersection of multiple systems of relations, the traditional internal–external ontological dichotomies (immanent–transcendent, public–private, freedom–power or autonomy–heteronomy) can no longer be assumed but have to be rethought.

A second fundamental assumption for this understanding of our meaning-making systems is their absence of necessity and naturalness: what I call here 'contingency'. This results from the impossibility of an extra-discursive centre that orders the system, since this centre would have to determine the relations from somewhere outside those relations while being itself made possible, i.e. intelligible and visible, only *within* them.[3] As such, the centre can only be thought of as transcendent through the erasure of the relations that make it meaningful. What this tries to suggest is that there are no constraints on meaning-making from outside the systems of meaning-making; those 'extra-discursive' determinants, including the material–ideal dichotomy, are created as such within discourse. It is precisely their lack of external determination that allows the dislocation of discourses: any fixation of meaning, i.e., any setting of boundaries within the field of relations, delimits not only an 'interior' (the system of differences or discourse) but also an 'exterior' (a 'surplus of meaning' that is outside discourse but not extra-discursive) that permanently threatens the 'interior' with dislocation[4] (Laclau and Mouffe, 2001). On the other hand, while the total fullness of meaning seems unattainable, being able to negotiate life presupposes the stability of meanings: a world whose rules, categories and identities shift permanently would be incomprehensible and unmanageable. Thus, social reality results from practices of power/knowledge that attempt to fix the meaning of objects by creating systematic configurations of relations, ordered by perpetually de-centred and redefined master-articulations or nodal points. The true object of social inquiry must

with other objects, taxonomies, concepts, theories, methodologies, trials and experiments, and thus structure what can be truthfully uttered about the object and the place of those truths in the wider hierarchies of truth.

3 This follows the Derridian erasure of the 'transcendental signified' (but as a non-locus and a desire); see, for example, Derrida, 1978, 278–293.

4 The possibility of dislocation is thus created *within* the discourse, not as an accidental effect of incorrect knowledge-formation but as a systematic effect of *any* process of knowledge-formation in the context of reality's lack of ultimate finality.

therefore be the permanent individual and collective effort to create meanings that resist dislocation, and that are, therefore, 'real'.[5]

The question of the techniques through which statements that in and by themselves have no epistemic status are ordered in clear-cut epistemic categories – i.e., of how *effects* of truth are created within discourses that themselves are neither true nor false (Foucault, 1980, 118) – cannot be exhaustively addressed here. I shall only mention that if everything could theoretically be said but 'everything is never said', then social reality is produced by 'regimes of truth' that regulate the means and techniques for realizing truth: the possible, observable, measurable, classifiable objects (the range of objects to be known); the possible position, function, type of gaze of the knowing subject; and finally the 'material', technical level where knowledges have to be invested to prove their utility (see Foucault, 1980; 1981). Hence, far from embracing relativism, this ontology asserts that not all truths are equal, that not all evidence and experience is possible, and that not everyone is allowed to speak in the name of 'truth'. It is an analysis of the mechanics of power[6] that create and impose truth (Foucault, 1982, 114), and considers that contemporary power-struggles take place for the ability to speak in the name of truth or to resist the imposition of truth, since when we represent the world we make statements about it, authorize views of it: in a word, *rule* over it (Said, 1996, 21–22). This ability often reflects resource[7] inequalities: in the contemporary onto-epistemic configuration, constructing reality is only available to a restricted group of individuals, professions, institutions or countries that possess the means required to restrict the range of possible statements about an 'object' to the 'true' ones, i.e., to make the cost of selecting a statement from outside this range prohibitive (Latour and Woolgar, 1986, 241–242). It is because the immense concentration of resources relevant for this purpose in the West gives it an increased ability to describe what the us and the other 'are', and to rule them accordingly, that all contemporary identities, i.e., the formation of all truths about subjects, are determined within the West–rest relationship.

---

5 For examples of how this is achieved in the case of scientific knowledge, see, for example, Latour, 1987; Latour and Woolgar, 1986.

6 There is not enough space for a discussion of power either; suffice to say that I generally subscribe to a Foucauldian characterization (see, for example, Foucault, 1980; 1981; 1982; 1990).

7 Resources here do not represent some extra-discursive objectivity, but rather point at the ways in which the systems of relations that construct our world create and distribute value through operations that deprive certain groups of access to what they consider to be valuable. It is always as a consequence of the modalities in which those systems of relations are fixed that some groups are denied access to the resources we call 'primary': food, water, shelter, medical care and so on.

Identities without substance

Continuing this line of reasoning, identities – i.e., the modalities in which we are made intelligible and meaningful to ourselves and to others – result from placing the person in various systems of relations. All possibilities for an assertion of the 'I' are created and regulated exclusively *within* the structure of signification: there is no pre-formed 'I' that encounters its environment in an oppositional epistemological frame (Butler, 1990, 181–183). Or, any truth about oneself – including agency and the possibility to think of oneself as autonomous – arises from the system of relations established between the conditions allowing one to become the legitimate subject ('knowing' and 'self-knowing') and the conditions forming it as a legitimate object ('known') of a type of knowledge (Florence, 1994, 315–316).

Like all knowledge formation, identities manifest an anti-entropic tendency to exclude chance and contingency, to establish extra-discursive centres (sex, gender, race, ethnicity, culture), to close around a 'substance'. However, identity cannot be definitively captured as a 'substance'; at most it represents the simulation of an essence within discourse, an effort to think and enact ourselves and the world so as to appear identical with the self presented to us as transcendent by discourse. Each of the subject-positions we negotiate is a regulative ideal; although the subject is pressured to completely identify with it, complete identification seems impossible.[8] As such, all identity that is completely assumed is ideological, i.e., represents the 'will to "totality" of a totalizing discourse' (Laclau, 1990, 92). Of course, while identities do not have 'substance', they do have content: we all like to think of ourselves as 'being' someone/something. This content can seem 'real' to the extent that it is assimilated with a natural substance, partly because all the possibilities of asserting the 'I' we have are formed within regulatory frames of intelligibility that actively constitute and assert identities as transcendent. To paraphrase a famous formula, no one is born a man, black, Muslim or heterosexual; they are made so by the relations they enter and are entered into. Those are non-ambivalent identities only to the extent that the relations that relentlessly attempt to make them transcendent – those practices that interpellate and make one significant only as man, black, Muslim or heterosexual, and that

---

8 There is an ongoing debate concerning the nature of this impossibility of fully closing meaning: is it due to the nature of the processes of meaning-making (the always already-incomplete knowledge of hegemony) or to the constitution of the subject (e.g., the Lacanian primordial 'lack' as resistance to full subjectivation)? Although central to the general debate, this question can be disregarded within the context of this chapter; for an insightful discussion of these issues as well as of the particular–universal dichotomy any contemporary theorizing has to navigate, see Butler et al., 2000.

reduce all social relations to a central us/them division – are still able to define the 'truth of being' for those subjects. It must nevertheless be clear that, in and by themselves, those nodal points of identity mean nothing; once closely scrutinized, substances supposed to determine identity univocally and exhaustively disperse in a multiplicity of articulations. They show themselves as composite entities, as empty signifiers that gain meaning only through their wavering connections with a plethora of heterogeneous elements that forever attempt to fix what the person 'is' or 'does'. What is more, in the same way that any knowledge production creates a 'non-knowledge', the other is formed as an intrinsic part of the I, since fixing what an identity *is* simultaneously fixes what it *is not*. Slightly twisting a certain Marxian understanding of the subject, we could say that the contemporary practices of signification mystify relationality and posit the individual and the relations that form him/her as such in opposition, i.e., make relations seem *external* to the individual's 'being'. It is through the 'naturalization' of the immediate, through the reification as 'eternal' laws of nature of what is the result of historically contingent systems of relations (Lukacs, 1978, 47), that individualism and more generally identities can become substances. Moreover, it is only when identities are understood as pre-relational substances that the 'I' and the 'other' become monadic singularities in opposition, excluding the concern for this 'other' from the practices of the self. It is in this sense that the interpersonal relations perceived as 'objective' in capitalism are alienated (Marx in Lukacs, 1978, 50).

'Woman', to take this example, is hegemonically constructed to mean the possession of a phenotype (genitalia, chromosomes), of certain desires (for the male), or of a multiplicity of psychosomatic traits (fragile, weak, beautiful, caring, maternal, neurotic and so on); but has no possible meaning outside those articulations. At the same time, 'woman' has no possible meaning outside its relation with 'man' as 'that which it is not'. This suggests that gender identity is a system of *relations* at the intersections of which a dispersion of objects/subjects (i.e. women) emerge; and that the only thing all 'women' have in common is that they are made intelligible by the signifier 'woman'. Nevertheless, this relationality is reversed, in that being designated as 'woman' is supposed to indicate the fundamental attributes of the person so signified and 'man', while intrinsic to any understanding and self-understanding of 'woman', is represented as a fully independent and antagonistic identity. The effect of a system of articulations (i.e. 'woman' as identity) is made to appear as the cause that explains those articulations, masking that there is no gender behind the expressions of gender and no subject of gender before its creation within a gendered system of differences (Butler, 1990, 33). The same logic can be applied to any identity. On the other hand, gender represents such a fundamental nodal point for the intelligibility of the social, a 'law of truth' that orders social relations, bodies, sex, sexuality, identities and so on, because it *can* (still) be truthfully designated as a substance. By this I do not mean some metaphysical conditions of possibility, but very pragmatic operations of knowledge formation and relations of power: the sway of gender over the systems of social intelligibility results from the repetition of a plethora of heterogeneous but gendered practices of power and knowledge. In other words, gender is so deeply seated in our mechanisms of meaning and identity formation partly because every (re)assertion of truth, the self and the world reiterates it. In this sense, it is only when left unquestioned that our identities might seem 'real', while exposing their relationality[9] and contingency when contested. What is crucial here is that we 'are' not only the result of the direct social interactions we participate in, but also of the wider epistemic-ontological systems of relations that make it possible to think and engage meaningfully in those daily interactions, and which always transcend any *one* subject (for an example of the threat to identity posed by the dislocation of such systems, see Chapter 9, this volume). I shall return to this argument later, to found the normativity of a solidarity without substance on it.

So far I have suggested that to 'be' an identity is to be made intelligible, and thus placed in specific networks of social practices, by a signifier purporting to indicate fundamental characteristics of the person; if, on the contrary, identities are understood as contingent practices of truth-formation, what political possibility for solidarity is there? Solidarity must be accorded a central position in those ontological problematiques because, while being deter-minant for the forms political struggles take, it is conceptualized as representing practices prompted by something that makes participants think of each other as 'one of us'. It is the nature of 'us' that has therefore to be engaged with when refining political understandings. The 'us' of solidarity can be abstract and universalistic, e.g. 'humanity' or 'human nature', in its diverse guises. Universalism is attractive since it tends to dissolve all identity-related boundaries – and probably represents an ineluctable moment in the contemporary attempts at theorizing (see Butler et al., 2000) – but is also potentially dangerous, since it homogenizes subjectivizations and replaces them with the definitive knowledge about what makes subjects 'human'. The critiques of the totalization exerted by such universalistic grand narratives are

---

9 I shall use this neologism to signify the ontological understandings of the self presented above (partly because I find its phonetic closeness to 'rationality' suggestive from a sociological point of view).

sufficiently well known; I shall just mention that a 'solidarity of humans' singles out but cannot accommodate ontological difference.[10] Hence, it is always imagined as 'containing' what makes individuals 'particular' but without this relation being fully explicated. Consequently, this imagining allows itself to oscillate freely between the universal and the particular, and thus to exert a plethora of exclusions from solidarity and withdrawals of solidarity in the name of either the event or identity in question being too particular to qualify as universally human enough; or the 'us' too universal for one identity to receive solidarity in the name of its specificity. The case of gender in the liberal understanding of the individual illustrates this tendency: the demand for gender 'equality' implies equality with men and *as* men, seeing that the latter are formed to represent the prototype of the average individual able to perform appropriately the public practices required of a citizen. The result is that equality demands erasure of difference: the conundrum here is that this difference is precisely what the patriarchal discourse attempts to fix as 'being' gender. Thus, engineering this system of differences otherwise than by transforming one of the existing polarities into the other would mean the dislocation of the system of differences itself, i.e., losing the intelligibility of either gender or of the liberal understanding of citizenship.

Alternatively, the 'us' of solidarity can be specific: nationality, ethnicity, gender, sexuality, culture, geographical community.[11] It is with this latter case that I shall engage, since it seems to be central not only for a wide range of contemporary politics but also, as already mentioned, for the definition of Western and specifically European solidarities (for discussions of solidarity defined in terms of European or religious identity, see Chapters 8 and 11, this volume). Once identity-bound, solidarity depends on the construction of an 'I' in relation with an 'us', both understood as substances. That is, if the normative demand for and justification of our conduct[12] towards each other stems from a characteristic that makes us 'same', then for this conduct to be sustainable the characteristic must be a-relational, immutable and determinant. Those identities have to expurgate all polysemy from their make-up, since if one's every conduct, including solidarity, is determined by one's womanhood, whiteness, Christianity, heterosexuality or European-

---

10 Without being able to expand on this point here, a solidarity in the name of the interdependence caused by difference of the type Durkheim advocates creates a whole set of boundaries of 'us', not least as a result of his understanding of society/community. See Nancy (1991) for a critique of the community understood as 'worked entirely from the inside'.

11 I shall not keep on presenting this – always deemed to remain incomplete – list of nodal points of identity; I hope I have managed to suggest what I mean by the 'us' of solidarity.

12 'Conduct' is here understood in the largest sense, i.e., as encompassing thoughts, emotions or desires.

ness, then all conduct deemed atypical of this identity is a sign of deviance and pathology, making the 'us' akin to the 'other', and must be erased when this identity is represented.[13] Therefore, such solidarities always exclude from the political game some part of the constituency it claims to represent (a type of politics that reduces identities to common essential attributes) as well as those it does not claim to represent (a type of politics that posits 'you have to be one to deserve our solidarity'). I shall not insist on those points: suffice to say that, once accepted as true by the subjects, such solipsistic–metonymic politics trap subjects 'under' their own identity, in the sense that since identity stops being a system of relations and appears to simply 'be', the critical interrogation of the (power) relations that create it is made to seem impossible. Such a move excludes from critical analysis and intervention precisely the practices that regulate the coming into being of the subject and its agency, thus hiding the vulnerability of all identities and creating some identities as open to being hurt.

In what follows, I shall start outlining a concept of 'solidarity of contingency' founded on the absence of substance and on the necessity to prevent any identity from being understood as a substance.

The politics of 'I'/'us'/'other' in 'post-substance' solidarity

If the identities we experience are never full, then any profound self-reflexive exercise must highlight that both the 'I' and the 'us' scrutinized are formed in relation with an 'outside'; it results that even when my reflexive practices concern the 'within', the relational nature of this 'within' directs my view towards my 'outside', towards the power operations that form the self always in relation with other selves. Critical ontology is always looking outwards. This is why I called identities 'vulnerable': if vulnerability means being wounded (*vulnere*), and if we understand 'wound' as a breach in one's boundary, then a vulnerable identity is one that is always open, never fully closed. Vulnerability comes to express the normative ideal of identity as relationality, the realization of discontinuity as the always already presence of the 'other' in the 'self'.[14]

Hence, the 'solidarity of contingency' must operate on this inside–outside

13 Of course, one's identity remains composite even when ruled by such Manichean signifiers. Thus, one can always say: 'I am a European, a Christian and a man!'. What the same person cannot say is 'I am also an African, a Muslim and a woman!'.

14 To reiterate, the possibility of exposing any identity as less then full partly results from the fact that any identity 'Y' gains meaning within a system of differences with a 'non-Y', i.e., the assertion 'I am Y' necessitates an 'I am not non-Y' assertion. Thus, 'non-Y' can be shown to always be part of the 'Y', and since the 'other' is never completely external to the 'I', the assertion 'I *am* Y' is fraudulent.

102

tension that is constitutive of the contemporary subject, so as to become a subsidiary of the line of analysis studying the link between the reflexivity of the subject and the discourse of truth (Foucault, 1988, 40). This involves a critical approach to the 'I' and 'we', one understood as striving to access a different way of dividing up the true and false (Foucault, 1991, 82), i.e., as a 'practice of the self' proceeding through an essentially social practice (truth-formation) and thus being aimed at the life in common.[15] Since the rules that regulate the intelligible assertion of the 'I' operate through repetition, i.e., since signification is not a founding act but a process of repetition made compulsory (Butler, 1990, 182), agency can be located within the possibility of variation of this repetition. And since those practices of truth, i.e., the games of signification and power that form any one subject, extend beyond the immediate, my practices either confirm or contest the articulations that fix what subjects and things 'are'. They either follow or disturb this repetition, but always impinge on all those introduced in specific systems of power relations by those fixations; thus, we are always already more (or less?) than ourselves and our immediate communities. An exclusive focus on the individual 'self' and its immediate practices becomes impossible to justify: our solidarity as political concern for the wellbeing of others can no longer be confined to 'close' others, but must include the 'remote' others as 'us'. Of course, this doesn't mean we are 'all the same': we are indeed singular and different and only intelligible as such; but we are formed as singular only through relationality, meaning that our differences are also always 'open', contingent. This is a 'care of the self' that not only assimilates cruelty with incuriosity (Rorty, 1989, 158), but assimilates the lack of solidarity towards the 'other' with irresponsibility and cowardice.[16] To exemplify, the meaning of Europe and the European (as well as of modernity, progress and other elements those empty signifiers articulate) was created in direct relation to the meaning of the non-European. The ontological category of 'European' depends directly on this relationship, i.e., it necessitates this 'other' to make sense of itself; in the process it imposes on the 'other' a 'law of truth' that will make it known and thus possible to affect. Those processes have been intensively investigated, so I shall not insist on their mechanisms; I shall only point out that any 'other' formed and ruled as a particular 'non-European' identity demands our solidarity. As mentioned, this involves a wide array of

---

15 Also see Foucault, 1988 for an account of how the practices of the self are always an element of the management of our relations with the others.
16 By 'cowardly' I mean avoiding the practice of the permanent critical ontology of the 'I' and 'us' that would characterize a responsible and courageous – i.e., unafraid of its own contingency – subject.

solidarities, since it is virtually impossible for a non-European subject to escape the relationship with Europe and the West when making itself known to itself and the others. Evidently, besides the West–rest dichotomy there is a myriad of 'others' that we need in order to make sense of the multiple subject-positions we negotiate within the multiple systems of differences forming our daily practices.

Such a dispersion of the practices of solidarity raises the question of guiding principles: since there are a plethora of power relations, creating a myriad of shifting subjects, is there a way of deciding between them? There is no a priori (and maybe no ultimate) answer to this question, since aspiring to univocal decisional criteria suggests the world could ever be exhaustively thought, moralized or reduced to the operation of a few formal principles. Moreover, a priori principles or blueprints of solidarity become insufficient in this analysis, since they abstract from the particular relations that make practices and subjects occur and become intelligible. Once nomothetic necessity is eliminated from socio-historical analysis, we have to renounce the idea of solidarity as arising spontaneously and inexorably from historical evolution; on the contrary, solidarity must be actively and continuously practised within our present historical circumstances: it becomes a continuous 'practical critique that takes the form of a transgression' (Foucault, 1984, 45–47). Therefore, rather then becoming preoccupied with the necessity of a blueprint, I would insist on the necessity to engage in a permanent reflection that always includes the 'other' in the question 'Who am I now?'. The politics of solidarity transcend the 'socio-technical element of forces and needs' (Nancy, 1991, 41) and thoroughly invest the 'everyday' as a permanent attitude to our thinking of the world:[17] I shall refer to those politics of solidarity in what follows.

The politics of solidarity – understood as struggles against the privilege to impose 'certain ways of speaking and seeing' (Foucault, 1980, 112) – have at least two salient characteristics. First, they are politics of the 'within': while it always has to look outside the self, this gaze also has to acknowledge that it is power/knowledge practices that make possible any intelligibility of the 'I', thus acknowledging that political engagement cannot grant us access to our 'true' identities or to a power-free utopia. Secondly, it is resistance to the substance of identities that becomes the principal form of political action. Since the aim of such politics cannot be to discover what we 'really' are, it must be to refuse what we are made to be now (Foucault, 1982, 213–214), to expose our being

---

17 As for Marx, therefore, emancipation is the realization that political power *is* social power and should not be separated from the domain constructed as 'private life' (Sayer, 1991, 64–66).

as a historically-contingent product and to thwart the ambition of social identities to constitute 'a full presence' (Laclau and Mouffe, 2001, 127). Community becomes resistance to immanence, 'to all the forms and all the violences of subjectivity', and mainly to the assumption that singular beings 'are' (Nancy, 1991, 31–35).

That means that solidarity can no longer be elicited by an unequivocal identity defining what the person 'really is', but only by the inability of any assumed identity to fully define what this person is, while at the same time positioning this person in particular power relations, precisely because it claims to exhaustively define him/her. In other words, solidarity is not elicited by an identity, but by what it always leaves out; it is directed towards the ways subjects' identities are formed, designated and ruled to appear as substances.

What are the political consequences of an always reactive solidarity, i.e., of solidarity as resistance? Would it be more desirable to think of a 'solidarity principle' that precedes the establishment of any particular power relations? Is a struggle to refuse what we are – rather than to define what we should become at the outcome of the political struggle – a retrograde form of politics? Wendy Brown (1995) suggests so when she claims that resistance – which she identities as the prevalent contemporary political tactic – is an 'effect of power not an arrogation of it'.[18] In this reading, resistance aims to avoid rather then to revise power relations, and is exclusively local, positioning without mapping. Brown is indeed right when pointing out that 'identity as resistance' can become short-sighted. To use Foucault's example of homosexuality, upon which Brown draws: on the one hand 'being gay' can become a mirror reversal of 'being heterosexual', reproducing its exclusions and regulations of performance. On the other hand, in its simplest form it cannot transcend a reduction of the identity of its members to the defining trait of what they 'are', in this case to their sexuality. The political options are, first, to 're-appropriate' the identity imposed on one by the dominant power relations and to make it 'positive', in the way that identity-politics does. Since this identity continues to carry within it the 'kernel of truth' of the discourse it contests (race, gender, sexuality and so on), and thus reiterates it with every reiteration of its own 'positive' identity, it is never able to fully escape being made 'other' by the dominant power/knowledge systems. Identifying oneself as 'gay' in this manner will place the person in a 'susceptible to being hurt' position for as long as the dominant sexual model remains heterosexuality. The second

18 Brown invokes here Foucault's (1990) remark that resistance is an effect and prolongation of the power relation that forms the subject as 'other'. His example claims that homosexuality asserted its legitimacy and neutrality using the same vocabularies and categories by which it was disqualified as pathological (medically, socially) (Foucault, 1990, 101).

political option is to attempt to dislocate the articulations of the dominant discourse by contesting the determining and ineluctable character of this substance for the identity of the subject: to erase genitals, skin pigment, place of birth or sexuality as signifiers of what a person 'is'. Continuing to think the world in terms of gender, race or sexuality, while constructing an ultimately untenable identity, also reproduces the discursive practices that make those identities pathological.

In my understanding, though, the issue at stake when defining resistance is rather the possibility and desirability of politics that precede, ignore or transcend the modalities in which the subjects are formed and performed within various systems of power relations, i.e., the desirability of engaging in politics outside power and discourse. Since both oppression and the possibility to dislocate appear as an effect of the fixation of meaning, specifying politics before the creation of such boundaries seems impossible. Moreover, imagining we can create successful politics using a vocabulary that runs parallel to that of power brackets the extent to which knowledge-formation and power are symbiotic in our societies. There isn't a discourse of power and a discourse running counter to it: rather, the vocabulary of power is the only one available to resist power (Foucault, 1990, 98). This is not meant in the sense that we must accept or flee from the nodal points power fixes, but in the sense that we have to engage with them, expose them as ideological if we can ever hope to dislocate them. Moreover, that resistance is always 'inside power' shouldn't mean that we are forever dominated, never to be 'free'; it rather means that the terms we use to think freedom – as something the individual 'has' and in opposition to the systems of relations creating the subject – hamper our political options. Freedom can be both imagined and attained, if by it we mean the possibility of transformation, i.e., of dismantling specific relations of signification and power once their attempts to form substances make them visible and vulnerable.[19] To return to the universal–particular dichotomy, it is in the virtual fracture between the assumed universalism and self-evidence of substances and their exposure as precarious and contingent constructs that the space of concrete freedom is created (Foucault, 1988, 36). Summing up, since power is itself a relation, and since it is only through such power relations[20] that identity is formed, then yes, all solidarity is reactive. Setting the parameters of

---

19 Freedom is thus possible only within discourse; once discourses are applied to fix identities, they transmit power and reinforce it, but also undermine and expose it, render it fragile and make it possible to thwart it (Foucault, 1981, 50–51).

20 Namely through the productive form of power that is '...implanted in bodies, slipped in beneath modes of conduct, made into a principle of classification and intelligibility, established as a raison d'etre and a natural order of disorder' (Foucault, 1990, 44).

my solidarity previous to the power relation that forms both myself and the other subjects I am solidaristic with is but a dream. That doesn't mean resistance is 'always passive, doomed to perpetual defeat'; even a theorist as non-committed to the idea of revolution as Foucault ventured to say that it is only the strategic codification of the dispersed points of resistance that makes revolution possible (Foucault, 1990, 96).

Far from being a universalistic and solipsistic exercise, such solidarities as resistance tackle any system of relations that fixes identities, including economic processes that trap people in poverty and exploitation. The work of Katherine Gibson and Julie Graham (Gibson-Graham, 1996) provides an interesting example of the anti-capitalist tactics made possible by such a political approach. Their argument is that the current representations of 'capitalism' – from both the right and the left – make it seem impossible to dislocate. They draw on feminist critiques of gender to point out that while the naturalness, determining role and reality of signifiers like 'woman' are contested to the extent that their ambiguity and openness is exposed, the same analytical process is never applied to 'capitalism', a signifier still closed upon itself, designating and determining reality as the hegemonic – or even only – form of economy. Gibson-Graham's alternative reverts to the less deterministic impulse in Marx's theorizing by aiming to expose the impossibility of the full presence of capitalism and its hegemony as a social articulation, always incomplete and vulnerable.[21] There are two points I would like to make before concluding.

First, this form of political action needs to avoid the 'politics of resentment' that Wendy Brown warns about, i.e., to reduce politics to a moral critique that claims a privileged access to truth by nature of the oppressed status of the actors involved[22] and, while denouncing the power of the opponent, denies having itself any involvement with power (Brown, 1995, 45–47). Second, since any identity results from a multiplicity of power relations, the relation that we direct our solidarity towards is probably not the only facet of this oppressed identity that can always accommodate racism, patriarchy, homophobia and so on. Any manifestation of political solidarity will therefore emphasize a particular set of relations in which the actors are enmeshed and ignore a whole set of other relations defining those subjects; we must accept

21 For example, no capitalist 'site' (e.g. a firm, industry) can be the concretization of an abstract capitalist essence, an invariant 'inside', but has to be understood as constituted by continually changing and contradictory outsides, practices, processes, events (Gibson-Graham, 1996, 16).

22 The experience of society's most exploited and devalued is here hailed as holding not only the truth of oppression, but also the truth of human existence and needs: a new universal class with a singular purchase on the truth and the good (Brown, 1995, 45–47). This is also Spivak's (1988) critique of Foucault and Deleuze.

that politics and solidarity are themselves intrinsically exclusionary, in the same way that any formation of knowledge is. We must nevertheless keep on critically exposing and amending our vulnerabilities and exclusions.

Finally, does advocating solidarity as the resistance to substances mean imposing our views of the world on the 'others'? This is when a critique of the reification of difference must counterbalance the critique of its erasure within a discourse of sameness. It is evident that if 'difference' is made absolute, it becomes identical to transforming an identity into a substance.[23] Similarly, if respect of difference is understood as non-interference with the other's worldview and identity, then it posits dialogue as a relation between two fully constituted entities, two self-referential singularities becoming 'one' in an ontologically post-hoc attempt to 'attach' to each other, rather than as a relation that creates the two entities in interaction. This is why the problematic of the 'recognition of the other' is a futile one: I do not recognize myself in the other, nor do I 'discover' the other, but rather I experience simultaneously 'the alterity in the other and the alteration that sets my singularity outside me' (Nancy, 1991, 33). Hence, a post-substance solidarity, rather than fetishizing difference, affirms that differences must be continuously dismantled and reassembled.[24] Since reality is but a struggle for discourses, maybe it is indeed time to stop shying away from normative assertions and use the only ontological anchor we have – fluidity and contingency – in order to condemn every 'care of the self' done for the sake of oneself. If all is relational, then there are no incommensurable onto-epistemological claims: my conduct affects the others, and should be assessed accordingly.

Conclusion

I argued for a solidarity of contingency that refuses to appeal to any 'we' in order to set the framework for thought and to define the conditions under which it can be validated. Instead of positing the problem as the necessity to place ourselves in a 'we' in order to be able to assert principles and values, we should rather focus on making other future forms of 'we' possible (Michel

---

23 The exclusions performed in the name of an unbridgeable difference, even more so in its guise as 'equal but different', are multiple and include, for example, racist segregation and a variety of European new right rhetoric (see, for example, Betz, 2003).

24 In a similar vein, Judith Butler affirms that constructing the 'I' *against* the 'other', as opposed to construing it as being formed *within* the relation with the 'other', is the specific effect of an ontology that postulates a subject that *precedes* agency (including political interests and action). Once this separation has been effected, the whole 'artificial set of questions about the knowability and recoverability of the other' ensues (Butler, 1990, 184).

Foucault cited in Rorty, 1989, 64). I hope I have managed to convey that, far from leading to political paralysis, such an understanding of solidarity as resistance makes the political co-extensive with the social, understood as 'life in common'. In my reading, it is rather an ontology of substances and a politics of utopia that makes resistances impossible (if substances exist they cannot be transcended), wrong resistances possible (if they deviate from the form of resistance that would accomplish the historical destiny foreseen by theorists), and totalization (of identities, struggles, resistances, subjects) under a law of truth desirable. Even if the solidarity of contingency advocated here has been, for particular reasons, expressed in terms of the 'subject' and the 'self', I hope that I have managed to argue that starting to think the world from the 'I' and 'us' is only a modality of turning our gaze outwards, towards other 'I's and 'us'-es. Hence, this understanding of a post-substance solidarity insists that if there is a responsibility, it is to represent 'remote' processes and 'remote' others as an intrinsic part of 'us'.

References

Betz, H.-G. (2003), 'Xenophobia, identity politics and exclusionary populism in Western Europe' in *Fighting Identities: Race, Religion and Ethno-nationalism, Socialist Register*, London, Merlin Press.

Brown, W. (1995), *States of Injury: Power and Freedom in Late Modernity*, Princeton, NJ, Princeton University Press.

Butler, J. (1990), *Gender Trouble: Feminism and the Subversion of Identity*, London, Routlege.

Butler, J., Laclau, E. and Zizek, S. (2000), *Contingency, Hegemony, Universality: Contemporary Dialogues on the Left*, London, Verso.

Derrida, J. (1978), *Writing and Difference*, London, Routledge and Kegan Paul.

Florence, M. (1994), 'Foucault, Michel, 1926–', in G. Gutting (ed.), *The Cambridge Companion to Foucault*, Cambridge, Cambridge University Press.

Foucault, M. (1980), *Power/Knowledge* (ed. C. Gordon), Brighton, Harvester Press.

Foucault, M. (1981), 'The order of discourse' in R. Young (ed.), *Untying the Text: A Post-Structuralist Reader*, London, Routledge and Kegan Paul.

Foucault, M. (1982), 'The subject and power: afterword' in H. L. Dreyfus and P. Rabinow (eds), *Michel Foucault: Beyond Structuralism and Hermeneutics*, London, Harvester Wheatsheaf.

Foucault, M. (1984), 'What is enlightenment?' in P. Rabinow (ed.), *The Foucault Reader*, New York, Pantheon Books.

Foucault, M. (1988), 'The ethic of care for the self as a practice of freedom' in J. Bernauer and D. Ramussen (eds), *The Final Foucault*, Cambridge, MA, MIT Press.

Foucault, M. (1990), *The History of Sexuality Volume 1*, London, Penguin.

Foucault, M. (1991), 'Questions of method' in G. Burchell, C. Gordon and P. Miller (eds), *The Foucault Effect: Studies in Governmentality*, Brighton, Harvester Wheatsheaf.

Foucault, M. (2002), *The Archaeology of Knowledge*, London, Routledge (first published in 1969).

Gibson-Graham, J. K. (1996), *The End of Capitalism (As We Knew It)*, Oxford, Blackwell.

Hindess, B. (1977), *Philosophy and Methodology in the Social Sciences*, Hassocks, Harvester Press.

Laclau, E. (1990), *New Reflections on the Revolution of Our Time*, London, Verso.

Laclau, E. and Mouffe, C. (1990), 'Post-Marxism without apologies' in E. Laclau, *New Reflections on the Revolution of Our Time*, London, Verso.

Laclau, E. and Mouffe, C. (2001), *Hegemony and Socialist Strategy: Towards a Radical Democratic Politics*, London, Verso (first published in 1985).

Latour, B. (1987), *Science in Action: How to Follow Scientists and Engineers through Society*, Cambridge, MA, Harvard University Press.

Latour, B. and Woolgar, S. (1986), *Laboratory Life: The Construction of Scientific Facts*, Princeton, NJ, Princeton University Press.

Lukacs, G. (1978), *History and Class Consciousness: Studies in Marxist Dialectics*, London, Merlin Press (first published in 1968).

Nancy, J. L. (1991), *The Inoperative Community*, Minneapolis, MN, University of Minnesota Press.

Nelson, L. H. (1993), 'Epistemological communities' in L. Alcoff and E. Potter (eds), *Feminist Epistemologies*, London, Routledge.

Rorty, R. (1989), *Contingency, Irony and Solidarity*, Cambridge, Cambridge University Press.

Said, E. (1996), 'Orientalism' in P. Mongia (ed.), *Contemporary Postcolonial Theory: A Reader*, Oxford, Oxford University Press.

Sayer, D. (1991), *Capitalism and Modernity: An Excursus on Marx and Weber*, London, Routledge.

Spivak, G. (1988), 'Can the subaltern speak?' in C. Nelson and L. Grossberg (eds), *Marxism and the Interpretation of Culture*, Chicago, University of Illinois Press.

Part II

Contemporary Boundaries of Solidarity in Europe

7   Obligations Versus Costs: Types and Contexts of Solidary Action

Claus Offe

I

'Solidary' actions (i.e., actions qualified as such by beneficiaries and/or third parties) have, from the point of view of the actor, often only affective or habitual 'motives'. At stake then are acts of spontaneous compassion or habitual generosity. For instance, a man falls on an uneven pavement, and a person passing by helps him to stand up. These are solidary acts by outcome, yet mostly not by conscious intention. Were we asked why we do such things, we would have little more to say than: 'Isn't it pretty normal to do so?' Such cases of unreflective solidarity will not be discussed here. I label them cases of 'type 0 solidarity'.

A different scenario applies when solidary actions are motivated by the idea that actors have a moral-political or legal obligation to practise sympathy, the fulfilment of which leads them to offer aid or assistance. To sharpen the concept of 'obligation', we need to realize that 'obligations' constitute the opposite of 'costs'. 'Cost', as any business textbook has it, is the consumption of valued resources, quantified in monetary terms, which is incurred in the intentional process of generating goods and services that are valued by markets (i. e., that carry a price). The differential between price and costs of a commodity is the profit that can be realized in its production and sale. If the price is 'given' (as in atomistic markets), this differential will be greater the lower the costs are. Competition thus induces the search for cost-cutting, i.e., efficiency-enhancing changes in the ways goods and services are being generated. In order to stay profitable, an entrepreneur acting in a competitive environment of other suppliers will do everything within his/her reach to economize on costs. Costs are, by their economic nature, items to be cut, avoided, reduced and minimized by rational actors.

The compliance with obligations, in contrast, typically also involves the spending of resources, as in the case of material assistance or donations. Yet, as such, resource use is recognized by the spender as a duty: trying to escape it or to minimize it would not be a rational act, but a violation of a normative rule to which the actor has committed him/herself by recognizing the obligation as binding in the first place. The distinction between costs that are essentially to be minimized, and ('costly') obligations that are to be fulfilled even in the presence of opportunities to avoid them, is all-important in social life. Whoever confuses the two by treating costs as obligations or obligations as costs commits a 'coding error' that typically will be sanctioned if detected. We shall see, however, that 'obligations' of solidarity are often such that they cannot easily be coded within the simplistic binary scheme of costs versus obligations.

Before addressing solidarity obligations and their scope, I would like to mention two other and arguably more basic types of obligation: the obligation to obey the law (i.e., the negative duty *not* to break positive legal norms or, for that matter, contracts) and those positive 'republican' obligations (consisting in various duties to practice loyalty with the political community and promote its collective wellbeing) whose reasonably reliable fulfilment by citizens is a precondition for the coming into being and the durability of a viable state authority. As regards the negative duty to obey the law (i.e., refrain from breaking it), it is assumed for the most part, at least in European political thought, that the bearers of rights and obligations are 'citizens', or members of a state-constituted political community. The organs of the constituted state authority serve to lay down rights through legislation, to protect them judicially and to enforce where necessary the fulfilment of (legal) obligations by means of sanctions.

This state-oriented conception of rights and obligations as those of citizens differs from one which is rooted in American legal thought. According to this conception, there exists a range of 'pre-positive' rights (and corresponding obligations to recognize these rights) that are not founded and granted by the state authority, but which are merely recognized and protected by it, as they derive from men's natural or divine original endowment. This conception of natural rights and duties, which can be traced back, in particular, to John Locke and his *Second Treatise on Government* (1690) (for example, a pre-state property right based on appropriation through one's own labour), is expressed in the assertion of the 'self-evident' quality of rights and of the reciprocal obligation to refrain from violating such rights.

The European conception of state-granted rights and obligations does not, of course, exclude the possibility that non-state associations (families, local and professional communities, religions communities, etc.) can also, through rules of association, more or less formally define rights and obligations for their members and sanction their compliance. There exists, however, a hierarchy such that state-constituted rights and obligations trump those of communal origin. Parents cannot place obligations on their children that contravene the personal rights of the child as laid down and protected by the state; likewise, religious communities cannot claim any rights for their members that go beyond and are not granted by the legal order of the state.

In the (European) framework of legal guarantees and rule of law, there arises a simple complementary relationship between rights and obligations. On the one hand, there is the liberal principle, according to which everything that is not expressly forbidden (through legally codified negative obligations) is permitted. On the other hand, there is the rule of law (*rechtsstaatlich*) principle: the rights of Person A are protected by the state such that all other persons (including state actors themselves) are legally obliged and can be compelled by means of the state's legal coercion – and beyond that motivated by moral norms – to desist from violating the rights of others or, in case a violation has actually occurred, to compensate by means of civil law or to suffer punishment administered to the violator by the means of criminal law. The freedom of action of any actor is thus constrained by the negative duty not to interfere with the freedom of action of others. By respecting the rights of everyone else (and by being forced to do so by the legal order and the means of coercion attached to it), an actor will eventually develop a measure of subjective reciprocal confidence that everyone else will, for their parts, respect his/her rights. Such practice of civilized conduct of affairs among private persons might be labelled 'type 1 solidarity', or liberal solidarity. Its practice rests on attitudes of granting the freedom of others and tolerating the use they are making of this freedom, while at the same time recognizing and complying with the constraints that are designed to hinder the use of freedom for the sake of interfering with the freedom of others.

II

This statist character of the law, which holds for continental European conditions, and its function of opening up (in the form of rights) and constraining (in the form of obligations) possibilities for action, rests for its part on the fulfilment of obligations that are not incumbent on a citizen vis-à-vis another concretely authorized citizen (for example, a contract partner), but rather refer to the state-constituted political community as a whole. The political system that issues or guarantees rights and obligations is dependent for its origin and continued existence on citizens fulfilling obligations that – unlike in the Weimar Constitution and many Länder constitutions – are only very cautiously specified in the Basic Law, the German constitution (c.f. Luchterhandt, 1988). Aside from obligations that are standardized for particular persons or organizations (for example officials, parents, property holders or political parties) or for particular situations (the emergency constitution's obligation to resist, the obligation to provide emergency assistance, the obligation to assume public honorary offices such as that of jury member), in the German constitutional tradition there are only three basic obligations that are 'state-founding' (and therefore characterized by Luchterhandt, 1988, 424, as 'state-ethical'): compulsory military service, or the obligation to defend the country as a professional soldier; the obligation to pay taxes; and the obligation to have children taught at public or state-recognized schools.[1] The fulfilment of these obligations differs from the obligations to obey the law and to respect the rights of others in that it takes place not 'in' the (already established) republic, but rather 'antecedent to' the republic, as it were as an individual contribution to its founding and continued existence. Whoever fulfils these three obligations thereby makes his/her solidary contribution to the achievement and the continuous implementation of a social and political contract, i.e., to the founding and the preservation of a constituted political community. At any rate, if sizeable sections of a population were categorically *not* willing (and could not be coerced) to risk their own lives in defence of the country, contribute parts of their incomes to common purposes through taxation, or teach children in the native language(s), as well as pass on to them collective cultural traditions, it would be scarcely possible to form and maintain a state-constituted political community.

This 'constitutive' type of solidarity, as it may be called, can be seen particularly clearly in non-state associations such as parties, associations or trade unions, although the legitimate use of physical force is absent in these cases. Such associations stand or fall with the preparedness of their members to subordinate individual material interests for the sake of collective goals and goods, and to make sacrifices for the sake of some 'common cause'. Cases in point are 'solidarity strikes' (one union going on strike in order to offer support for the industrial action of another union), or the observance of 'party

---

1 Interestingly, compulsory voting is not a feature of most European democracies. In Belgium, for example, the obligation on citizens to take part in general elections, which still exists and is enforced by sanctions, has the drawback of protecting political parties in their entirety from the discrediting revelation that a part of the electorate (in many countries or elections a relative majority) is insufficiently convinced by any of the competing parties to be willing to vote for one.

discipline' by dissenting MPs in parliamentary votes. The successful practice of such self-denial, self-restraint and sacrifice of opportunities for 'selfish' action is critically contingent on the perception members have of each other. The practice will thrive if (and to the extent that) individual members trust everyone else in the organization or movement to reciprocally subordinate individual advantage to the pursuit of the collective cause, thereby allowing the organization to be successful and durable. This constitutive, or organization-building and collective-goods-generating practice of solidarity will be labelled here 'type 2 solidarity'; it cannot be enforced by formal sanctions but is, at least in part, inspired by an ethos that we may call 'republican'.

This holds also for the state itself, i.e., its dependence upon the citizens' preparedness to self-subordinate and make sacrifices. The state, which is essentially thought of (according to liberal doctrine) as an agency dedicated to protecting the rights to 'life, liberty and property' (John Locke) or 'life, liberty, and the pursuit of happiness' (Thomas Jefferson, *Declaration of Independence*, 1776), at the same time requires individual citizens to sacrifice certain portions of exactly these three resources as a precondition of the protection being at all effective. So as to be able to protect the citizens' lives against foreign attacks, the state requires citizens to be ready to sacrifice their own lives for the defence of the country; likewise, the effective protection of property presupposes a deduction from property and income through taxation, and the protection of freedom requires children's and students' subjection to the curricula of the public school system, which can significantly interfere with the freedom of parents and their preferences.

In circular fashion, the fulfilment of these state-constitutive duties is itself entirely contingent upon an established state authority, which, on the other hand, comes into being only through the fulfilment of these duties on the part of citizens.[2] The readiness of citizens to pay taxes and to comply with the regime of military service is contingent not just on the 'fair' distribution of these burdens, but demonstrably also on every citizen being sufficiently certain - as the result of the state's capacity for coercion and a general evidence concerning the adequacy of this capacity – that no other citizen escapes his/her duties (by, for example, buying him/herself out of military service, or evading taxes through bribing officals, or cultivating linguistic, ethnic and religious identities in unlicensed private schools). Margaret Levi has used the concept

---

2   The EU finds itself, currently and for the foreseeable future, in a situation in which constitutive solidarity obligations on the part of national governments are largely required as a precondition of further integration steps, without however yet being enforcible on the basis of a supranational EU fiscal, security and particularly education policy competence.

117

of 'contingent consent' to describe this set of conditions: 'Contingent consent is a citizen's decision to comply or volunteer in response to demand from a government only if she perceives government as trustworthy and she is satisfied that other citizens are also engaging in ethical reciprocity' (Levi, 1998, 88; cf. Rothstein, 1998, 116–143). To be sure, the citizen's basic capacity for the practice of ethical reciprocity must already be presupposed here; is is only the extent to which this capacity is activated that depends on the perceived fairness of the legal distribution of burdens and obligations itself, and citizens' confidence that the legal norms specifying such burdens will be implemented fairly and effectively.

Both the capacity for and the activation of type 2 solidarity can deteriorate in a downward spiral of interaction. For instance, if 'I' perceive tax evasion to be easy to perform and hard to detect under conditions of intransparency of transactions and openness of borders, my ethical capacity for reciprocity and commitment to civic duty might decline due to the consideration that I will probably end up in the 'sucker' position if I unconditionally stick to my commitment. If, in addition, there is reason to argue (or a motive to invent such a reason) that not only the implementation of a legal norm is ineffective, but also that the norm itself implies an unfair allocation of burdens, the original ethical commitment will falter even further. It is not only in Germany that tax fraud and tax evasion, as well as perfectly legal patterns of tax avoidance, play (and are known to play) significant roles; the same applies to the avoidance of social security contributions through illegal employment, the shifting of gainful activities into the shadow economy, and similar strategies such as faked self-employment (*Scheinselbständigkeit*). Responding to the worsening situation, politicians appeal to the 'solidarity' of citizens and their willingness to pay taxes and contributions, pointing out that the failure to do so amounts to an act of unfairness towards all those who depend on social security funds – a moral argument that is likely to prompt the not entirely inaccurate claim that it is the biggest earners who have the greatest opportunities to minimize their tax burden or escape taxation entirely.

Apart from the failure to pay taxes and contributions, the violation of standards of solidarity is ubiquitous wherever two conditions coincide: that the benefits of violating the law are substantial, and the costs of monitoring and effective enforcement are high. To make things worse, there is often a third condition present that further undermines solidarity in the production of collective goods and the containment of negative externalities. Often, the benefits from violating regulatory rules are so great that they can be shared with those negatively affected who are thus turned into accomplices. Examples are to be found in the policy areas of environmental protection, the regulation of health and safety at work, and consumer protection: the work environment may be unhealthy, but present job security is of greater concern than health hazards that manifest themselves in the distant future. Some food product may violate a nutritional health standard, but the consumers, to the extent they are at all aware of the violation, may feel perfectly content as the product costs much less than its healthier alternatives. It is not clear how the enforcement techniques of the public administration can possibly cope with competition-driven snowball effects. They function according to a simple logic: more and more actors violate regulations because they believe that ever more actors do the same, without being hindered by effective enforcement mechanisms employed by the state.

III

Let us now turn to yet another kind of solidarity, 'type 3' solidarity. It is not identical to the liberal mutual obligation of individual actors to respect and protect each others' liberty; nor is it fully identical to the 'republican' notion of a duty to serve – and sacrifice in the promotion of – a common good or common cause. The third type of solidarity has to do with a social democratic notion of providing income, security and material freedom to those who are unable to gain these basic goods of human existence through their own means, even if such redistribution involves substantial losses and sacrifices not just for the rich, but for virtually every non-poor person. We are thus talking of solidarity as redistribution and, moreover, redistribution mandated and enforced by a democratic state, the redistributive activities of which are supported and tolerated by voters and collective actors within civil society.

There are two underlying dispositions that can support solidarity as the redistribution of material means. Firstly, an attitude that is cognitive and passive: the condition of my less fortunate fellow citizen is not a matter of indifference to me; instead, I am ready to take note of their deprivation, hardship and insecurity as a condition that is in conflict with my notion of justice and the wellbeing of the national political community. Secondly, motivational and active: I am ready to make a contribution to remedying this plight, even if my own material condition and my economic options will be negatively affected in the process, and even if those affected by inferior conditions can be blamed for having contributed to the coming about of these conditions. At the same time, however, solidary action differs from action driven by altruism or charitable compassion. In contrast to the latter, solidary action is driven by the activist attitude and confidence that misery cannot only be alleviated ad hoc and at the level of individual cases, but can be sustainably prevented from occurring at the collective level through the introduction of legal, political, educational and other institutional means and innovations that are designed to effectively preclude at least the more severe forms of poverty, exclusion and socio-economic precariousness. In contributing to this kind of change, even the net losers of redistribution can enjoy the pleasure of having contributed to the shaping of a society that is a little less unjust.

The sacrifices and contributions made can be of a voluntary nature or mandated, for the sake of universality and sustainability, by state policies that operate through taxation, legal entitlements, the establishment of collectivist security schemes and the provision of services, promotion and incentives (common resources, tax-deductible donation receipts), or legal obligations. Even if these state policies take the form of a legally decreed 'compulsory solidarity', a voluntary element to the fulfilment of solidary obligations remains significant to the extent that the citizenry submits to this coercion and refrains from attempting to use political resources for the purpose of cost-cutting relief from these obligations by the means of populist mobilization against 'welfare cheating' and 'excessive provision' that allegedly undermines work incentives.

The legal order of a welfare state imposes upon some categories of citizens and employees (and not just the 'better off') the legal obligation to contribute more than they get out of it, while others are made by design (and not just as the result of unpredictable events, as is the case in any insurance system) net recipients of transfers and services. For instance, single-person households tend to be net contributors, while large families are net recipients, almost regardless of their income bracket. What matters here is more than the liberal obligation to the freedom of others and to refrain from interfering with it, and also more than the 'republican' type of solidarity and the obligation to contribute to some common cause or common good. The practice of solidarity that consists in redistribution remains asymmetrical in terms of its distributive effects, which favour the less advantaged and impose burdens on everyone else. The questions this arrangement provokes are obvious. How much is enough to compensate for disadvantage? How much of a redistributive burden will be accepted by those who have to carry it?

Towards net receivers of solidarity benefits, the violation of (legal or moral) obligations of solidarity is frequently rationalized by voicing the suspicion that it is in truth *them*, the receivers, who conduct themselves in an unsolidary way: by making inordinate claims on the provisions, or by renouncing all efforts to make themselves independent of such offerings. The receivers, so the argument continues, are practically persuaded into such conduct by the solidary provisions of the net contributors. Such a reasoning leads to desolidarizing consequences, which can be avoided only – except through the moral (as opposed to solidary) commitment to follow altruistic norms – by recourse to two kinds of counter-arguments. First, one can refer to (or demand) particular constraints on behaviour, with which the net receivers must comply so as to rebut the suspicion of unsolidary use of the solidary offerings of others. Second, one can provide an interpretation of asymmetrical solidary offerings that demonstrates that solidary transactions create advantages not only for the receiver but, due to existing interdependencies, indirectly also for the net payer; advantages such as, for example, the preventive pacification of social conflicts, or the prophylaxis of epidemic health risks emerging from poverty-stricken habitats. The inclusion of receivers of solidary provisions, one could say, is here procured through imputations of interdependence. One needs to bear in mind, though, that the diffusion of negative effects of the misery of strangers on the neighbourhood can alternatively also be neutralized through the fortification of borders, rather than through solidary provisions, as one sees in the cases of gated communities or indeed of 'fortress Europe'.

As regards, first, the behavioural requirements placed on the net beneficiaries, the history of poverty offers rich material for contemplation. To put it succinctly, the poor must, in order to qualify at all as legitimate receivers of solidary offerings, be (locally) resident, worthy and humble. If they do not belong to 'our' political community; if they have, through their past behaviour, created their dependence on the solidarity of others in a reproachable manner; or if they have shown a lack of reasonable effort and self-responsibility and claim solidary offerings beyond the level of the 'necessary' (in amount or duration), net payers will subjectively feel exempt from their obligations to solidarity. Clearly, though, a wide and contested terrain opens up here, in which suspicions may be raised for reasons of interest. Suspicions of abuse are today ubiquitous not only because the administrative and juridical clarification of these three features is typically extremely costly; they arise also because the practice of solidarity in general exposes itself to the interested (and social-scientifically enlightened) public to the suspicion of its being counter-productive – the suspicion namely that solidary offering is truly nothing but thoughtless and misplaced generosity that creates perverse incentives (i.e., attracts non-residents, rewards the unworthy with gifts and discourages responsibility). As a result, according to a popular conclusion, solidarity would not assuage true need, but rather encourage the pretence of need.

As concerns the second of the two motivational pillars of solidary action for the benefit of the net receivers, a second-order solidarity problem arises with the shrewd consideration of interdependencies. This is indicated by the question: how sure can I be that those of my fellow citizens in a similar position will likewise make their due contribution to the enlightened prevention of negative interdependence effects that affect all of us? A collective goods problem clearly exists among those obliged to make solidary provisions: my contribution only carries weight if I can assume that a significant number of other actors will voluntarily engage in like-minded action, or can be compelled to do so by a third party.

Thirdly, consideration of the contextual circumstances plays a role in the recognition or relativization of solidarity obligations, in addition to reflections on the worthiness of the favoured and the scope of interdependencies. The readiness to fulfil such obligations can be strengthened or discouraged depending on the assumptions that are made about, for example, the competitiveness of the national economy, its prospects for growth, questions of sustainability, demographic developments, problems resulting from supranational integration, and political reform options and alliances. The typical question is: in view of changed contextual circumstances (of which the much invoked so-called 'globalization' is only one), can we all really still afford the continuation of solidary arrangements, even assuming the readiness to maintain the accustomed level of solidary behaviour and the pattern of distribution of competences? Here the argument of collective self-damaging plays a role, a self-damaging that is feared for the case that the hitherto valid standards of redistributive solidarity goals are maintained even under deteriorating pre-conditions to meet them. Those who are only putatively the beneficiaries of an existing solidarity arrangement will, as some like to warn, have the most to suffer from such collective self-damaging and from the heightened danger that all of us are somehow living beyond our means.

Such trains of thought, today lovingly modelled in sociology and public finance (cf. key words like 'welfare dependency', 'adverse selection' and 'moral hazard'), place effective doubt on whether the practice of solidarity is really worth it at all and whether it does not rather amount to an injury to the common good, or at the least exploitation of well-intentioned payers and donors. Solidarity has never been understood as pure and abstract obligation; an element of cunning was always mixed with it, whose calculus must be established empirically. Socio-political systems of provision have, since Bismarck's time, been justified and defended not only with reference to ethical obligations but also with reference to the desirable behaviour-conditioning effects on those who are the direct beneficiaries of the social security measures. Norbert Blüm, a former Christian Democrat Minister of Social Affairs in Germany, spoke of the valid claims of the 'decent and respectable contribution-payers'. True, generous subsidies for the agrarian sector and the coal-mining industry are just as costly as tax grants for pension insurance, but traditionally the gains for the nation state's autarchy (i.e., its non-reliance on imports in the case of international conflicts) and the integration of the labour force have been so positively considered that the solidarity sacrifice for such measures could be made to seem collectively beneficial in the light of the expected consequences. It is today probably more difficult to make recourse to such consequentialist motives for socio-political systems of solidary provision than in the not too distant past, when there was still a Communist 'alternative system' (certainly not something to be thought of with nostalgia) in the face of which the 'inner unity' of the nation state was to be strengthened by socio-political means, and when furthermore the West European economies were not as open and vulnerable to the mobility of factors of production as they are today. In these rather novel circumstances, it is difficult to estimate (i.e., it becomes a matter of hegemonic patterns of interpretation and their interested adoption) whether the social integrative effect of social policy solidarity stands in justified relationship with its economic cost or not.

The cunning motive for solidarity as a means of preventive conflict resolution or as the anticipated reward for future cooperation probably only works in the nation state framework. One presents oneself as generous in order to build up debts of gratitude and reciprocal obligations that will be paid off by the renunciation of opposition or through (electoral) political support. In this respect, there is a large grey zone between clear cases of socio-ethically motivated action, on the one hand, and competitive profit maximization on the other. Cases of ostentatious and well-timed generosity, such as President Bush's measures for illegal Mexican immigrants during the pre-election period in 2004, or former German Chancellor Schroeder's rhetorical commitment to Turkey's EU membership, lie in this grey zone. In both cases it would not be too much to presume that such initiatives were at least partly pursued to court strategically relevant sections of the electorate. Such a political exchange under the cover of allegedly solidary favours will have a chance of success only in relation to well-organized collectives, i.e., those equipped with a long-term memory, while those perhaps really in need of solidarity are organizationally rather less capable of presenting themselves as partners for political bartering in this sense.

All three social parameters of solidarity – the perception of inter-dependencies and of everyone else's readiness for solidarity, expectations about the behaviour-steering socio-integrative preconditions and effects of solidary behaviour, and conceptions of legal, economic and demographic contextual circumstances – appear difficult to establish objectively today, and

123

are accordingly heavily susceptible to the interpretations of interested parties, which, as surrogates for knowledge, are supposed to counteract overwhelming experiences of contingency. Problems and possible crises of solidarity should therefore be examined by social science methods like discourse analysis and the 'sociology of political knowledge' (*Wissenspolitologie*, Nullmeier, 1993), i.e., with procedures that assume that 'reality' and our action-relevant knowledge about it is the result of 'rhetoric', of strategic interpretations and negotiations. Such strategies of interpretation constitute the social and temporal horizon within which either the validity of shared identities, values, norms and reciprocal responsibility can be supposed, or within which interdependencies are perceived. The dominant depictions of such contexts of consolidated social integration and system integration can be exposed to a critique of ideology, which will often critically conclude that those contexts are conceived too narrowly. However, the opposing critical perspective can prove useful, for example in the case of a community of 'the West' that is too comprehensively cast as a community of values and interdependencies and can on good grounds be deconstructed (cf. Haller, 2002).

IV

Besides the obligations to obey the law and to keep contracts, the 'constitutive' fulfilment of obligations on which the political collectivity relies, and the largely context- and meaning-sensitive socio-political systems of social security in nation states, a 'type 4' solidarity can be distinguished that relates to members of other states or to categories of human beings beyond one's nation state. These are external solidary relationships into which national governments enter on the basis of political decisions (which then result in international contractual agreements), or non-state actors (such as national or international non-governmental organisations, NGOs) enter in a voluntary way (i.e., without the force of law or contract). These external solidarity provisions, which are overwhelmingly unilateral and discretionary – i.e., based on obligations that governments, NGOs and individual donors create for themselves – are mainly cross-border aid programmes, for which the interwoven relationship between obligations and costs – between moral imperatives and cunningly calculated effects – that is characteristic of all solidary actions is particularly hard to disentangle.

A practice of humanity-wide universalism entirely untouched by calculations of one's own advantage, purely altruistic and at the same time rational, would obviously result in the poorest inhabitants of the poorest countries being attended to most urgently with the resources that are available for solidary provision. This straightforward criterion might then be adjusted and balanced by further considerations regarding the human rights situation and other characteristics of the regime in the target countries. Such a purely altruistic practice of allocation would be rational, because with this allocation rule one could bank on the greatest poverty-relieving effect for the sum transferred. Certainly, though, the observable practice of supranational solidary provisions contrasts very markedly with this model of rational altruism. In what follows, I wish to put forward just a few indications of the extent to which the null hypothesis, namely that the scale of supranational solidary provisions corresponds to the level of the receivers' need for help, can be falsified.

The receivers of provisions of money, goods and services, to some extent also of privileges regarding citizen rights and social insurance rights, are often categories of foreign persons who, on the basis of their identity – namely, their ethnic-national, religious or class-defined similarity – stand in proximity to 'us', the givers of aid, and who for this reason assert and enjoy a claim on solidary provisions that is seen as worthy of recognition. Examples are the privileged status of citizens of the former East Germany and later of the Spätaussiedler (supposedly German people settling 'back' into Germany from Eastern Europe) in the Federal Republic of Germany; the special treatment by Hungary of Hungarian minorities in Slovakia, Serbia and Romania; the beneficiaries of the Israeli Law of Return; and the massive food aid contributed by German private households during the Polish economic crisis of the 1980s, which, on the output as well as the distribution side, was organized by the Catholic Church in both countries. Rather peculiar, perhaps, is the example of the money which was transferred by the Soviet trade union association in the mid-1980s to striking miners in the UK in the name of 'proletarian internationalism'. There is nothing peculiar, though, about the assistance that ethnic migrant communities offer to the new arrivals from their respective countries of origin. The transnational aid provisions, partly also in military terms, that the governments and NGOs of Islamic countries sent to their spiritual kin during the war in Bosnia, were religiously motivated. Transnational solidarity provisions are granted by nation states in the form of various graduated residency rights, such as permanent and temporary permissions to stay, connected with more or less restrictive work and social entitlements. These few examples show that principles of giving and receiving that connect to ethnicity, nationality, religion and class membership are at work in supranational solidary relations between states, their members and collective actors.

A second deviation from the model of rational-altruistic universalism, which we proposed for purposes of contrast, becomes evident when we consider the temporal structure of solidary provision. If they at all extend beyond the criterion of likeness just described, international solidarity transfers appear to be event-driven and guided by an acute deterioration in the receivers' situation of need, i.e., not by the intensity of an already long-existing need. On a large scale, the OECD countries and UN agencies engage in transnational aid in the event of natural disasters, climate-induced famines, wars, civil wars and the consequences of civil wars, and health catastrophes such as the HIV and SARS epidemics. Attention, strong sympathy and the corresponding willingness to help are aroused by a *suddenly* deteriorating situation of need, and not to the same extent by any constantly problematic situation. One could explain this difference by means of the assumption that sudden deteriorations in Country X create a stronger likelihood of negative externalities (for example, waves of immigrants) in the donor countries A, B and C than a consistently bad situation in Y. The media-relayed evidence of sudden emergency also lowers the cognitive demands on solidary action. The intensity of the actual aid provisions can probably be explained by the respective degree and persistence of media interest on the one hand, and on the other hand by the competition for reputation between national and supranational aid organizations.

Furthermore, the scale and direction of international aid efforts are co-determined by the constellation of historical ties and resultant obligations arising from the history of the nation states involved in today's solidary relationships. The special case of German–Israeli relations and the ever-present history of Jewish extermination by the National Socialists apart, the key cases here are wars and war crimes (Germany and Poland, Japan and Korea), post-colonial constellations (France and Algeria, Belgium and the Democratic Republic of Congo, Germany and Namibia), and the history of slavery (the USA and West African states). In such inter-state solidarity relations, characteristically, the questions of whether one is dealing with acts of restitution and compensation for past injustice on the basis of recognized guilt (as in the case of the German *Wiedergutmachung*), or whether efforts on the part of the donor countries are meant to defuse past conflicts and their long-term effect, remain suspended and contested.

Finally, solidary provisions on the international level may occur, analogous to the mechanism operating domestically within nation states as described above, in the form of veiled inter-temporal exchange relations, i.e., one-sided advance measures designed to pave the way for future alliances and cooperative relations with the receivers of solidary provisions. The continuous transfer of solidary 'gifts' is likely to sharpen the receiver's sense of what s/he must *refrain* from if s/he wishes to secure the continued flow of such transfers; this association is well known from both research on political corruption (Rose-Ackerman, 1999) and on the 'conditionality-based' promotion of democracy (Carothers, 1999). Supranational European acts of redistribution (e.g., structural funds) pursue as their goal the consolidation of EU member states. That said, it is clear that the transfer of financial resources from prosperous member states to relatively backward ones in no way functions reliably as a premium for later cooperation (Tarschys, 2003).

Lastly, back to solidarity within the nation state. Above, I argued that solidary obligations are a social construct composed of the reach of shared identities, values and norms, *and* of the reach of perceived interdependencies. Both together form a horizon within which obligations, on the one hand, and outcome-oriented calculations, on the other, come together to form the mix that is characteristic of the concept of solidarity. But this information is of little help if the two dimensions do not change in step with one another, and if the perceived interdependency extends so rapidly in post- and supra-national constellations that the corresponding expansion of social norms, and the readiness to observe them reciprocally, does not keep pace. In such situations – the present condition of European integration is probably an illustrative case – solidarities would be functionally necessary in the interests of system integration as a response to the increase of interdependencies to new orders of magnitude, yet at the level of social integration they would for the time being be insufficiently robust in motivation. The question is whether this gap can be expected to close gradually and automatically, or whether we are dealing with two developments that run counter to each other. In the latter case, which is in my view the more probable one, one should reckon with a future situation in which supranational interdependencies widen after the end of the nation state, but at the same time the potential for operative solidarity contracts to ever-narrower communities of protection and obligation (regional, sectoral, sub-national, linguistic, cultural, defined by historical experience, etc.).

References

Carothers, T. (1999), *Aiding Democracy Abroad: The Learning Curve*, New York, Carnegie Endowment for International Peace.

Haller, G. (2002), *Die Grenzen der Solidarität: Europa und USA im Umgang mit Staat, Nation und Religion*, Berlin, Aufbau.

Hirschman, A. O. (1988), *Shifting Involvements*, Frankfurt, Suhrkamp.

Levi, M. (1998), 'A state of trust' in V. Braithwaite and M. Levi (eds), *Trust and Governance*, New York, Russell Sage, 77–101.

127

Luchterhandt, O. (1988), *Grundpflichten als Verfassungsproblem in Deutschland: Geschichtliche Entwicklung und Grundpflichten unter dem Grundgesetz*, Berlin, Duncker und Humblot.

Nullmeier, F. (1993), 'Wissen und Policy-Forschung: Wissenspolitologie und rhetorisch-dialektisches Handlungsmodell' in A. Heritier (ed.), *Policy-Analyse: Kritik und Neuorientirung*, Opladen, Westdeutscher Verlag, 175–196.

Rose-Ackerman, S. (1999), *Corruption and Government*, New York, Cambridge University Press.

Rothstein, B. (1998), *Just Institutions Matter: The Moral and Political Logic of the Universal Welfare State*, Cambridge, Cambridge University Press.

Tarschys, D. (2003), *Reinventing Cohesion: The Future of European Structural Policy*, Stockholm, Swedish Institute for European Policy Studies.

8 Forms and Prospects of European Solidarity

Steffen Mau

In recent decades, much research has been undertaken to characterize the roots, distinctiveness and uniqueness of European society. This endeavour was set in motion because the process of European integration demanded arguments and reflections on the specific traits of Europe. Policy makers and social scientists have frequently referred to the nature of European society and the shared traits of the European nation states and people in order to justify the process of supranational community building. In their view, the European Union constitutes more than a random cluster of countries that have opted for a particular form of cooperation; it represents a particular identity and commonness that come together to support the integration process. Indeed, though the European continent has been the locus of the nation state and nationalism, it can also be argued that there is a common ground that unifies the European countries. As Giner (1993, 153) underlines:

> The lives and destinies of the European peoples have been inextricably intertwined for a very long time indeed, and no emphasis on internal varieties and variations can ever disguise the fact that the continent has shared one single civilization over centuries.

It can be argued that the Europeanization process is inspired and rests on this common history and interconnectedness of European societies. However, looking at the European Union, it is far from being clear what the 'nature of the beast' (Risse-Kappen, 1996) will eventually be. In the view of the most pronounced Euro-optimists, the European Union in the making represents the first 'macro-society' that will replace and supplant the nation states. The vision of Europe they conjure departs from the nation state concept; it will be a confluence of several societies into one though fusion, interpenetration and

129

mutual influence. Others, in contrast, insist that the constituent units of the European Union, the member states, maintain their predominant role in relation to the organization of social and political life, and that cooperation at the European level by no means implies that the nation states should dissolve. At the social level, too, the framework of national societies as clearly-defined unities and pivots of identity and belonging is seen as lasting.

Sociologists have always argued about the defining characteristics of a society. Though many meanings are ascribed to it and no conceptual agreement is in sight, many sociologists would agree that solidarity is one of the features that are immanent in the definition of society. However, solidarity itself is a nebulous concept with very different meanings, such as social cohesion and integration, demarcations of social inclusion and exclusion, group loyalty, special duties, social bonds or feelings of togetherness. Applied to modern mass societies, a fruitful understanding of solidarity can be developed if one focuses on the special role of institutions and the state in organizing relations of solidarity.[1] In contrast to private and small-scale solidarity, modern forms of solidarity rely on an institutional and legal framework that establishes and sustains social bonds between the members of a society. However, even within institutionalized arrangements the subjective dimension of solidarity is not entirely absent, since institutional stability and the ability of institutions to function depend on the mobilization of the capacities of the citizens for solidarity. This applies despite the fact that many institutionalized solidarity arrangements operate on a compulsory basis, e.g., by imposing tax or social contribution duties, because allegiance to and approval of these duties by citizens cannot be taken for granted. The institutional relations of solidarity will only survive in the long run if they are backed by motivational support and constantly reproduced. The welfare state can be seen as the prime example of the institutional organization of solidarity, since it collectivizes social risks and provides for occurring social needs. On this basis, some have defined solidarity as the 'preparedness to share resources with others by personal contribution to those in struggle or in need, and through taxation and redistribution organized by the state' (Stjernø, 2004, 2). This definition implies a readiness for collective action and 'a will to institutionalize that collective action through the establishment of rights and citizenship' (ibid).[2] Modern solidarity is inherently linked to the nation state

---

1   There are, of course, other contemporary concepts of solidarity, such as Habermas's discourse-ethical (1996) approach, or Honneth's critical theory (1992). However, for the analytical perspective taken in this paper it seems most appropriate to focus on material acts and institutional arrangements of solidarity, rather than problems of the immanent justification of solidarity.
2   Michael Hechter (1987) has proposed a simple indicator for solidarity. According to him, solidarity

as the dominant form of social and political organization in modern times. Indeed, the formation of the modern nation state did not only include territorial and administrative components, but also entailed the state taking over functions for collective and individual welfare (Rokkan, 2000, Ferrera, 2003). The concept of citizenship has evolved in the context of the nation state, with citizenship status incurring duties of tax payment as well as rights of social citizenship (Marshall, 1964).

Given this perspective on solidarity, the article will look at the emergence of a European solidarity space, or more specifically, at new institutional forms of solidarity that exceed the borders of the nation state. In this context, it has been claimed that the nation state can be regarded as the largest societal unit that is able to impose duties of solidarity, because only state-like entities have the authority and capacity to demand and enforce the fulfilment of citizenship duties, and it is only within the context of the nation state that ties between different groups and citizens exist which underpin institutional arrangements of solidarity (Offe, 1998). While agreeing with the general perspective that the nation state is and will remain the dominant organizational unit of solidarity, this article seeks to stress that it does not define the 'natural' boundaries of solidarity. In looking at the process of Europeanization this chapter will seek to demonstrate by which means and institutional forms the horizon of solidarity is currently expanding. To do this, the chapter proceeds in four steps. First, it introduces conflicting theoretical perspectives on the European Union as a new supranational political order. It demonstrates that authors tend to adopt quite different understandings of the possibilities and limits of transnational solidarity. Second, the chapter discusses in more detail some of the features of European integration that indicate the emergence of new forms of European solidarity. The third part uses survey data to examine whether European citizens view the EU as unit of accountability for different policy objectives related to solidarity and social sharing issues. The final section contains a brief discussion of the possible future of European solidarity.

Contested European solidarity

In most general terms, Europeanization can be understood as a process of supranationalization by which the member states as constituent units become

---

can be measured as the average proportion of resources that a member of a collective contributes for collective purposes. However, his definition has one disadvantage: it reduces solidarity to the quantity of resources given (in relation to what one has). Is also limits solidarity to individual actions, whereas one could also understand solidarity as something that characterizes collectives.

part of a larger unit acquiring its own political, economic and social competencies (Wessels, 1997; Ebbinghaus, 1998). Since the process of Europeanization has profound ramifications for the autonomy and self-steering capacity of the nation states, their ability to organize and to determine the scope and content of national solidarity is also affected. This development puts the theme of European solidarity on the agenda, and it is hotly debated whether the European Union can and should incorporate features of solidarity.[3] Drawing on the political functions of solidarity, for example, it is suggested that if the European Union were to turn its back on solidarity, it would also jeopardize the integration process. The argument runs as follows: since market integration also brings with it increased flexibility, privatization and new social risks, it also produces winners and losers. The losers, in particular, are prone to reservations about the integration process and will only be willing to support intensified cooperation if flanking measures are put in place to accompany the integration process. This type of argument has been lucidly characterised by Moravcsik (2002, 605) as follows:

> If – as Karl Polanyi and Joseph Schumpeter asserted – the legitimacy of democratic capitalism rests on an explicit compromise between markets and social protection, then the EU appears a dangerous exception... The most salient task of the modern state is to equalize life chances and socialize the risk faced by individual citizens, a goal to which the EU appears indifferent or even hostile. No wonder, then, that many Europeans – and disproportionately the poor, female, economically peripheral and recipients of public sector support – view the EU with scepticism.

Besides politico-functionalist arguments for the strengthening of social solidarity at the European level, normative arguments are also put forward. Habermas (1998), for example, understands solidarity as a specific European trait that can serve as an integrating idea across Europe. In contrast to market-driven or meritocratic societies such as the USA, the European identity encompasses elements of solidarity that also need to become part of the process of European integration. For the process of supranationalization, therefore, it would appear to be necessary for a specific relationship between

---

3 In one of the rare sociological studies on supranational community building, Amitai Etzioni (2001) has pointed out that a community is established only when it has self-integrative mechanisms that are able to contain centrifugal tendencies. Among other integrative mechanisms, he emphasizes that any political community needs a centre of decision-making that is able to affect significantly the allocation of resources and rewards throughout the community. This also facilitates a shift in public attention, and that of interest groups, from the component units to the unit of communities. By doing so, 'it leads to the formation of cleavages that cut across the member units and create community-wide interest groups that countervail centrifugal forces' (Etzioni, 2001, 4–5).

European Union member states and its citizens to evolve. Habermas (1998, 128) stresses that Europeanization implies that the solidarity previously reserved for the nation state needs to be extended to all citizens of the EU, so that Swedish and Portuguese people, for example, would take responsibility for each other.

However, if solidarity is determined predominantly at the national level, then the chances for a fully fledged concept of supranational solidarity seem to be rather flawed. In the discussion about the solidary resources of European unification, such scepticism has been fairly widespread. Authors have argued that Europe is not a 'community of sentiments' (Mann, 1998, 91) that rests on feelings of sympathy and commitment, but principally a special form of cooperation between nation states. The success of nationally organized solidarity, especially, is viewed as a hindrance to the extension of the boundaries of solidarity. Since the national welfare systems are already in place and provide security against the volatility of the market, national citizenries may have an interest in keeping their welfare states, rather than shifting responsibility to the supranational level. It has also been pointed out that the moral resources that underpin national welfare states and allow for a sharing of burdens and forms of redistribution are not present at the European level (Offe, 1998). The situation appears to be critical with regard to the 'demand side' of solidary help too. With a warning undertone, Lepsius (2000) states that the EU should not aspire to a normative integration similar to that of the nation state, because this might lead to considerable increases in claims on the regulatory and redistributive power at the European level.[4] Since the EU has only limited means to address such demands, this could result in frustrations and disappointments on the part of European citizens.

The role of solidarity in the policy framework of the EU

If one reads the official documents of the EU, one finds a clear commitment to the social responsibility of Europe. The concept of solidarity is first mentioned in the Treaty of Rome of 1957, and it entered the Charter of Fundamental Rights in the year 2000, together with other rights such as

---

4 'The central achievement of the nation state is the creation of moral orders that are not just the result of political institutions but need the support of a linguistic community, internal toleration and solidarity, and self-allocation of responsibility for shortcomings and lags in development. Downgrading nation states, limiting their possibility of action and fragmenting their formal competencies, would have considerable consequences, especially for a territorially extended sovereign territory with highly aggregated interest representation in the decision-making centres' (Lepsius, 2000, 220)

liberty, equality, justice and citizenship. In the EU documents, the term 'solidarity' is used in two ways: on the one hand, it refers to a quality that is ascribed to Europe as a kind of central virtue; on the other hand, it refers to specific policies designed to enhance the European solidarity. Whereas the first version frames solidarity as one of the founding values of the EU – in other words, as something that is common to all member states and will therefore also characterize the EU as a whole – the latter relates solidarity to certain measures that are supposed to put solidarity into practice (see Demertzis, 2005). In many policy areas, such as employment or regional policy, the term solidarity features prominently as one of the key objectives of these measures.[5] In the Treaty of Maastricht of 1991, a turning point in the European integration process, the economic objectives of the European Economic Community, such as building a common market, were complemented by a distinctive political vocation of the integration process. Article 2 of the treaty proclaims an 'ever closer union' among the peoples and member states of the EU. Although the treaty signified a noticeable advancement in the field of monetary and economic integration, it also laid the foundations for the Cohesion Fund, created in 1994. Article 117 even states that the objective of the EU is to harmonize living conditions in Europe. With the Maastricht Treaty, the EU also introduced the concept of European citizenship, and departed from the concept of the 'market citizen' (the consumer, employee, etc.). The rights associated with European citizenship guarantee the freedom of mobility, the right to choose a place of residence within the EU, political rights, such as the right to vote in local elections and European parliamentary elections, and the right to diplomatic support. European citizenship works as a supplementary form of inclusion, being partly derivative of national citizenship and partly a new and independent source of status rights (Faist, 2000; Wobbe, 2000).

Within the context of Europeanization there has been a lively debate on the extent to which the European Union can and should get involved in social policy issues. Though there is much talk about the social dimension of Europe, whether this implies social convergence between the member states, a harmonization of the different welfare systems or even the establishment of

5 Jacques Delors, the former President of the European Commission, propagated a social dimension of Europe combining both aspects by saying that since solidarity is a deeply entrenched social value in European societies, this also needs to be reflected at the pan-European level. Hence, solidarity is not just something that should be respected and protected by the EU; the EU itself should promote inter-state solidarity as part of its integration policies. As a proponent of regulated capitalism, he was committed to policies that empower the less well-off, such as policies designed to increase the potential for indigenous economic growth in poorer regions, and employment policies to bring the long-term unemployed, low-skilled and youth back into employment.

pan-European welfare schemes is disputed.[6] For the time being, the organization and financing of collective social security schemes is still the domain of the member states. At the European level, no legislation has yet been adopted that 'involves actual social transfers to the citizen from the EU, and such transfers after all constitute the core of social policy' (de Swaan, 1992, 568). Indeed, redistributive policies at the European level are only of secondary importance or even negligible, so that the EU relies on regulatory measures rather than redistributive measures (Majone, 1996; Scharpf, 2002).[7]

However, there is no denying that the EU increasingly affects national welfare state arrangements. Though the states still occupy the central place in the provision of welfare benefits and the organization of collective schemes, there are also signs of a growing shift of responsibility to the European level that makes it increasingly difficult for the member states to preserve autonomy and to act independently of each other. The emergence of a single social area entails 'individual member state control slipping or being given away, mostly in favour of pooled sovereignty' (Threlfall, 2003, 135). In particular, the principle of territorial sovereignty – the exclusive say in determining insiders and outsiders and restricting access and consumption to nationals – has been seriously undermined (Leibfried and Pierson, 1995). With regard to social rights (eligibility, entitlements), new membership spaces opened up with increased opportunities for European citizens to enter the welfare systems of other member states (Ferrera, 2003). Although this does not imply the emergence of transnational solidarity in the sense that resources cross borders, it significantly diminishes the external closure against other citizens and the locking in of a state's own citizens. In principle, European citizens are free to choose their place of residence and to access social institutions (such as labour markets and social security systems) in a similar way to nationals.[8]

There is, however, a difference between the European social space relating

6 Most advanced is Schmitter and Bauer's (2001) idea of a Euro-grant to fight poverty in the EU. It proposes that the EU pays €1000 per annum to all citizens and denizens of the EU living in extreme poverty (those with less than a third of the average income of everyone living within the EU borders) by using CAP and Structural Fund resources. They argue that the envisaged scheme holds even for enlargement, when the EU comprises 27 members. Such a pan-European grant would truly constitute a substantive commitment to European social citizenship and solidarity.

7 While the EU controls less than 1.3 per cent of the EU GDP (gross domestic product), member states can spend up to 45 per cent of their national domestic product for public purposes.

8 This shows that in principle, citizenship rights are also open to other determinations than the national membership status. For example, one can define citizenship rights as participatory status rights granted to those people who take part in the social and economic life of a given territory (Schnapper, 1997).

to access to (and equal treatment within) social insurance schemes, and access to social assistance schemes. Whereas barriers related to social insurance schemes that hinder the mobility of workers and employees have been removed, the need-related forms of provision are still shielded from free and unrestricted access. Eligibility for social assistance in another member state of the EU still requires relatively long periods of residence or previous employment in the respective country. Ferrera (2003, 635) comments accordingly:

> It is not surprising that member states wanted to reserve these rights to their own citizens. The sphere of asymmetrical solidarity (i.e., public support purely based on need considerations) presupposes, in fact, those ties of 'we-ness' that typically bind members of a national community – and them only.

Apparently, coordination works best with individualized, 'earned' rights of the employed, but not so well with provisions that are conditional upon certain needs or that are universal (see Leibfried and Pierson, 1995, 57).

The most recent policy invention of the EU, the Open Method of Coordination (OMC), entails a softer approach towards integration in social policy matters (de la Porte and Pochet, 2002). The OMC is intended to improve coordination between the member states. However, rather than adopting a top–down approach, the European Commission and the member states have developed common objectives and benchmarks, which the member states seek to accomplish with their own means. Setting up common goals and a system of common qualitative and quantitative indicators for different policy areas and periodic monitoring and reporting is understood as initiating a process of policy learning and increased coordination. Though the states retain the prime responsibility for policy measures, a common acceptance of good practice can be promoted. It is hoped that such a voluntary approach may have the potential to overcome the many difficulties of harmonization without heavy reliance on centralized measures. In this policy context, the Commission acts as a 'norm-entrepreneur' (de la Porte, 2005) supported by different political and civil society actors. However, it is still rather unclear what significance this development may have for the issue of solidarity, especially if solidarity is defined in terms of social responsibility and mutual assistance.

With its regional policies, the EU has established a policy par excellence that aims at promoting social cohesion and reducing social disparities. In order to accomplish this, the EU spends a large part of its budget on regional policies intended to stimulate growth in the most backward regions or in regions with specific developmental problems. The Regional and Structural

Funds realise investments in infrastructure and human capital in member states or regions with a GDP below a fixed threshold, or that are confronted with severe problems of economic transformation, unemployment or poverty. De facto, these are institutionalized forms of transnational redistribution that establish bonds of solidarity between the richer and the poorer parts of the EU (Ross, 1998). For the development of the EU, it is of foremost importance that existing disparities are mitigated and that the objective of long-term convergence is accomplished. Only on this condition can the EU be assured of the support of its participants, because the voluntary nature of the integration process does not allow for a very unequal distribution of burdens and benefits. Indeed, for the legitimacy of the EU it is essential that the interests of the weaker and economically underprivileged members are also taken into consideration. This is why some have viewed regional transfers as side-payments to the losers of the integration process, by which they are 'brought into' the EU (Pollack, 1995). The motives of the net payers to the regional funds have been understood as 'self-interested help' (Vobruba, 1996). However, one also needs to emphasize that without the commitment of the EU to the political objectives of solidarity and territorial cohesion, these policies would not have succeeded. The claims of the economically weaker member states and regions could also call on norms of fairness and solidarity. The regional policies are financed out of the EU budget, and amount to 35 per cent of overall social expenditure. Between 1992 and 1999, the EU spent around €170 billon on structural policy; for the period from 2000 to 2006, expenditure amounted to €210 billion (at 1999 prices, not counting spending for the new member states). The budget contributions of the member states are calculated according to the principle of equivalence: in other words, the more prosperous countries contribute more than the poorer member states. The spending criteria are oriented towards targeting need and entitling the most deprived regions and countries to transfers (Mau, 2004). The EU deploys indicators such as GDP, unemployment rates and employment structures to measure relative deprivation. However, the regional funds are not confined to some less developed countries; money is given to regions with difficulties in all member states. That means that all member states finance the schemes, and all derive benefits from it. In some senses, the programmes are measures by all members for all members; this fact diminishes potential distributional conflicts and increases a sense of reciprocity (Begg, 1997). However, this by no means implies that all countries are net beneficiaries. The collective mode of financing, in combination with the principle of expenditure according to need, produces a scheme with groups of net payers and net receivers.[9]

In its own studies, the EU points to the success and effectiveness of the Structural Funds (European Commission, 2001). The experiences of Ireland, Portugal, Spain and (partially) Greece indicate that, in some central areas such as living standards, social security and life satisfaction, important improvements have been made (Delhey, 2002). With European enlargement comes new challenges for EU regional policy, because the 'welfare gap' between the old and the new members is relatively great. If one takes the threshold of 75 per cent of the EU GDP as the decisive indicator for entitlement for development aid, nearly all regions in Eastern and Central Europe are eligible for EU funding. During the negotiations over the terms and conditions of the enlargement, it became clear that the net payers of the EU were not willing to shoulder additional burdens, and the new member states could not count on significantly increased resources. The EU had granted financial help prior to accession, and included the new member states in the schemes, but the money spent per head is significantly lower than in the previous enlargement rounds. It is reasonable to assume that, with enlargement, the resources of pan-European solidarity have reached their limits and the member states need to renegotiate a system of fair burden-sharing. It seems that the readiness to support backward regions does not increase in proportion with the needs, but evolves in relation to a state's own problems and resources. It will also become more and more important that the givers within the system see the success of these measures in terms of those lagging behind catching up, and that they believe that the recipients of help are making bona fide efforts to overcome their problems.

Attitudes of solidarity

In defining the term 'solidarity', it has been emphasized that the concept not only features an objective relation of providing assistance, but also entails a subjective dimension (Bayertz, 1998). This means that solidarity also requires motivation on the part of the benefactors, or a specific moral commitment. Within the framework of the nation state, we take for granted a readiness to engage in solidarity and to contribute to the common good. However, one should not forget that the national welfare state represents a system of

9 The transnational transfers of the regional policy do not intend to redistribute income as national welfare schemes, for example, do. Instead, they aim to stimulate economic growth by investing in infrastructure or human capital. The recipients of the transfers are countries and regions, not individuals or households. The transfers, therefore, realize solidarity between socio-spatial units rather than between social classes or groups.

compulsory solidarity that does not rest on the voluntary contributions of the citizens, but on tax duties or compulsory social contributions (Kersting, 1998, 442). Europe, in contrast to nation states, is not a state-like entity that can impose such duties, but a voluntary project highly dependent on the member states' interests. The respective governments of the member states, however, are compelled to take the majority preferences of their electorates into consideration if they seek approval of their engagement in European integration. If we understand Europe as an undertaking that depends on the agreement of citizens as well as on the will of political elites, then the question arises as to whether national citizenries are in favour of an EU that takes on more responsibility for social issues. The question is whether the EU is increasingly regarded as a unit of accountability in matters of collective welfare.

Eurobarometer survey data can give some indication as to people's preferences with regard to the allocation of competences between the national and the European level (Table 1). It is interesting to note that a significant majority of Europeans favour a joint European responsibility in the policy areas of poverty and social exclusion, as well as regional aid. A transfer of competence from the national to the European level in the area of health and social welfare, in contrast, finds little support. It seems that here, a pan-European welfare policy in the traditional areas of welfare state activities comes into conflict with existing national programmes. People in the advanced welfare states, such as the Scandinavians, exhibit the greatest reservations towards the Europeanization of welfare responsibility in the core areas of welfare state activity (see Mau, 2003). It seems that the much-touted 'passion for equality' of the Scandinavians does not necessarily pave the way for a social Europe, and that egalitarian preferences are more national than European or universal. For the Scandinavian countries, this effect is probably due to the level of welfare their citizens are accustomed to, and the belief that European integration would lead to a reduction in social benefits. That the Southern Europeans express such strong support for the Europeanization of health and social welfare policies relates to their relative backwardness and the positive experiences associated with catching up with the other member states since joining the European Union (ibid). In the area of unemployment, the number of those who take the nation state as the unit of accountability is a bit larger that the number who think joint European policy-making is necessary. In this policy area, it is not just a question of which level should be responsible but also which level has the competence to deal with the existing problems. As far as poverty and social exclusion are concerned, the respondents prefer joint policy action rather than leaving each European member state to act on its own. In additon, this might also suggest that greater horizontal links between the members of the European Union induce a demand for supranational policy solutions.

That a majority perceives the EU as the addressee responsible for the provision of support to regions facing economic difficulties indicates that the EU has, in the view of its citizens, also evolved as a new level of political and social responsibility. Since building a common market may cause pressure on backwards regions, it seems to be fair that the European Union should compensate the 'losers' of integration and support a catching-up. This entails a bond of solidarity between the stronger and the weaker parts of the EU, which is, according to the responses, largely accepted. Of course, the degree of support is highest in the beneficiary countries such as Greece, Ireland, Spain and Portugal, where three-quarters of the respondents are in favour of joint European policy action in support of regions facing economic difficulties. Nonetheless, the level of support is also high in countries that make net payments.

Table 1: *National or European responsibility?*

	National government	European Union	Don't know
Health and social welfare	65.2%	30.5%	4.3%
Fight against poverty and social exclusion	39.0%	56.7%	4.3%
Fight against unemployment	53.0%	43.2%	3.7%
Support for regions with economic difficulties	37.7%	57.1%	5.2%

N=15,443.

Weight according to the proportion of the population.

Source: Eurobarometer, October/November 2004.

Every enlargement has led to fears and resentment against an ever-growing Europe. In the Eurobarometer survey of 2003, nearly 42 per cent of the respondents feared that enlargement would bring about more unemployment in their own country. The survey also asked whether people believed that as the result of the enlargement, the current beneficiaries of regional aid would receive less, because more money would be transferred to countries in Central and Eastern Europe. People in countries like Finland, Sweden, Ireland, Denmark and Portugal took this view. It is not, therefore, surprising that they prefer to give accession priority to those countries that are able to contribute to the EU budget, and where the welfare gap is relatively small. However, irrespective of the existing fears, there are also positive signs of solidarity. For example, nearly 30 per cent of the respondents in the old member states supported pre-accession aid to the candidate countries. It is interesting to note that those countries that profited heavily from the regional programmes of the EU in the past are those most in favour of an engagement on the part of the EU (Figure 1, to the right of the dotted line). It is possible that their own past experiences have a positive effect on their willingness to behave with solidarity, or that they are more ready to accept a redistributive role for the EU. In addition, one could also argue that approval of such a role on the part of the EU also reaffirms their own claims on EU resources.

Figure 1: *Help for the candidate countries*

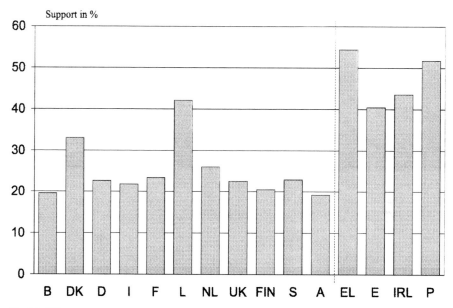

N=16,409.

Question: Thinking about the enlargement of the EU to include new European countries, do you tend to agree or disagree with the following statement: The EU should help future members financially, even before they join?

Weight according to the proportion of the population.

Key: B = Belgium, DK = Denmark, D = Germany, I = Italy, F = France, L = Luxembourg, NL = Netherlands, UK = United Kingdom, FIN = Finland, S = Sweden, A = Austria, EL = Greece, E = Spain, IRL = Ireland, P = Portugal.

Source: Eurobarometer, March/April 2003.

What does the future hold for European solidarity?

There are indeed good reasons to argue that utilitarian expectations alone can hardly bolster the far-reaching project of European integration, and that it also requires a normative appeal (Habermas, 2001). The question remains, however, whether and how such normative and solidary flanking of the Europeanization process is possible. As reflected in the theoretical discussion, two types of answers are given: the first points to a lack of solidarity at the supranational level, and the second assumes that one can indeed identify notions of community and solidarity. The first perspective sees the nation state as the dominant entity in the organization of solidarity, because only states 'make' societies through inclusion, citizenship, legislation and policy making, and therefore are able to impose duties of solidarity (Offe, 2001). Europe, in contrast, cannot count on a sense of belonging and conformity to social norms that emanate from the social and spatial identity of state and society. The second perspective principally doubts that solidarity always requires a strong sense of community. The idea of solidarity with strangers, for example, as put forward within the framework of inter-subjective social philosophy, aims at overcoming the particularistic notions of solidarity so as to broaden the horizon of solidarity (e.g., Brunkhorst, 1997). Habermas (1996) proposes a concept of solidarity arising from ideas of an inclusive and non-coercive discourse of free and equal participants. Under these conditions, generalizable interests and universal norms will develop and overcome particularistic notions of solidarity. Here, solidarity appears to be detached from the idea of community, as it does not presuppose mutual familiarity or belonging, but rather a common political culture, a public sphere and the power of self-determination.

Rather than giving a priori preference to one of these positions, this chapter has empirically considered the relationship between supranational community building and the emergence of solidarity. In reaction to the prevailing views that the nation state is the keystone of modern solidarity and that Europe is characterized by a solidarity deficit, it has been argued that the nation state is an unsuitable benchmark for understanding transnational solidarity. Neither the extent nor the density of solidary relations at the national level are good points of reference when dealing with supranational entities. Since the relationship between states or within supranational communities is a categorically different issue than solidarity within nation states – be it in the socio-moral respect or with regard to the political and constitutional organization – it is fairly clear that supranational solidarity is unlikely to resemble national solidarity. As the chapter argues, it would also be misleading to diagnose European integration as being characterized by an absence of any form of solidarity, or infer that solidarity beyond the nation state is impossible. With reference to different policies and institutional regulations, it has been demonstrated that the EU has adopted features of institutionalized solidarity, and that the 'monopolistic control of the state over both the membership and the territorial boundaries of social sharing started to be undermined from within and from without' (Ferrera, 2003, 631). There is also empirical evidence that a significant proportion of Europeans have started to approve the idea of the EU becoming a unit of accountability for the organization of solidary or welfare-related policies.

Given this finding, one could suggest a third theoretical position that neither confines solidarity to the nation state nor fully frees solidarity from the concepts of society or community. It seems that the creation of an ever-closer union with denser networks of social, political and economic relations and the growing governing capacity of the European Union may be able to facilitate European solidarity. The link between interdependence and solidarity has, since Durkheim's (1960) classic book *The Division of Labour in Society*, been one of the core theorems of the sociological analysis of the genesis of solidarity. Durkheim's theoretical programme assumes that intensified exchange and entanglement engender social and emotional bonds between the interacting actors. With regard to European integration, one has to concede a growing degree of interpenetration and dependency between the member states. Following Durkheim, it stands to reason that solidary bonds are increasingly likely to develop as the European member states become more intertwined. Durkheim (1960, 405–406) himself indicated such a possibility:

> among European peoples there is a tendency to form, by spontaneous movement, a European society which has, at present, some idea of itself and the beginning of organization. If the formation of a single human society is forever impossible, a fact which has not been proved, at least the formation of continually larger societies brings us vaguely near the goal.

However, though such a mechanism might be at work, one should not take for granted a positive association between interdependency and solidarity. Such a functionalist fallacy would not be able to account for instances of solidarity withdrawal, or regionalist or nationalist tendencies within the process of Europeanization. Therefore, the supranationalization of solidarity is by no means a simple function of the depth of integration, but requires the building up of trust relationships, a sense of interrelatedness, and positive experiences of cooperation. Accordingly, solidarity needs to be institutionally facilitated and politically supported in order to become viable. Though political action will fail if it attempts to create solidarity from above, it indisputably sets the conditions which make solidarity thrive or deteriorate. Within the context of European integration, much depends on the way in which the project is conveyed to the general public in the different member states, the conditions of solidarity in terms of participation, and the institutional solutions found. Moreover, what applies to the generation of solidarity within Europe is also valid for relations of solidarity beyond Europe.

References

Bayertz, K. (1998), 'Begriff und Problem der Solidarität' in K. Bayertz (ed.), *Solidarität: Begriff und Problem*, Frankfurt am Main, Suhrkamp, 11–35.

Begg, I. (1997), 'Reform of the Structural Funds after 1999', *European Planning Studies*, 5, 5.

Brunkhorst, H. (1997), *Solidarität unter Fremden*, Frankfurt am Main, Fischer.

de la Porte, C. (2005), 'The emergence of the open method of co-ordination in social inclusion', paper prepared for the annual ESPAnet conference, Fribourg, Switzerland.

de la Porte, C. and Pochet, P. (2002), *Building Social Europe through the Open Method of Coordination*, Brussels, P.I.E.-Peter Lang.

Delhey, J. (2002), 'Die Entwicklung der Lebensqualität nach dem EU-Beitritt: Lehren für die Beitrittskandidaten aus früheren Erweiterungen', *Aus Politik und Zeitgeschichte*, B1-2.

Demertzis, V. (2005), 'Solidarity inside the EU: European solidarity without European Welfare State', paper presented at the Espanet Conference, 22–24 September, University of Fribourg.

Durkheim, E. (1960 [1983]), *The Division of Labour in Society*, Glencoe, IL, Free Press.

Ebbinghaus, B. (1998), 'Europe through the looking-glass: comparative and multi-level perspectives', *Acta Sociologica*, 41, 301–313.

Etzioni, A. (2001), *Political Unification Revisited: Building Supranational Communities*, Lanham, MD, Lexington Books.

European Commission (2001), 'Unity, solidarity, diversity for Europe, its people and its territory', Second Report on Economic and Social Cohesion, Brussels, European Commission.

Faist, T. (2000), 'Soziale Bürgerschaft in der Europäischen Union: Verschachtelte Mitgliedschaft' in M. Bach (ed.), *Die Europäisierung nationaler Gesellschaften, Sonderheft 40, Kölner Zeitschrift für Soziologie und Sozialpsychologie*, Opladen, Westdeutscher Verlag, 229–250.

Ferrera, M. (2003), 'European integration and national social citizenship: changing boundaries, new structuring?', *Comparative Political Studies*, 36, 6, 611–652.

Giner, S. (1993), 'The rise of a European society', *Revue européenne des sciences sociales*, 95, 151–165.

Habermas, J. (1996), 'Gerechtigkeit und Solidarität: Eine Stellungnahme zur Diskussion über Stufe 6' in W. Edelstein and G. Nunner-Winkler (eds), *Zur Bestimmung der Moral. Philosophische und sozialwissenschaftliche Beiträge zur Moralforschung*, Frankfurt am Main, Suhrkamp.

Habermas, J. (1998), *Die postnationale Konstellation*, Frankfurt am Main, Suhrkamp.

Habermas, J. (2001), 'Why Europe needs a constitution', *New Left Review*, 11, 5–26.

Hechter, M. (1987), *Principles of Group Solidarity*, Berkeley, CA, University of California Press.

Honneth, A. (1992), *Kampf um Anerkennung: Zur moralischen Grammatik sozialer Konflikte*, Frankfurt am Main, Suhrkamp.

Kersting, W. (1998), 'Internationale Solidarität' in K. Bayertz (ed.), *Solidarität: Begriff und Problem*, Frankfurt am Main, Suhrkamp, 411–429.

Leibfried, S. and Pierson, P. (1995), 'Semisovereign welfare states: social policy in a multitiered Europe' in S. Leibfried and P. Pierson (eds), *European Social Policy*, Washington, DC, Brookings Institution, 43–77.

Lepsius, R. M. (2000), 'The European Union as a sovereignty association of a special nature' in C. Joerges, Y. Mény and J. H. H. Weiler (eds), *What Kind of Constitution for What Kind of Polity? Responses to Joschka Fischer*, Florence, European University Institute, 213–221.

Majone, G. (1996), 'Redistributive und sozialregulative Politik' in M. Jachtenfuchs and B. Kohler-Koch (eds), *Europäische Integration*, Opladen, Leske & Budrich, 225–247.

Mann, M. (1998), 'Is there a society called Euro?' in R. Axtman (ed.), *Globalization and Europe: Theoretical and Empirical Investigations*, London, Pinter, 185–207.

Marshall, T. H. (1964), *Class, Citizenship and Social Development*, New York, Doubleday.

Mau, S. (2003), *The Moral Economy of Welfare States: Britain and Germany Compared*, London, Routledge.

Mau, S. (2004), 'Transnationale Transfers in der EU-Regionalpolitik: Die institutionelle Lösung eines verteilungspolitischen Problems' in S. Liebig, H. Lengfeld and S. Mau (eds), *Gerechtigkeit und Verteilungsprobleme in modernen Gesellschaften*, Frankfurt am Main/New York, Campus, 331–360.

Moravcsik, A. (2002), 'In defense of the "democratic deficit": reassessing legitimacy in the European Union', *Journal of Common Market Studies*, 40, 4, 603–624.

Offe, C. (1998), 'Demokratie und Wohlfahrtsstaat: Eine europäische Regimeform unter dem Stress der europäischen Integration' in W. Streeck (ed.), *Internationale Wirtschaft, nationale Demokratie: Herausforderungen für die Demokratietheorie*, Frankfurt am Main, Campus, 99–139.

Offe, C. (2001), 'Is there, or can there be, a "European society"?' in A. Koj and P. Sztompka (eds), *Images of the World: Science, Humanities, Art*, Krakow, Jagellonian University, 143–159.

Pollack, M. (1995), 'Regional actors in an intergovernmental play: the making and implementation of EU structural policy' in C. Rhodes and S. Mazey (eds), *The State of the European Union*, Boulder, CO, Lynne Rienner Publishers, 361–390.

Risse-Kappen, T. (1996), 'Exploring the nature of the beast: international relations theory and comparative policy analysis meet the European Union', *Journal of Common Market Studies*, 34, 53–79.

Rokkan, S. (2000), *Staat, Nation und Demokratie in Europa: Die Theorie Stein Rokkans* (edited by Peter Flora), Frankfurt am Main, Suhrkamp.

Ross, G. (1998), 'Das "Soziale Europa" des Jacques Delors: Verschachtelung als politische Strategie' in S. Leibfried and P. Pierson (eds), *Standort Europa: Europäische Sozialpolitik*, Frankfurt am Main, Suhrkamp, 327–368.

Scharpf, F. (2002), 'The European social model: coping with challenges of diversity',

Journal of Common Market Studies, 40, 4, 645–669.

Schmitter, P. C. and Bauer, M. W. (2001), 'A (modest) proposal for expanding social citizenship in the European Union', *Journal of European Social Policy*, 11, 1, 55–65.

Schnapper, D. (1997), 'The European debate on citizenship', *Daedalus*, 126, 3, 199–222.

Stjernø, S. (2004), *Solidarity in Europe: The History of an Idea*, Cambridge, Cambridge University Press.

Swaan, A. de (1992), 'The receding prospects for transnational social policy', *Theory and Society*, 26, 561–575.

Threlfall, M. (2003), 'European social integration: harmonization, convergence and social single areas', *Journal of European Social Policy*, 13, 2, 121–139.

Vobruba, G. (1996), 'Self-interested help: belated modernization and interwoven interests between East and West', *Crime, Law and Social Change*, 25, 1, 83–93.

Wessels, W. (1997), 'An even closer fusion? A dynamic macropolitical view on integration processes', *Journal of Common Market Studies*, 34, 267–299.

Wobbe, T. (2000), 'Die Koexistenz nationaler und supranationaler Bürgerschaft: Neue Formen politischer Inkorporation' in M. Bach (ed.), *Die Europäisierung nationaler Gesellschaften*, Opladen, Westdeutscher Verlag, 251–274.

9 'Catching Up with the West': The Impact on Eastern European Solidarity

Raluca Parvu

This chapter explores aspects of the production of the social in the post-Communist context, namely the re-drawing of boundaries among social groups with the emergence of new collective identities and the reconfiguration of social ties. It addresses the implications of this restructuring in regard to concepts and practices of social solidarity. It draws on fieldwork performed in Bucharest, Romania during 2002–04, consisting of 78 in-depth interviews, observation and a survey of the media.

The analysis focuses on the discursive structures that underpin these processes, and proposes an understanding of the reconfiguration of the social (as processes of articulation: cf. Laclau and Mouffe, 2001 [1985]; Laclau, 1990) in post-Communist Romania as inseparable from the societal project of 'catching up with the West'.

First, I will outline the context or explanatory framework of the reconfiguration of the social in the shape of a 'mythical space' that grounds the new hegemonic discourses; subsequently, I will look at some of the processes that have affected the practices and the conceptualization of solidarity in the post-Communist social landscape. The new discursive regime has created new lines of division and social categories (according to the criterion of material status), meaning the old social ties have been largely broken. Various practices of solidarity enacted through these relationships have been lost. On a more profound level, the new discourses are forging a novel normative frame at the societal level, with a deep impact on understandings of solidarity as a social norm on the part of social actors.

As Outhwaite and Ray (2005) put it, it seemed that after 1989 everything was tossed up in the air, but fell down in familiar patterns of social and economic organization: post-Communist countries have largely adopted

147

Western political and economic forms. In opposition to theories of 'convergence' as deterministic views of social change through 'laws' of social evolution or the natural superiority of the Western model, I propose an account of the adoption of the discourses[1] of capitalism and democracy in Eastern Europe that draws on the notion of mythical space (Laclau, 1990) and focuses on configurations of discourses and operations of power that made possible certain social evolutions while precluding others.

Re-suturing the social: the role and form of the mythical space

The issue of social change after 1989 in Eastern Europe has provided social scientists with endless material for analysis and commentary. How to best conceptualize what happened after the disintegration of Communism (as well as inquiring into the causes of this rather unexpected collapse) is still part of a heated debate in the expanding field of post-Communist studies. An 'entire scaffolding of normal routines, trusted assumptions and certainties has collapsed, whose intrinsically equivocal nature nevertheless provided a basis for stabilized everyday habits' (Thomas, quoted in Segert and Zierke, 2000, 241). I wish to emphasize here a dimension of change as the collective breakdown of orientation, the dispersion of meaning, as many discourses lost their power to define and order social reality.[2]

In the early 1990s, the ground was left open for alternative ways of meaningfully organizing the social world in Romania, under circumstances of substantial social dislocation. New discourses had to hegemonize the social space, mainly by providing conceptual guidelines and norms for the political and economic re-organization of society, but also at a micro level. A fixation of meaning was needed regarding how to envision personhood, and the relationship with others and society, including ideas of human nature, social hierarchies, sociality and social solidarity. A re-working of the normative underpinnings of society took place as well; new criteria for social stratification and social worth emerged as the ones upheld during the Communist period faded. A discursive approach helps to explain the disorientating features of everyday life – a common theme in post-Communist societies that have found themselves at the intersection of competing discourses and possibilities for reality-making – and the salience of individual and collective identities in these societies, together with the importance and intensity of boundary creation.

---

1 I use here an understanding of 'discourse' that encompasses practices, as opposed to a purely linguistic approach.
2 Sztompka (2002) goes as far as describing the change as 'cultural trauma'.

In the case of Eastern European countries, including Romania, the fall of Communism has represented a moment of profound and generalized dislocation; a new principle of ordering the social was provided by a 'mythical space' in the form of certain discourses that can be grouped under the label 'the need to catch up with the West'. According to Laclau (1990):

[T]he 'work' of myth is to suture that dislocated space through the constitution of a new space of representation. Thus, the effectiveness of myth is essentially hegemonic: it involves forming a new objectivity by means of the rearticulation of the dislocated elements. (61)

As a 'principle of reading of a given situation' (Laclau, 1990, 61), the mythical space defined the state of affairs post-1989 as the collapse of an 'evil' system and the need to move away from its legacy towards a 'good' or 'appropriate' socio-economic order. The project of 'catching up with the West' can be seen as the first principle of societal reorganization and mobilization that sutured the generalized social dislocation. Its role in the production of the social has not stopped there: as mentioned, 'catching up' involves the adoption of 'democracy' and 'capitalism' (seen as the very essence of the West), but the exact meaning of these signifiers was not fixed. The production of the social proceeded in the years following the collapse of Communism through the struggle to invest signifiers with specific meanings, accompanied by the creation of policies, laws and institutions, a whole range of practices inseparable from 'the struggle over meaning'. Social actors in Romania (from powerful institutions to ordinary citizens) have contributed to the production of the social by engaging in articulatory practices involving a wide array of signifiers, among which solidarity is central, along with democracy, freedom, the market, social rights, social responsibilities, competition, work, meritocracy, human nature, the state, the West, etc.

Next, I will set out in detail two interrelated aspects of the production of the social post-1989 that have affected the nature of social ties, and impacted on forms of solidarity. On the one hand, the emerging criterion of material status is assigning to different strata (collective subject positions) people who used to belong together in various guises under Communism, and in the process it displaces pre-existing social relationships; this means that networks of relations between people sharing similar positions under the previous regime have been largely dismantled, thus dissolving the practices of solidarity and reciprocity that these networks had supported and circulated.

On the other hand, the production of the social associated with the project of 'catching up with the West' – or becoming more Western and shaking off the Communist ways of being, as respondents put it – has entailed the adoption of 'adequate' or 'desirable' outlooks, norms and values codifying personhood and interpersonal relationships, in the form of a strong individualistic stance and 'Western' modes of interaction that actually preclude both notions and practices of solidarity.

Concepts and practices of solidarity under Communism

We used to care for each other. (56-year-old man)[3]

It would be difficult to deny that with the fall of Communism in Eastern European societies, a major shift has taken place in the form of the dislocation of routines and practices, and ways of conceptualizing society and one's place in it. This quotation, the sentiments of which recur over many accounts, suggests a decline in mutual help and forms of solidarity in the post-Communist period.[4]

I will not detail here the self-understandings on the part of social actors under Communism that were involved in the conceptualizing of solidarity, but will focus on tactics or strategies of solidarity that were present at the time. Although it is possible to identify various forms of 'we-ness' under Communism – notions of 'us' and 'them' through boundary construction,[5] that fostered and legitimized forms of both social solidarity and exclusion – it is difficult to present a coherent picture of social identities under Communism.[6] I will point to the ways in which certain arrangements under Communism imposed norms of solidarity, or facilitated the emergence of reciprocity networks.

3 All quotations are from fieldwork material (in-depth interviews).
4 This section focuses on forms of social solidarity (some actively promoted) under the Communist regime, a view that contrasts with the dominant political science literature on the atomized nature of Communist societies.
5 One of the frequently invoked lines of division in Communist societies separated the higher echelons of the Communist Party members from the rest of the population, with the former enjoying a monopoly of political decisions, privileges and access to goods and services that the latter were denied in a context of widespread scarcity. Another line of division that belied the official propaganda and notions of a homogenous society often associated with socialist societies was that between intellectuals and workers. Fuller (2000) asserts that the homogeneity paradigm frequently employed by analyses of Communism glosses over a deep rift in Communist societies between the categories above, with the intellectuals enjoying more privileges and being deeply involved with the Communist ruling and management structures. This view is in line with the famous thesis formulated by Szelenyi (1982), which identified a 'new dominating class' in Communist countries, the intelligentsia. This thesis was received with hostility by the said Eastern European intellectuals.
6 This is due to the limitations of the data on which the chapter is based. I reject here the popular image of the 'Communist' (atomized, apathetic, passive, dependent on the state, unresourceful) that emerges across numerous studies on Communism. It is inadequate for the purpose of grasping social actors' self-understandings or identities.

It can be argued that specific practices of the Communist era forged forms or sites of togetherness and enforced strong norms of social solidarity in these sites (along a more abstract notion of societal-level solidarity). The workplace,[7] the school, and, to a certain extent, the place of residence were such sites. The workplace was designed as a unit where everyone was expected to perform their tasks, but also to help out and coordinate with fellow workers and make the good functioning of the unit a priority, which required down-playing personal ambition and career goals. The dilemma of choosing between the success of the work collective and individual fulfilment was relentlessly enacted in plays and movies in the Communist era, together with a strong moral lesson: the 'good' character chooses invariably to 'sacrifice' superficial individual gains for the more profound rewards linked to the achievements of the group, and in the end this form of solidarity always pays off.

The school similarly functioned as a site of group identity and solidarity. While individual pupils were rewarded at the end of the year in special ceremonies, their performances were framed by the 'points' or prestige they brought to their classes. Good pupils were expected to spend time every week tutoring less successful ones outside teaching hours, a practice (one of many) that served to reinforce the norm of duty towards fellow students and induce solidaristic behaviours. Images of 'pulling together' pervaded school settings, from the content of the curriculum to school-organized 'civic' activities.[8]

Finally, wide ranging *blat* networks (Ledeneva, 1998) had an impact on social lines of division and emphasized interdependence and reciprocity. Most of the population in scarcity-ridden Communist societies had to rely on networks of favours. These networks comprised a wide range of people from a variety of occupations. The concept of *blat* covers very diverse practices:

> *Blat* was an exchange of 'favours of access' in conditions of shortages and a state system of privileges... It served the needs of personal consumption and reorganized the official distribution of material welfare... Intertwined with personal networks, *blat* provided access to public resources through personal channels. (Ledeneva, 1998, 37)

Therefore,

> *blat* is a distinctive form of non-monetary exchange, a kind of barter based

---

7 The workplace was also the source of welfare distribution, subsidized flats, holiday tickets, healthcare and other services (Harloe, 1996).
8 Both schools and workplaces were involved in organizing compulsory civic (or, in official parlance, 'patriotic') activities, such as cleaning parks and streets, visits to old people's homes, and so on.

on personal relationships. It worked where money did not. In the planned economy, money did not function as the main element in economic transactions; things were sorted out by mutual help, by barter. (Ledeneva, 1998, 34)

One of the main features of the *blat* was the importance of personal relationships. It was different from informal economic practices (the 'grey' informal economy, bribery or 'fiddling') because it was based in ties of reciprocity within personal networks, rather than profit-oriented activities and market-type exchanges.

There was no clear-cut quantification of reciprocity within such networks: there was a more intuitive sense of mutual obligations, supported by eagerness to belong to the system and fear of being excluded from it. (Ledeneva, 1998, 115)

Blat practices blurred to a certain extent social boundaries and hierarchies between occupational groups.[9] Importantly, they were intertwined with a rhetoric of friendship, including 'sharing', 'helping out', 'friendly support' and 'mutual care' (Ledeneva, 1998).[10] It is in this sense that these practices are relevant to the topic of solidarity: the *blat* system accentuated notions of interdependence, which are discursively related in respondents' accounts to friendship and human solidarity. Other respondents distance themselves from these 'inadequate' ways of doing things.

To sum up, the Communist past was pervaded by certain practices of solidarity (some of them intertwined with strong 'official' societal discourses of solidarity and social responsibility, others embedded in strategies for overcoming scarcity)[11] that have been radically modified post-1989. Ideas and practices of solidarity have been reconfigured: while defining social goals such as emulating the West through democracy, the free market, free enterprise and competition, discourses grounded in the 'catching up' project have

9   The scarcity of consumer goods and services resulted in a mutual need for resources. For example, a shoe salesperson's importance and status in the network could compensate for a relatively low-prestige job.

10 Ledeneva (1998) discriminates between two types of ties implied by *blat* practices: horizontal ones, composed of people of the same status (sometimes sharing workplace or leisure activities, similar values and lifestyles), where routine 'help' was given; and vertical ones among people of different social strata, which were accessed intermittently for special favours, and had a more instrumental character.

11 In this context, the (simplistic) question of whether people 'really believed' in the official discourse concerning social solidarity is irrelevant: the engagement with this discourse was uneven among social actors, and of an ambiguous, situational nature, while the practices of solidarity were indeed present and often reinforced through state bureaucratic mechanisms.

facilitated the adoption of values, norms and models that have impacted on forms and practices of togetherness. Social change has entailed a questioning of identity and belonging ('with whom do we belong?' is a central question that respondents engaged with in their accounts), and a reflection on what the 'appropriate' relations among people and groups should look like.

The issue of social solidarity in the post-Communist landscape will be approached through an analysis of new forms of stratification that have cut across old ties and old practices of solidarity, and through a discussion of the new norms that make up the social, reconfiguring its moral outline.

The redrawing of social boundaries and its impact on social ties and forms of solidarity

A central aspect of the production of the social post-1989 is represented by the way hegemonic discourses restructure concepts of 'us' and 'them', creating boundaries between social categories, attaching to these groupings valuative connotations, and placing them in hierarchical relations. The issue of social differentiation was overwhelmingly formulated throughout the interviews, and other types of fieldwork material, in material-financial terms:

[Interviewee] People are in different strata, we belong to different strata.

[Interviewer] What sort of strata do you refer to?

[Interviewee] Well ... we don't belong to the same ... I guess money, and what people do with it. (38-year-old man)

The respondents associate stratification with the emergence of the free market, which has allowed for sharp differences in material situations to surface. With the end of state control over the job market and private property, money becomes a strong criterion for assigning individuals to different categories, thus creating subject positions.

No, it's not like before. People have come to realize that you cannot have everything planned by the state. They've tried, and what did it lead to? It didn't work. I know what they say: there is too much poverty because of the way things are organized now, with private property and private companies and competition for jobs. But this is it, you cannot have the past, you have to live in the present. (35-year-old man)

These comments are illustrative of a widespread conceptualization and acceptance of the centrality of free-market arrangements as a societal structuring principle. Romanian society and ordinary life cannot be thought of as divorced from the workings of the market. In this sense, the articulation of capitalism as the only viable socio-economic arrangement is a hegemonic one, which does not allow for other conceptualizations to take form or gain legitimacy. The main criterion or basis for assessing one's general situation and for grasping the surrounding social reality is material status. People assess their material situation in terms of finance (sources of income and ability to cope with expenses), material possessions and consumption patterns.

Money has acquired a different meaning in post-1989 Romanian society. It has 'real' value because one's material wellbeing 'really' depends on it, as opposed to the past, when money was not of much use, under conditions of scarcity in which products were obtained through *blat* rather than purchase, and money alone could not ensure a good lifestyle. (Similarly, social status was also almost insignificant.) 'Money can buy you anything here' and 'everything revolves around money' are common phrases in today's Romania. The only legitimate individual striving in the post-Communist society seems to be related to the improvement of financial status.

> people are obsessed with money. Everything is about money, about how much money you make. I get asked all the time by my mates how much I get paid, and they compare and assess you. (19-year-old man)

> If you have money, you're sorted! You don't need brains, education or manners. (64-year-old man)

'Money' emerges as the single most important factor determining status in contemporary Romania. Following Bourdieu (1986), it can be asserted that economic capital has overshadowed other forms of capital, such as cultural (education) or social (networks), which had played such an important role under Communism. 'Money' is signified by the possessions people surround themselves with and strive for. During Communism, certain practices of consumption (such as purchasing books, foreign jeans, toiletries or cigarettes) were performed as small acts of defiance of the system and the values promoted by the Communist discourse. In the capitalist order, money, consumption and social status are brought together by pervasive articulations and carve out clear subject positions.

The structuring power of the material criterion in the face of other potential principles for binding people together and separating them from other social groups, and of alternative criteria for prestige and status, is grasped by a strong materialistic outlook. The latter seems to be a generalized norm that channels life choices and individual aspirations. Goals in life, or 'the things that matter' for social actors, are overwhelmingly formulated in the material realm.

The most important things for me? I don't know... Well, affording things. So, my job is important; I couldn't live on any job. And it's important to have a good life, a car so that you don't have to squeeze onto public transport, and a comfortable house, and the basic things... furniture, a TV, electronic equipment, a dishwasher, those things. If I have kids they need to go to a private kindergarten, because I don't trust the state ones, obviously, with all the diseases and all... Bringing them up, that's money. (32-year-old man)

New 'public definitions for the general desirability of occupations' (Wegener, 1992, 266) are worked out in contemporary Romania. The prestige of jobs tends to be assessed through earning potential, while occupations that previously had some prestige are now looked down upon because of their meagre salaries (teachers, performers, artists and so on). Chapter 10 in this book is illuminating with respect to the importance of occupational status in the post-Communist landscape.

One aspect of the creation of strata and social divisions according to material status (forms of 'us' and 'them') is the awareness of belonging together in a certain category, an acknowledgement on the part of social actors of their positioning (within broad categories such as 'rich', 'comfortable', 'struggling' and 'poor'). Collective identities are cemented as social actors take up the newly established subject positions. In addition, respondents felt that they had to regulate and filter socialization and interaction in order to demarcate the social group or stratum to which they belonged by interacting with people of a similar status or comparable social standing.

[Interviewee] You can't just stop in the street and talk to everyone. I do socialize in my circle. Some neighbours have invited me for celebrations or such things, but...

[Interviewer] Did you go?

[Interviewee] No, I didn't. They are not my class. (64-year-old man)

Symbolic divisions according to financial status are reinforced by separations according to ways of life and daily practices, from types of jobs and work environments, to patterns of consumption that correspond to distinct sites for shopping, leisure and housing. This 'emplacing' of material status means that certain categories of people have very limited contact, as they use physically distinct spaces that do not overlap. Spaces that are 'for the rich only' or 'for the poor only' take the form of opulent company offices, exclusive clubs or holiday resorts, expensive restaurants and gated neighbourhoods, or second-hand shops, cheap convenience stores and run-down neighbourhoods.[12]

One of the effects of this type of stratification can be seen at the level of social ties, as illustrated by the interview material. The issue of new social categories defined by material status was narratively integrated with accounts of the changed nature and content of human relationships. Social ties were addressed in relation to the 'concrete' circle of friends, acquaintances and neighbours, and at the more abstract level of 'people in this society', as examples of 'what has changed' since 1989. Taking as an anchoring point one's life circumstances and experiences, respondents described the changed nature of sociality. Interviews were replete with statements like this:

> [Interviewee] I had more friends before. Now people have been drawn into other things, or have changed. My friends have changed, there isn't any of the old feeling left.
>
> [Interviewer] In what way have they changed?
>
> [Interviewee] They are just different. Some got rich, and it's all about their business. Others, on the contrary, are not doing that well. So, we just don't feel comfortable together anymore, it's obvious. (53-year-old woman)

The general picture that emerged from a multitude of accounts was of people who used to be linked by ties of friendship, reciprocity and solidarity now being placed in different categories, characterized by different resources and expectations, and divergent practices (such as leisure and consumption). Many respondents perceived the present content or nature of sociality as impoverished. The metaphor of being 'pulled apart', frequently used by respondents, suggested that forms of 'we-ness' were being destroyed. This historic 'we-ness' was usually deployed to critique present arrangements, part of a resistance tactic in the face of re-stratification processes and their perceived consequences.

An important issue that has implications for the emergence of new ties and norms of solidarity in the post-Communist landscape is a widespread feeling of resentment over what is perceived by some as 'unfair' fates. This arose in many of the respondents' accounts, especially those who had not fared very well in the post-Communist period. People who used to be in a similar material situation had found themselves in different categories post-1989, sometimes

---

12 It can be argued that during the Communist period, this type of spatial segregation was less prominent: for example, workers and company directors had subsidized tickets for the same seaside resorts; state-run restaurants had prices that placed them within most people's financial reach; blocks of flats were occupied by people with a mix of occupations, from manual to professional jobs.

with dramatically divergent social trajectories. Questions such as: 'How come they have made it?', or 'Why did they became rich while I am struggling?' indicate the bitterness that characterizes the outlook of many social actors. As many 'new rich' have achieved their new status through bribery, illegal activities (or bordering on the illegal, in the context of a changing and ambivalent legislative framework) and insider knowledge, often capitalizing on their positions under the old regime, their success is met with suspicion and distrust. This type of distrust on the part of the 'losers' tends to extend to anyone who has 'made it', or who is slightly better positioned in material terms. This feeling precludes any orientations that could bond people together, and, implicitly, future practices of solidarity.

Distrust is often accompanied by rancour, an acute feeling of antagonism that imbues social actors' understandings of the social. Rancour and bitterness are directed towards either specific categories or people, or towards more diffuse and pervasive forms. A sense of social injustice is entwined with these feelings: after all, the new social order (capitalism) was supposed to make everyone more prosperous and enable them to achieve Western standards of life, rather than reward some and allow others to sink into poverty. The other side of the coin is the view of the 'winners', the ones who live relatively comfortable lives and who distance themselves from the 'envious' and resentful 'others'. With social relations marked by widespread distrust, resentment and envy, it is difficult to see how cross-cutting networks and practices of solidarity could emerge.

To round off the picture of forms of solidarity in the post-Communist landscape, I will next address the emerging normative make-up that plays into the nature of sociality and conceptualizations of solidarity, and the new norms and values that are articulated in various configurations as part of the production of the social in contemporary Romania. For this purpose, I will look at possessive individualism, competition and freedom as central signifiers in the discourses that are part of the societal project of 'catching up with the West'.

Normative transformations and their reflection on notions of social solidarity

The new norms regarding the individual in relation to society and governing interpersonal relationships are, as asserted throughout this paper, intertwined with notions of catching up and becoming 'Western-like'. Dominant understandings of the social will focus on a departure from the past (anti-Communism) and an embracing of self-reliance, freedom, individualism and competition. The meaning of these signifiers emerges through articulations that social actors perform, as detailed below. While the discursive space is colonized by these concepts, there are attempts to contest their social desirability or legitimacy; they are not self-evident in the way they tend to be in some Western societies.

A strong norm that plays into notions of personhood is that of self-reliance or autonomy; the individual who 'makes it happen' and succeeds on his/her own has become a dominant model for fashioning identities.[13] An awareness of one's dependence on and duties towards others was prominent and constantly reinforced under Communism, and it played into conceptualizations of personhood. Self-understandings at present are rejecting those particular constructs as part of the effort to become 'Western'. The implications of this contemporary understanding of personhood are familiar in the Western context, and visible in the post-Communist one as well. Such implications include: individualized social strategies that are at odds with practices of social solidarity; placing responsibility for social success and failure with the individual; and an unwillingness to engage in practices that would assist less successful people.

> You can only take care of yourself. One should focus on oneself. (31-year-old man)

This form of structuring is reinforced through other concepts, among which 'freedom' is prominent. One conception of freedom was put forward by some respondents who actively distanced themselves from the Communist networks of relations and practices, their normative underpinnings, and the social control element of the gaze of the co-workers, party cadres, neighbours and so on:

> Yes, I would say we're definitely freer now. I mean, we're not entangled in all that mutual ... doing things together, in the same way ... and if you didn't do it [in the same way] as everyone else, someone would tell on you. (60-year-old woman)

A slightly different articulation of freedom refers to freedom from responsibilities towards the others:

> Well, I don't care about X. If he cannot pay his share of the bills, it's not my problem, is it? I'm free, I don't have to care about everyone. (29-year-old man)

---

13 For similar findings in the post-Communist order, see Ule, 2004; Buchowski, 2005.

This statement is part of an individualistic stance that many respondents embrace; being free means not having to care for others, or to feel responsible – a step in the direction of 'the West', and at the same time a move away from the past. The issue of responsibility was constantly emphasized by the Communist regime, through schools, workplaces and the media. There is a clear understanding of 'freedom' as meaning 'freedom from practices of solidarity' that coagulates in the post-Communist setting. There is also a valorization of this norm, mainly in contrast with Communist 'impositions'.

The issue of competition is not so much addressed in the general terms of economic competition as a principle of the free market, but rather in terms of everyday life experiences, especially linked to employment:

> What has really changed is the way you need to really fight for jobs. (31-year-old woman)

The image of scarce resources is often invoked in relation to competition, forging the powerful metaphor of survival in a hostile environment through a ruthless struggle against others.

> In the jungle we live in, one has to fight. (28-year-old man)

This construction invites reflection on appropriate behaviour in a 'jungle'-type society: what is the best strategy for this type of competition? The lack of success in securing a reasonably paid job can mean ending up in the street.

> Nobody cares about anybody; I could drop dead in the street or be sick, and people wouldn't stop. This wouldn't have happened before, but people have changed; they care only for themselves, and do not look around. At all. (64-year-old woman)

What emerged in the interview material was the strong association of competition with individualism and less solidarity in social relations. Understandings of human behaviour that centre on self-interest and egoism were prominent, and images of social life as competition gave them support.

> Yes, I do feel sorry for all these people out there who cannot make ends meet, but you have to keep your focus and try to provide for yourself and your family, if you have one. It's a very tough society, and some will not make it... And because it's so tough people are less caring, less helpful. (58-year-old woman)

The norms underpinning social relations are highlighted in almost all interviews as 'something that has changed' in contemporary Romania, in comparison to the 'past'; self-interest and retreat from certain type of ties, while positing the family as the legitimate focus of one's concerns and efforts, emerge as dominant social strategies.

> Relationships were important; people cared about friends. Now it's definitely more a case of everyone for himself. (34-year-old man)

The new norms concerning interpersonal behaviour have transformed relationships and sociality, through their accent on individualism and independence rather than reliance on others in solving problems, and through introducing a more contractual type of interaction, as opposed to the personalized networks of the past that were necessary for obtaining preferential treatment in conditions of scarcity and for participating in *blat* practices.

The appropriate shape of association and content of relations emerges through the labelling of gregariousness and openness to others as 'Communist' or 'Balkanic', and an embracing of 'efficient', goal-oriented relationships with people of one's choice. This latter mode of interaction is closer to (what is perceived to be) a Western (and 'capitalist') cultural model.

A prominent feature mentioned in relation to sociality is the lack of time for engaging in social relationships, which becomes a device for legitimizng the new norm of 'keeping to oneself' and cutting down on types of interaction that are not directly relevant to one's material wellbeing.

> To be honest, I don't have time for the others. All of it, I put it into my family. (46-year-old woman)

The leitmotif of lack of time, employed by the majority of respondents – whether employed professionals, housewives or retired persons – seemed to become a marker of social worthiness. Not having time to waste reflects adherence to the dominant materialistic discourse and its slogan 'time is money', and indicates people's commitment to activities that could improve their material status: one's worthiness is tied up with the material situation. An image of personal merit as 'lack of time' or 'being busy' is part of an emerging cultural model that valorizes the workplace or the company (materialized in time spent at work). Lack of time is also invoked as the reason for reducing socializing activities: it rationalizes unavailability and unwillingness to commit or make oneself available to others. The meaning of time is central to the new discourses, and it is articulated with both the individualistic and the materialistic outlooks.

Ideas of social solidarity seem marginal in contemporary Romania compared to a normative ideal of privatized, self-sufficient individuals and self-interested social relations. As illustrated here, notions of independence surface powerfully in the context of concepts of interpersonal relationships. By portraying autonomy as the most appropriate arrangement in the present capitalist order, and interdependence and mutual exchanges as characteristic of the Communist period, a contrast is set in place that valorizes independence and clear boundaries (physical and social) at the expense of cooperative behaviour.

In a similar manner, social solidarity and social justice are associated with 'imposed equality' or 'forced homogeneity' and with 'Communism', as opposed to inequality being associated with capitalism. The clear rupture with the past and the discarding (or devaluation) of everything associated with the 'old regime' results in the discursive marginalization (including both modes of thinking and practices) of a set of concepts and ways of doing things, of which cooperation, interdependence and egalitarianism are parts.

Solidarity with the poor and disadvantaged becomes very problematic, as it translates into personal loss or disadvantage. Helping others, for example, means sharing resources (materials or time), and in the present climate of possessive individualism this is often perceived as an unacceptable depletion of one's assets. Solidarity is seen as having no use, as one has to protect personal interests in a world of competition; cumbersome relationships with people of inferior material status, for example, can entail demands for help or favours, which in the long run are considered to work to one's disadvantage.

> I am keeping it at the level of 'Hello', and that's it, because neighbours always know loads about you, so they know I earn well, and might come to me if they can't pay the water rates or God knows what. (33-year-old man)

The poor cannot expect much compassion and help, not only because of the issues outlined above, but also because of the dominant belief that responsibility for personal fate lies with the individual rather than society. Moreover, those who flounder are burdened with the accusation of 'slowing down social progress', and they tend to be stigmatized as the undesirable 'others' who keep 'us' from becoming more 'Western'.

To sum up, independence from social obligations and responsibilities (associated with the 'freedom' that the fall of Communism has yielded) has become a dominant normative ideal that has a deep influence on the way interpersonal relationships are conducted; social solidarity cannot take shape as a norm or social strategy in a discursive landscape dominated by self-reliance and the assuming of individual responsibility for one's wellbeing. The norms, values and conceptualizations that social actors tend to uphold, as presented above, impact on the nature of social ties, including forms of social solidarity. Such norms tend to be articulated as a move away from the 'wrong' ways of doing things, or mentalities of the past; or, conversely, as 'appropriate' when they chime with free-market capitalism and more generally with the 'Western' way.

Conclusion

This chapter has been written to illuminate, using interview material, the ways in which the new hegemonic discourses of the post-Communist period penetrate ordinary ways of thinking and daily practices, and the consequences in terms of sociality and social solidarity. The dominant cluster of discourses on the social that claims to appropriately frame social processes and provides guides (motives and justifications) for action (a 'new culture') coagulates around the signifiers of 'materialism' and 'individualism', and has the power to marginalize alternative ways of thinking the social world. The worldview sustained by the local dominant discourse envisages a society structured by competition for material gain (the marker of social status or position in social hierarchies), which produces winners and losers, separating the ones who make it from the ones who flounder. The lines of division between these strata appear unbridgeable, in the absence of mechanisms that would weave networks of mutual dependence, such as the Communist-era *blat*. This trend is accompanied by norms of individualism that made it difficult to support notions of social responsibility, common fate and associated forms of social solidarity.

At the same time, one can detect forms of resistance to the emerging dominant norms that contest the desirability of using the material criterion to assign social worth, and that support a communalist or collaborative model of social action. The alienating effects of an individualistic stance are emphasized across a significant number of interviews, and some respondents take these reflections a step further by mounting a social critique of the present situation and by sustaining an alternative image of solidarity and collective action as the best strategy in the face of a traumatic social transition.

While this particular articulation could legitimize different ways of thinking and acting on the social, including the reconstitution of forms of 'us' or togetherness associated with claims for social justice, it remains a marginal one in the Romanian post-Communist discursive economy.

References

Bourdieu, P. (1986), 'The forms of capital' in J. Richardson (ed.), *Handbook for Theory and Research for the Sociology of Education*, New York, Greenwood Press.

Buchowski, M. (2005), 'The exoticisation of new others in the neo-liberal "scientific" discourses in Poland', paper given at the Dilemmas of the Post-Communist Condition conference, 23–24 June, Wolverhampton.

Fuller, L. (2000), 'Socialism and the transition in East and Central Europe: the homogeneity paradigm, class, and economic inefficiency', *Annual Review of Sociology*, **26**, 585–609.

Harloe, M. (1996), 'Cities in the transition' in G. Andrusz, M. Harloe and I. Szelenyi (eds), *Cities after Socialism*, Oxford, Blackwell.

Laclau, E. (1990), *New Reflections of the Revolution of Our Time*, London, Verso.

Laclau, E. and Mouffe, C. (2001[1985]), *Hegemony and Socialist Strategy* (second edition), London, Verso.

Ledeneva, A. V. (1998), *Russia's Economy of Favours: Blat, Networking, and Informal Exchange*, New York, Cambridge University Press.

Outhwaite, W. and Ray, L. (2005), *Social Theory and Postcommunism*, Oxford, Blackwell.

Segert, A. and Zierke, I. (2000), 'Metamorphosis of habitus among East Germans' in P. Chamberlayne, J. Bornat and T. Wengraf (eds), *The Turn to Biographical Methods in Social Sciences*, London, Routledge.

Szelenyi, I. (1982), 'The intelligentsia in the class structure of state-socialist societies', *American Journal of Sociology*, **88**, Supplement: Marxist Inquiries: Studies of Labor, Class, and States, S287–S326.

Sztompka, P. (2002), 'Cultural trauma: the other face of cultural change', *European Journal of Social Theory*, **3**, 441–465.

Ule, M. (2004), 'No time for complacency: sociology after socialism', *European Societies*, **6**, 2, 159–166.

Wegener, B. (1992), 'Concepts and measurements of prestige', *Annual Review of Sociology*, **18**, 253–280.

163

10 Non-solidarity and Unemployment in the 'New West'

Herwig Reiter

East-Central European transformations take place in the dual context, or 'cognitive frame of reference', of 'the West' and 'the past', as Offe (1996, 230) programmatically noted some ten years ago when describing the fundamentally different starting conditions for the development of political economies in post-Communist countries. A few years later, it seems that images of the future of social cohesion within the extended West in Europe must shift their perspective towards 'the East', and see what has become of it. There is concern that the 'post-Communist solidarity crisis' (Outhwaite and Ray, 2005, Chapter 3) might be a critical, perhaps contagious feature of the somewhat vague European social model. One particular phenomenon that I want to introduce and discuss in this chapter could be called 'the post-Communist paradox of desolidarization', i.e., the coincidence of persistently egalitarian values with low levels of involvement in solidary activities. This chapter strives to contribute to a refined understanding of post-Communist solidarity dilemmas faced by people living in former Communist countries who are confronted with the new phenomenon of mass unemployment.

There is increasing evidence that testifies to the challenge of living in former Communist neo-capitalist countries, and the ambivalent findings point to the complex nature of this issue. Generalizations across contextual varieties seem obvious, but risk becoming as inappropriate as the transfer of Western research tools, concepts and interests. What further complicates research into an issue like solidarity is the fact that, despite the many claims proposed, nobody knows what it is. The notion of solidarity is hardly consolidated; it can mean everything, from a prerequisite of the social to a good reason for redistributive taxation and welfare (see Baldwin, 1990; Crow, 2002; Mau, 2003). In my view, solidarity is first of all one of the ways of synthesizing the general question of chances, beyond individual freedom and (dis)advantage, of moral as well as material integration, and in line with standards shared by members of a community.

The chapter discusses the constitution of post-Communist (local) solidarities with regard to the new but fundamental threat of mass unemployment associated with the capitalist organization of work in the 'new West'. Focusing on the recent establishment of a frequent image of 'the unemployed', the chapter considers the nature and sources of knowledge about unemployment and the unemployed that might engender feelings of suspicion towards 'the other'. The notion of 'knowledge' applied is that of everyday life suggested by Berger and Luckmann (1967); it is contextual, taken-for-granted and action-relevant. For the purpose of this chapter I conceptualize solidarity indirectly, as being constituted from below by the performance of activities by members of a certain community by virtue of their 'knowledge' about what establishes full membership in society. The constitution of knowledge is my principal focus.

I do this on the basis of an interview with a young man from Lithuania, a context in which the social transformation has been most radical. The interview is part of a qualitative research project[1] exploring the 'new meanings' of work and unemployment from the perspective of young people. The perspective of a young person provides an opportunity to contrast the intergenerational transfer of knowledge relating to 'the past' with the second 'cognitive frame of reference' of 'the West' (Offe, 1996). Both of these aspects are represented by important family members. It should also enable us to observe how these two perspectives come together in the work-related and unemployment-related criteria of a young post-Communist EU citizen, and how they help to organize social space and establish images of 'outsiders' in the new society.

In order to contextualize this case, I will first develop a research perspective on the basis of the post-Communist paradox of desolidarization, which is characteristic of the solidarity triangle of mutual relations between individuals, 'the other' and the state. The presence of essentially unknown social figures, like the unemployed – a result of the mainstreaming of society and its institutions in line with Western standards– could lie behind this paradox. I will also briefly consider work-related changes in the context of the social transformation in favour of the market economy. Finally, I will introduce and discuss our young man from Lithuania, and the way he negotiates the meanings of work and unemployment.

---

1   The research was carried as part of a PhD project at the European University Institute in Florence.

The post-Communist paradox of desolidarization and beyond

Civil society research and surveys in post-Communist societies provide an ambivalent picture and allow for the identification of what could be called a 'post-Communist paradox of desolidarization'. Survey research indicates a generally higher level of sensitivity to and rejection of forms of injustice among citizens of former Communist countries than among those of the European West. Public opinion does not converge in a linear way towards Western standards, nor is this strongly facilitated by the values of 'the younger generation' (e.g. Arts et al., 2003). Research into civil society development, on the other hand, shows that this does not correspond to a high level of citizen involvement in the activities of civil society.[2] The readiness to participate in forms of common activity for the sake of some more or less specifically-defined 'other' is weak. Howard (2003), for instance, studies civil society development in East Germany and Russia, and finds that people are tired of any form of commitment to collective activities, and frustrated by the slow pace of change for the better in their societies. In addition, their social relations suffer from the changing preconditions of socializing under post-Communist conditions.

This last element points towards a more fundamental transformation in interpersonal relations: People increasingly focus on their own personal lives, and distance themselves from one another for reasons of survival or a lack of alternatives. Money, which now represents 'real value' and possesses a power of distinction, has a 'newly prominent and destructive role' (Howard, 135) with regard to relations between people and within families. Social inequalities and polarization have both increased dramatically. Interpersonal relations in the workplace have been transformed, for instance by the increased turnover of the workforce, the introduction of formal codes of interaction between colleagues at work, and the elimination of the workplace as a platform for making and meeting friends.

Research of this kind penetrates the deeper layers of the eroding preconditions for social bonding in post-Communist contexts. Sennett (1998) views the contemporary capitalist West in a similar light, concluding that traditional social bonds are at risk from an apparent decline in mutual dependence. In view of findings such as those described above, I would tentatively argue that a similar conclusion – namely, that social bonds are under threat – can be reached in respect of the former Communist contexts, precisely as a result of the *introduction* of mutual dependence. In the past, the

---

2 For a recent argument in favour of a close association between solidarity and civil society, see Muenkler, 2004.

state mediated interpersonal relationships. Moreover, although people were equally replaceable (in terms of their place in the labour force), they were not replaced, as this did not make sense within the logic of a socialist shortage economy.[3] Thus, Sennett's conclusion with regard to the erosive effect of 'shame about dependence' (1998, 141) might also apply to the post-Communist condition, but as a result of opposite causes.

Generally speaking, the rebuilding of civil society in the context of solidarity must consider the fact that 'the socialist state was programmatically an individualizer, trying to break all other kinds of social relations', as Peter Wagner (1994, 102) notes, against the prevailing consensus. Now that this state is no more, reciprocity has become a prerequisite of the common. Searching for a definition of the 'other' is part of coming to terms with the sudden possibility *and* necessity of intra-society relations. This process seems most difficult, and might yield the most painful outcome, where the features of the 'other' are radically new, such as in the case of the 'unemployed' or, to take another example, the immigrant.[4]

Biographical research into the social transformation associated with the market economy provides some answers to this paradox of persistent solidarity in attitudes and values versus weak solidarity in practice. It does this by confronting individual trajectories of (non-)solidary action with the trajectory of public (non-)solidarity (i.e., welfare). Struck (2003) reports on a study into coping and decision-making within the life course of adults under the 'new conditions' of the 'individualized market economy' in the former East Germany.[5] He concludes that the observable 'signs of desolidarization' among the respondents are not due to the mere loss of an over-protective state or deficient socialization (Struck, 2003, 212).[6] Instead, they have their roots in the fact that a 'willingness to succeed', where it is observed among individuals as having survived the process of social transformation, does not have 'counterparts at the level of the social system' (Struck, 2003, 221). Against the background of one of the research interests, the study finds that 'habitual dispositions' remained stable after the social transformation, but triggered

---

3 Of course, there were other ways for the system to identify the unworthiness of a person.
4 For an account of 'welfare state xenophobia' (solidarity violence?) in the shape of skinhead violence in the unified Germany, see, for example, Ostow, 1995. For a hint that this concern is not implausible, see paragraph 140 of the interview in the appendix.
5 Sackmann et al., 2000.
6 This latter argument is, for instance, proposed by Sztompka (1996). In a strongly normative argument, he identifies a 'cultural lag' between institutional transformation and cultural resources. It is on account of this 'incongruence of institutional and cultural levels' that a whole generation of people socialized in the old system would be at once devalued.

divergent and pragmatic patterns of behaviour, directed in this case towards occupational security. Disappointed expectations of a continuation of the state's responsibility for the welfare of citizens thwart individual readiness to undertake solidary action. On the basis of these findings, one could hypothesize that by virtue of the different pressures of immediacy, the asynchronous trajectories of individual versus public action that occurred through the transformation did not facilitate the activation of still-available notions of a good life and moral behaviour.

An alternative but non-exclusive hypothesis, and this is the one I want to pursue throughout the rest of the paper, adds the dimension of knowledge to the puzzle partly solved above. Desolidarization might actually have some of its roots in the confusion, caused by a lack of knowledge, concerning the possible beneficiaries of articulations of solidarity within the individual–'other'–state triangle. As far as social groups that ultimately depend on support (e.g., the unemployed) are concerned, it could be due to this knowledge gap that, as the above research indicates, state action is expected, although in the end it is regarded as inadequate. More specifically, and in relation to post-socialist transformations in the world of work, one could assume the following: in order to be able to be acted upon as either a companion or an outsider, the contemporary figure of the unemployed person might still need to be constituted conceptually, and knowledge related to the unemployed might still need to be consolidated.

Changing notions of work and the advent of the unemployed

The breakdown of Communism and the 'catching-up' (e.g. Zapf, 1994) of many former Communist societies with Western standards brought an end to the socialist policy of full employment, where the state's commitment to providing jobs for everybody went hand in hand with the citizens' obligation to work. Starting from the 'complete elimination of unemployment' announced by Soviet leaders in the autumn of the year 1930 (Davis, 1986), and the criminalization of resigning from a job without the employer's permission in the Soviet Union ten years later in view of the coming war (Filtzer, 1986), the world of work in the Communist half of Europe remained characterized for decades by what Baxandall (2000; 2004), in his study of Hungary, identifies as a 'Communist taboo against unemployment' in ideological, economic and political terms. Once established, the system's achievement of full employment had the status of an irreversible 'acquired right' of the worker (Kornai, 1992, 210) within socialist ideology. Economically, unemployment did not exist, at least not officially.[7] Politically, the policy of unemployment was maintained as officials, leaders and workers could equally benefit from supporting the systemic rule against unemployment.

As was the case in so many other areas, the official line did not fully match the reality, and 'unemployment', according to a Western understanding of people changing jobs or a mismatch between jobs and job-seekers, did in fact exist in the Soviet Union and in socialist countries in general. However, unemployment was banned from public discourse, its scope was not 'measured', and institutions of unemployment (such as labour exchanges or unemployment registration) were not established. Instead, people outside work were clearly identified; non-participation in work was considered either a temporary interruption of work due to good (mostly private) reasons, or it was associated with social outcasts and even criminalized.[8]

Following the collapse of Communist regimes, unemployment was one of the side-effects of the prescribed 'shock therapy' of economic reform that intensified the social policy difficulties associated with the transition to a market economy (e.g. Standing, 2002; Ferge, 2001). The low level of social benefits, together with a massive decline in employment and the emergence of the new phenomenon of mass unemployment, undermined the traditional expectations of citizens towards the state. As unemployment, in terms of its meaning and experience, became part of this new arrangement between state and citizens, the meaning of (formal) employment in the life course changed (Kohli, 1986; Leisering and Leibfried, 1999). Employment has remained a 'key access point to social benefits', as Deacon (2000, 147) describes it, for the socialist system; but the efforts necessary to enter employment and to remain a gainfully employed insider are much greater within a capitalist context.

Lithuania is one of the countries that, following the collapse of the Soviet Union some 15 years ago, underwent a social and economic transformation that brought it closer to the Western European model of economy and society. In 2004 it joined the European Union. The Lithuanian march westwards has covered a long distance, and Lithuania is among those that have ventured furthest. A recent World Bank report (World Bank et al., 2005, 2) announced that Lithuania, together with Slovakia, 'broke into the list of the 20 economies with the best business conditions as measured in this year's report'. However, there is a darker side to liberalization, and some of its adverse effects are work-related: EUROSTAT statistics (Bardone and Guio, 2005) assessing the

---

7 Unemployment was 'negligible in scale' (Kornai, 1992, 530); the exception was Yugoslavia (Woodward, 1995).

8 A view of the practical aspects of the obligation to work and the difficulties of dealing with 'parasites' is provided by Granick, 1987, 23–28.

poverty risk of employed and unemployed people show that in Lithuania, as well as Slovakia, more than 40 per cent of the population above the age of 15 and at risk of living in poverty are actually employed. The average in the EU's 15 most long-standing members is 26 per cent.[9]

In the meantime, new definitions of 'right/good' or just 'appropriate/ tolerable' behaviour with regard to employment are negotiated against the background of the recently introduced institution of the labour exchange. Apart from its function as an interface between labour supply and demand, it has, as Juska and Pozzuto (2004) remark, become a bureaucratic institution reproducing rituals of supervision, discipline and control. Based on an ethnographic study of labour exchange clients and practices in Lithuania, the authors argue that the labour exchange has become a crucial player in the new, post-Soviet establishment of patterns of exclusion and marginalization, by operating with the moralizing distinction between the 'deserving' and the 'undeserving' unemployed/poor. The labour exchange draws the unemployed into a continuous search for non-existing jobs in order to assure their (moral) eligibility for benefits, while having a negligible impact on the actual situation of the unemployed.

Therefore, it appears that young people in the 'new West' receive mixed messages concerning the shift in meaning of formal employment and unemployment. On the one hand, and according to the prevailing opportunity structures, formal employment is defined as only one option for survival; formal unemployment does not necessarily entail actually being out of work. On the other hand, the individual orientation towards successful employment performance and continuous contribution to the social security system has become a new 'requirement' for both the reproduction of the system and for individual wellbeing. Recent policy-driven changes in the assessment of this orientation among young people have contributed to an upsurge in the contradictory character of the entry of young people into the labour market (Reiter and Craig, 2005). The advent of the figure of the unemployed in the 'new West' is framed by these tensions characterizing the redefinition of the role of work in one's life, and by the struggle concerning the constitution of what can be called 'a socially recognized contribution to social reproduction' (Honneth, 2002, 54).[10]

Young people occupy a particularly delicate position in this process of knowledge renewal, as it is largely up to them to negotiate 'old' meanings and

9 Altogether, the number of working poor in the 25 members of the EU amounts to 14 million people.

10 For an assessment of the concept of recognition in Honneth's version in the context of research into changing meanings of work in post-Communist contexts, see Reiter, 2005.

to carry them further into the new society. This is a common but usually gradual process. In the case of post-Communist transformations, the devaluation of the knowledge represented by the parents' and the grand-parents' generation can be expected to be more profound. However, while the (legal) framework of institutions together with official discourses might have changed within very short periods of time, the socially available patterns of interpretations, together with the moral readjustment of the people to the new circumstances, cannot. What Srubar (1998, 131, referring to Parsons, 1951, 96–101) calls the 'latency of values' operates in the background, with a certain stabilizing (or at least decelerating) effect. Representatives of the old system, whether perceived as such or not, will still be around for some time, both physically and in terms of ideas. The particular case presented below can be read as an illustration of this struggle.

Negotiating meanings of work and unemployment: the example of Saulius

Saulius[11] was one of the participants in a qualitative study exploring the 'new meanings' of work and unemployment from the perspective of young people making the transition to working life. He belongs to the group of young people in 'linear transitions'; they are mostly still in education and, like the majority of young people, 'on track'. Saulius is a 16-year-old student in the tenth and last year of compulsory education. He is 'on track' in the sense that there is no indication that he will drop out of school; his environment is supportive and at least until finishing upper secondary education, his plans are certain. Saulius is an interesting case for many reasons. The nature of his family relations makes him a particularly suitable candidate for an illustration, though not an explanation, of how new meanings are established between different worlds, and the way in which they are represented. In summary, when his parents, both of whom had received a university education, divorced ten years ago, his mother left to work in the USA. Since she did not want him to live with his father, Saulius, their only child, moved away from the capital Vilnius to a small town to stay with his maternal grandparents, both of whom had retired.

His family relations might be considered exceptional and not 'common' enough. However, his parents' divorce was not unusual, and his mother's employment abroad in order to maintain the family back home, was, and still is, very common. In general, it is not out of the ordinary to know somebody

---

11 'Saulius' is the pseudonym the interviewee chose. The interviews were carried out in Lithuanian and subsequently translated.

who works abroad. However, the closeness of his contact with his grandparents, and in particular his grandmother, is probably greater than average, and might make him an exceptional case. Nevertheless, it is precisely this that allows us to reconstruct what I call the 'dialogue with the past'. His mother, who returns from her work in the restaurant of a cruise ship for one or two months every year and then stays together with him in the same room, is the second significant reference person. She is his main partner in his 'dialogue with the West'.

The discussion of the material in terms of 'dialogues' is analytic, and follows Offe's (1996) suggestion of studying post-Communist transformations in the dual 'cognitive frame of reference and comparison of "the West" with "the past"' (Offe, 1996, 230). Obviously, these are imaginary dialogues and heuristic tools here, which are without exclusive character. At the same time, it is not possible to reduce knowledge constitution to a transfer between family members, as this would underestimate its complexity. Nor does knowledge originate only in the West or the past, as this would put into question the availability of knowledge in the place under discussion. The spatial and temporal *present* needs to be considered as the primary arena of meaning negotiation and frame of reference of both acting and time structuring.[12] However, it seems appropriate to emphasize the significance of family members in this case: Saulius himself stresses the importance of this inter-generational transfer of knowledge for the constitution of his own opinion and public opinion in general.

With regard to the issue of unemployment, the second forum of knowledge (i.e., the dialogue with his mother) seems less relevant, at least in terms of a direct influence on his opinion, which is determined mostly by what he can observe in his immediate environment. Unemployment is here and now; what is abroad is his mother and her successful career. However, his mother's experiences and what he learns from communicating with her about the new world of work in the 'West' are part of the constitution of his developing professional persona.

I will therefore first take a brief look at what Saulius thinks about the world of work and the requirements for success, as well as, implicitly, failure. This is confronted with his image of the unemployed. The conclusion is that the world of work, like his mother in the West, is closer to him than the world of unemployment and his grandmother, who is a source of knowledge from which he tends to dissociate himself.

12 Cf. Reiter, 2003 on biographical time structuring for young people.

The dialogue with the West

His mother is Saulius's role model of success in the Western world of work, a world that he generally describes as demanding and hostile:

> I wouldn't like to go to America. My mum has told me terrible things: terrible people are there, they require a lot. That is why I don't like it. People are better in Lithuania, more sincere, not spoilt yet. [He is laughing.]

His mother left after divorcing his father, and over the years she worked her way up from waitressing to being a restaurant manager on a cruise ship.[13] Although Saulius obviously misses her, he recognizes her accomplishment. In fact, he cannot even visit her because she needs to make sacrifices in her private life: 'She doesn't work on the continent, she is on the ship all the time, so she doesn't have a permanent place to live – that is, she has a cabin.' He understands that she sustains him financially and that, in spite of her promises, she will probably not come back 'because here there is no work for her' that would be equally well paid.

The idea of (labour) mobility is something he easily integrates into his own life plans. In view of his family's plans to move back to Vilnius, where he grew up, he demonstrates his willingness to move house, as he expects this to be a natural feature of working life: 'Somehow I want to change the environment, because ... as one goes through life, anyway, one will change workplaces. So I need to get used to that.'

The expression of his readiness to adapt to the anticipated requirements of the new world of work is not unique. He gives the impression of an attentive observer with broad 'knowledge', and throughout the interview he keeps associating his plans, priorities and perspectives with expectations of this kind.

Referring to his mother's stories about working abroad as well as to job advertisements that he has read, he understands that what counts these days in applications, job interviews and recommendation letters is 'experience, experience'. Experience might be the 'foundation for the future', although it may come at the cost of 'working for nothing' at the beginning. Another reason why it has become so difficult to find a job is that many well-educated people compete for the same jobs, but only the 'the best ones are chosen'. His reply to a question about whether he intends to study is emphatic:

> Of course I do. How can I do without studies? One is not hired to clean streets without having studied these days. [He is laughing.] Studies are necessary. In general, a person studies all his life.

---

13 It is important to note that Saulius never claims that the cruise ship actually sails under a US flag; however, his generalizations address 'America'.

He strives for a 'good education', and when he thinks about all the 'dumb people' in the USA, whom his mother mentioned to him, he feels the obligation to become educated and smart, in order 'not to be the only stupid one among many clever people' in 'a small country like Lithuania', where 'it is possible to get a good education'. What counts is education as such, not the specific course of study; in particular, a knowledge of languages is important in the European Union.

He knows that education has become a minimum job requirement, and that specialized professional skills need to be constantly updated. Asked whether a career would be important for him when he starts working, he specifically emphasizes virtues like flexibility, ('natural') ambition and lifelong learning:

> Of course it is important. You would not work in one position for your whole life. It is necessary to climb the career ladder and try to reach the top, because ... people who are bosses, they will leave one day, and someone has to take their positions. So everything is always moving forwards. I hope to always move forwards like this. Of course, a career is important. One needs to put in a lot of effort, and to study all your life; study in order to climb up to the next step of the career ladder.

Finally, he learned that, apart from education or simply communicative slickness, 'contacts' – acquaintances and friends – can be essential for success. Furthermore, having contacts is most powerful as a complementary feature: for talented or intelligent people who 'have a couple of contacts ... everything is fine, life is in order'. Saulius seems to deal with his 'contacts', friends mostly, very consciously. He collects them, and leaves some behind. Very early in the interview, he says, 'I have sifted out my friends' as his interests and priorities changed over the course of time. Many of his friends are older, by about five years, and he has more in common with them than with his peers. He likes to attend and participate in theatre productions and he is interested in art, and he 'chooses' his friends accordingly. Reflecting on what is important about work, he illustrates his understanding of how contacts operate:

> Most important, it seems to me, is making new contacts, getting acquainted. In the future ... these contacts will become very useful. Sometimes, when you need some help or a favour, contacts are important. And in general, nowadays, if you listen to people, it seems that it is impossible to get anywhere without contacts.

The dialogue with the past

His grandmother is Saulius's strongest and most tangible link to the past, and he refers to her throughout the interview. She is an ambivalent source of knowledge, which he rejects in principle but appreciates when alternative interpretations are not available. Saulius describes his grandmother as 'too conservative'. Unlike his parents, who let him find his way, she can be very straight about her 'stupid wishes' for his career. When she states that she would like him to become a doctor, he just 'laughs at her, and that's it, nothing else'. This is also how he would, to her embarrassment, stop her from telling stories about how it used to be 'when [she] was young'.

Saulius's assessment of unemployment and unemployed people in Lithuania is a complex articulation tying together many associations. I restrict my discussion to three main issues relevant for the present chapter. They are interwoven, but analytically separated here:

1 unemployment and the unemployed,
2 the assumed role of the state, and
3 general opinions about the unemployed, as well as Saulius's own attitude.[14]

Unemployment and the unemployed

Although Saulius recognizes the problem of a lack of jobs, as well as the state's responsibility in this respect, he does not accept unemployed people who do not even try to find a job, but instead appear to exploit the system of welfare by, for instance, living on child benefit. He is convinced that work can be found with the appropriate attitude. He repeatedly calls unemployed people 'lazybones', and dissociates himself explicitly from them: 'I don't support such people. I somehow do not like such people'. Asked for his opinion about unemployment and its reasons, he answers:

Hmm. [These] people are lazybones. [He is laughing.] ... Those who want [one] can surely find a job. It is not that ... there is no work ... [as though one were] in some village: 'I came here and cannot find a job.' You have to look for it: those who look for work, find it. If you lie on a couch with a glass of brandy [laughs], life will surely not get better because of that. The state, of course, cannot create work for everybody, but for many. If you cannot find a job, so what? You can go abroad. I don't think that it is

14 See the appendix for the relevant interview passage.

absolutely impossible to get a job. Of course, it is possible. But sometimes people are very demanding and lazy, exactly those who do not have [work]. They think that it is much easier to live out of the state's pocket by having lots of children, that that is much easier than to work like normal people.

Saulius's general image of the unemployed is associated with idleness, reluctance to take chances and a form of social parasitism that lies outside social normality. The unemployed are discouraged citizens who complain, but do not articulate this through democratic participation. Furthermore, unemployment goes hand in hand with alcoholism. Most of the unemployed people he knows drink, 'and employers do not want such people'. He has little sympathy for them in general, and does not consider them 'common people, like others but simply without jobs'. The only exception he can think of, and this indicates the possibility for alternative behaviour by the unemployed, is his aunt's husband, who actually 'does something' (taking care of their share of a formerly collective garden). Nevertheless, the general image of the unemployed is that of filth and scum, associated with a 'shabby home', and 'asocial families who do not take care of anything'. Referring to his aunt's husband, he says:

> ... even though he drinks, at least he does something, [which] is good, because there are [people] who don't do anything. It is absolutely terrible. Shabby home. These social workers, when they enter [such homes], it makes them wrinkle their noses. It is terrible. Or like [some things] they show on TV ... so many famous people are forgotten [or] disabled, it is terrible. The state doesn't take care [of them] properly. It is still young as a state, it [can't] take care of everything yet. That is why people are cheerless and disappointed with life sometimes.

The assumed role of the state

In the final part of this last quotation, Saulius articulates the disappointment of people in post-Communist countries with the state's failure to take responsibility. It is similar to that described by Struck (2003, see above). Saulius identifies insufficient state support as the reason for people's general dissatisfaction. However, he considers this to be a temporary problem associated with a 'young' state. Within the context of the whole passage related to work and unemployment, this statement has the status of a conclusion based on related accounts made before.

Saulius indicates that there is a state responsibility with regard to unemployment, but that it is necessarily limited; moreover, there is a risk of abuse. He supports the idea of paying unemployment benefit, because there are people who simply could not live otherwise, for instance 'people without education' or those with qualifications that are less in demand. On the other hand, he has faith in public support on the municipal level, and refers to offers of voluntary work that should be accepted. However, he considers benefit levels to be too low ('a person wouldn't survive'), and is upset with the low level of retirement pensions. The state's inadequate answer to a life of hard work is a case of mis-recognition, in the sense of Honneth (1995); again, it is considered a temporary problem.

> (...)the pensions, altogether, are nothing but a mockery. [He is laughing.] A person works hard all his life and then gets some pennies, and is not able to live on them. But Lithuania is a growing state, everything will be fine in the future.

Apart from 'ridiculous pensions', Saulius laments the low level of health expenditure and doubts the state's readiness to take responsibility for education, despite its actual benefits in terms of a capable labour force. Altogether, the state's responsibility for coordinating institutionalized forms of solidarity like pensions, health provision, education and job creation is not questioned.

Opinions about the unemployed

The other source of support for the unemployed is potentially sympathetic individuals within a generally indifferent or even hostile social environment. 'Pity' is the people's general attitude towards the kind of unemployed person Saulius has in mind. The example he gives is a woman in manifest misery who, distinguished by a 'swollen face' from drinking, successfully approaches his grandmother for a pittance. Saulius adopts this attitude of pity towards some, especially long-term, unemployed people. Furthermore, he assesses them against his own situation on the basis of what could be called a 'reflexive sense of equity'; they are less lucky than him and live less well than he does:

> (...) especially those who haven't become unemployed recently, but who have not found a job for a long time: I feel pity for these people most of all, that they are not lucky in life, that they cannot live well and have all that ... I have.

Nevertheless, his final assessment takes him back to where he started: the unemployed are the 'lazybones' he described before. He is not alone in holding this opinion, and explicitly acknowledges the strong influence of other people, especially his grandparents and parents. Reflecting upon the general popular opinion, he says:

> How do they look at them [the unemployed]? First of all, they call them lazybones, like I do. [He is laughing.] I agree with their opinion. Maybe they made us get used to the idea that they are lazybones, so they think the same as I do. People always think the same way that adults do – their grandparents or parents.

Unemployment between 'the past' and 'the West'

The world of work beyond his immediate surroundings, associated with his mother working in the West, appears to be closer and more real and relevant to Saulius than the present world of unemployment surrounding him, which he associates with his grandmother, who represents a source of distant knowledge. Saulius's dialogue with the West is about getting work, keeping it and moving upwards within it. It is not unlikely that these have become the most important features of work in the 'new West'. Partly as a result of his mother's experiences, he adopts a perspective that is necessarily future-oriented; work is ahead of him, and now is the time to prepare. Good education and the right contacts, which were important criteria of social mobility in the old system, are complemented by other requirements, like 'working for nothing', mobility, flexibility, and the willingness to continuing learning. All this facilitates upwards mobility, which is an inbuilt feature of the system of work as well as of individual efforts. Finally, work and career – as in the example of his mother working on a ship –go hand in hand with sacrifices in one's own private life. Those companions previously regarded as friends or acquaintances are now 'contacts' (sources of potential favours), or competitors in the race for good jobs. Saulius seems to have learned and understood this part of life extraordinarily quickly, and the availability of a close and 'successful' representative of the new world of work certainly contributed to it. However, he does not establish a link between the transformation of people's priorities towards individualistic career-orientated goals and the image of 'terrible people' that his mother provides in her account of contemporary 'America'.

On the other hand, Saulius's account of unemployment and unemployed people evolves out of a dialogue with the past, while the connection between the issue of unemployment and what he knows about the West remains implicit. In his perception, the unemployed are either redundant, old or ill-qualified; alternatively, they are miserable and reluctant to work. For them, finding and keeping work under the new conditions is necessarily problematic given the presumed lack of necessary basic personal qualities. According to Saulius, the state is not released from its life-course responsibilities; education, job availability and creation, post-work pensions and citizens' survival are still part of the state's solidarity burden. State support is described as remedial and requires voluntary involvement; it offers only a minimal contribution to the re-establishment of a person's 'status of worth'. The social environment, on the other hand, is characterized by a basic suspicion of this caricature of 'the unemployed'; this is overcome by occasional sympathy. Suspicion seems to be the common attitude, and sympathy is not unconditional but depends on the moment of attention, as well as comparison and 'discrimination', in the sense of the establishment of difference. While a sense of equity is in principle also evident in Saulius's account, the question is whether stable and reasonable criteria for the assessment of unemployed people will crystallize on this hollow basis, and if so in which direction it will develop.

Conclusion

The two perspectives on the past and the possible future of post-Communist societies that I suggested for analytic purposes produce largely inconsistent accounts. While the dialogue with the West overtakes reality and advances larger-than-life expectations, the dialogue with the past lags behind and becomes bogged down in outdated stereotypes about unemployed people as social outcasts, or the role of the state as a responsible actor. The reality of mass unemployment, the working poor, poverty and social polarization is somewhere in between, but it remains a blank field inasmuch as appropriate patterns of interpretation are unavailable. The case of Saulius illustrates the current struggle for a consolidation of knowledge about unemployed people by negotiating and confronting available yet inconsistent claims. As a representative of young people in former Communist countries – one who has presumably incorporated particularly sensitive filters of knowledge – he needs to make sense of what could be thought of convergent and path-dependent bodies of knowledge.

The stereotypical figure of the contemporary unemployed person seems anachronistic within the post-Communist context. It has inherited features from Soviet ideology: an idle, asocial alcoholic trying to exploit meagre state benefits. 'Real' victims of the (labour) market – for instance, the elderly, the ill-qualified – are perceived as exceptions. Given the scope of the unemployment problem, such a caricature is both false and inadequate. It certainly portrays one aspect of the post-Communist social landscape, but it is inappropriate for a general representation of market-induced mass unemployment.

A rapid knowledge turnover in the 'new West' cannot be expected; habitual knowledge is still in place and continues to be reproduced. Furthermore, it will be of crucial importance to observe the direction in which the balance within the solidarity triangle (individual–'other'–state) will further develop due to the new representatives of the state, such as institutions of (un-)employment management, and their criteria of inclusion/exclusion.[15] However, undefined relations between potential strangers within this triangle seem to account for some of the enigma of post-Communist non-solidarity.

Generalizing beyond this case study, one could assume that, for the time being, the inaction of both the state and the individual are in principle legitimized by a biased representation of the unemployed, the establishment of boundaries around them, and a strong and largely inappropriate dissociation from them. On these grounds, it seems unlikely that solidarity based on a persistent basic attitude of supportiveness within a community of shared realities and values will develop. By contrast, the circle of solidarity is temporarily extended in order to embrace those who manage to catch the attention of the insiders.

Acknowledgements

Many people contributed to improving earlier versions of the text. I want to thank especially Nathalie Karagiannis, Michael Vorisek, Thomas Fiegle, Annika Zorn, Thomas Fetzer, Jaap Dronkers and Martin Kohli for helpful comments and discussions.

References

Arts, W., Gelissen, J. and Luijkx, R. (2003), 'Shall the twain ever meet? Differences and changes in socio-economic justice norms and beliefs in Eastern and Western Europe at the turn of the millennium' in W. Arts, W. Hagenaars and J. Halman (eds), *The Cultural Diversity of European Unity: Findings, Explanations and Reflections from the European Values Study*, Leiden, Brill.

Baldwin, P. (1990), *The Politics of Social Solidarity: Class Bases of the European Welfare State 1875–1975*, Cambridge, Cambridge University Press.

Bardone, L. and Guio, A.-C. (2005), *In-work Poverty: New Commonly Agreed Indicators at the EU Level, Statistics in Focus – Population and Social Conditions*, Volume 5, European Communities. http://epp.eurostat.cec.eu.int/cache/ITY_OFFPUB/KS-NK-05-005/EN/ KS-NK-05-005-EN.pdf (accessed 4 May 2005).

15 For instance, identified by Juska and Pozzuto, 2004.

Baxandall, P. (2000), 'The Communist taboo against unemployment: ideology, soft-budget constraints, or the politics of de-Stalinisation?', *East European Politics and Societies*, 14, 597–635.

Baxandall, P. (2004), *Constructing Unemployment: The Politics of Joblessness in East and West*, Aldershot, Ashgate.

Berger, P. L. and Luckmann, T. (1967), *The Social Construction of Reality: A Treatise in the Sociology of Knowledge*, London, Penguin.

Crow, G. (2002), *Social Solidarities : Theories, Identities, and Social Change*, Buckingham, Open University Press.

Davis, R. W. (1986), 'The ending of mass unemployment in the USSR' in D. Lane (ed.), *Labour and Employment in the USSR*, Brighton, Wheatsheaf.

Deacon, B. (2000), 'Eastern European welfare states: the impact of the politics of globalization', *Journal of European Social Policy*, 10, 146–161.

Ferge, Z. (2001), 'Welfare and "ill-fare" systems in Central-Eastern Europe' in R. Sykes, B. Palier and P. M. Prior (eds), *Globalization and European Welfare States: Challenges and Change*, Houndmills, Palgrave.

Filtzer, D. (1986), *Soviet Workers and Stalinist Industrialization: The Formation of Modern Soviet Production Relations, 1928–1941*, London, Pluto Press.

Granick, D. (1987), *Job Rights in the Soviet Union: Their Consequences*, Cambridge, Cambridge University Press.

Honneth, A. (1995), *The Struggle for Recognition : The Moral Grammar of Social Conflicts*, Cambridge, Polity Press.

Honneth, A. (2002), 'Recognition or redistribution? Changing perspectives on the moral order of society' in S. Lash and M. Featherstone (eds), *Recognition and Difference*, London, Sage.

Howard, M. M. (2003), *The Weakness of Civil Society in Post-Communist Europe*, Cambridge, Cambridge University Press.

Juska, A. and Pozzuto, R. (2004), 'Work-based welfare as a ritual: understanding marginalisation in post-independence Lithuania', *Journal of Sociology and Social Welfare*, 31, 3–24.

Kohli, M. (1986), 'The world we forgot: A historical review of the life course' in V. W. Marshall (ed.), *Later Life: The Social Psychology of Ageing*, Beverly Hills, CA, Sage.

Kornai, J. (1992), *The Socialist System: The Political Economy of Communism*, Princeton, N.J., Princeton University Press.

Leisering, L. and Leibfried, S. (1999), *Time and Poverty in Western Welfare States: United Germany in Perspective*, Cambridge, Cambridge University Press.

Mau, S. (2003), *The Moral Economy of Welfare States: Britain and Germany Compared*, London, Routledge.

Muenkler, H. (2004), 'Enzyklopaedie der Ideen der Zukunft: Solidaritaet' in J. Beckert, J. Eckert, M. Kohli and W. Streeck (eds), *Transnationale Solidaritaet: Chancen und Grenzen*, Frankfurt, Campus.

Offe, C. (1996), 'The politics of social policy in East European transitions: antecedents, agents, and agendas of reform' in C. Offe (ed.), *Modernity and the State: East, West*, Cambridge, Polity Press.

Ostow, R. (1995), '"Ne Art Bürgerwehr in Form von Skins": Young Germans on the streets in the Eastern and Western state of the Federal Republic', *New German Critique*, 64, 87–103.

Outhwaite, W. and Ray, L. (2005), *Social Theory and Postcommunism*, Malden, Blackwell.

Parsons, T. (1951), *The Social System*, London, Routledge & Kegan Paul.

Reiter, H. (2003), 'Past, present, future: biographical time structuring of disadvantaged young people', *Young: Nordic Journal of Youth Research*, 11, 253–279.

Reiter, H. (2005), 'The concept of recognition as a tool for researching changing meanings of work in post-socialist youth transitions to working life', background paper for a workshop on 'Recognition: Theoretical Perspectives and Empirical Research', European University Institute, San Domenico di Fiesole, 27–28 May.

Reiter, H. and Craig, G. (2005), 'Youth in the labour market: citizenship or exclusion?' in H. Bradley and J. van Hoof (eds), *Young People in Europe: Labour Markets and Citizenship*, Bristol, Policy Press.

Sackmann, R., Weymann, A. and Wingens, M. (2000), *Die Generation der Wende: Berufs- und Lebensverläufe im sozialen Wandel*, Wiesbaden, Westdeutscher Verlag.

Sennett, R. (1998), *The Corrosion of Character: The Personal Consequences of Work in the New Capitalism*, New York, W. W. Norton.

Srubar, I. (1998), 'Phenomenological analysis and its contemporary significance', *Human Studies*, 21, 121–139.

Standing, G. (2002), 'The babble of euphemism: re-embedding social protection in "transformed" labour markets' in A. Rainnie, A. Smith and A. Swain (eds), *Work, Employment and Transition: Restructuring Livelihoods in Post-Communism*, London, Routledge.

Struck, O. (2003), 'Trajectories of coping strategies in Eastern Germany' in R. Humphrey, R. Miller and E. Zdravomyslova (eds), *Biographical Research in Eastern Europe: Altered Lives and Broken Biographies*, Aldershot, Ashgate.

Sztompka, P. (1996), 'Looking back: the year 1989 as a cultural and civilizational break', *Communist and Post-communist Studies*, 29, 2, 115–129.

Wagner, P. (1994), *A Sociology of Modernity: Liberty and Discipline*, London, Routledge.

Woodward, S. L. (1995), *Socialist Unemployment: The Political Economy of Yugoslavia 1945–1990*, Princeton, N. J., Princeton University Press.

World Bank, International Finance Corporation and Oxford University Press (2005), *Doing Business in 2005: Removing Obstacles to Growth*, Washington, DC, World Bank.

Zapf, W. (1994), *Modernisierung, Wohlfahrtsentwicklung und Transformation: Soziologische Aufsätze 1987 bis 1994*, Berlin, Sigma.

Appendix: Interview with Saulius, extract

129 **Interviewer:** Ok, now, look, regarding this work theme, but something a bit different: when there's no work. The fact is that there are many unemployed in Lithuania; unemployment is high. What do you think could the reasons for that be?

130 **Saulius:** Hmm. [These] people are lazybones. [He is laughing.] ... Those who want [one] can surely find a job. It is not that ... there is no work ... [as though one were] in some village: 'I came here and cannot find a job.' You have to look for it: those who look for work, find it. If you lie on a couch with a glass of brandy [laughs], life will surely not get better because of that. The state, of course, cannot create work for everybody, but for many. If you

cannot find a job, so what? You can go abroad. I don't think that it is absolutely impossible to get a job. Of course, it is possible. But sometimes people are very demanding and lazy, exactly those who do not have [work]. They think that it is much easier to live out of the state's pocket by having lots of children, that that is much easier than to work like normal people.

131 **I:** When they get all kinds of benefits …

132 **S:** Yes, but I don't support such people. I somehow do not like such people.

133 **I:** What about the unemployed? Let's [talk about] those benefits that they get … there is this state support, the state benefit. What do you think?

134 **S:** My reaction to benefits … of course, benefits are necessary, because how can a person live otherwise? But, let's say, painters …, it is difficult for them to find a job according to their qualifications. To draw posters for companies does not make sense. I do understand that such people are unemployed. Or, let's say, people without education, well, volunteers can work at the municipality…

135 **I:** [To return to the subject of] support…

136 **S:** Well, that is the state's support. 'At the municipality, go to work as, let's say, as a volunteer, and they will really help you.' I don't think that the municipality would remain indifferent and not help. But benefits are too small in my opinion; a person wouldn't survive. And the pensions, altogether, are nothing but a mockery [laughs]. A person works hard for all of his life and then gets some pennies, and is not able to live on them. But Lithuania is a growing state, everything will be fine in the future.

137 **I:** What do you think the state should take care of? What else [should] the state should give to a person? How should it help?

138 **S:** Healthcare, it really should… Well, healthcare in our state is normal… but regarding prescription refunds; I don't know anything in detail, but, as far as I have heard, half of the people do not get it, and that is bad, because the elderly have ridiculous pensions and their medicine is not paid for, so this is a real mockery, this is terrible. I think that the state should pay for medicine for all the old people who cannot afford to buy it. And the state, in my opinion, has to take care of young people, and education has to be free for everyone. Well, let's say, not everyone, but, let's say, those who are talented and those who entered universities, they shouldn't have to pay all that money to get education, because it is not them who need it, but the state that needs people who could work. When you think like this…

139 **I:** And a person, does he have any duties towards the state? What should a person…?

140 **S:** A person? His labour, of course. And a person has to fulfil his duties, for example, to vote. I don't understand those who do not vote and then rail against the authorities: 'We elected the one who shouldn't have been elected'. 'So why do you sit on your couch then? Get off your ass and vote.' This is nonsense, when they sit at home and laze about, and they shout, 'Not this

one and not that one!' So this is also a duty, to vote. Then, what else, other duties? It seems to me that it is a duty to raise children for the state, because, for example, the population is decreasing in Lithuania now. It is terrible, what might happen in many, many years. If there was no Lithuania, then all kinds of black people would overrun it, and I think that would not be too much fun [laughs]. That is why I think that every person has to leave one person... at least one. What else? What other duties can there be? To create a nice environment [laughs]. Not to leave untidy things around your house, so that it is nice in Lithuania, so that people who visit will remember that here, people live really nicely, they don't idle, but they work. For example, those unemployed, people in the countryside, let's say, and also some of my relatives, they do not work. But if you think about it, if you come to their (collective) garden ... well, it doesn't look like he is unemployed. Everything is nicely fixed, all the surroundings. He works there. And for me it is, for example, pleasing. And sometimes there are asocial families who do not take care of anything, they do not look after their children, but some other unemployed people manage very well. It means that people can live in another way. That's it. It is a duty to live tidily [laughs].

141 **I:** We also talked about your relatives who do not work, so I would like to come back to the unemployed. Do you know any unemployed people? What kind of people are they, and why don't they work?

142 **S:** Yes. My godfather, who is also the husband of my aunt, he doesn't work – I think that he doesn't work. He doesn't work because he likes drinking ... and employers do not want such people. And he is qualified as something like a crane operator [laughs]... I think that people like that are not too much wanted these days. Whereas constructors, here in X (town) and everywhere else, they are wanted... but he, somehow, he didn't know his job well or something like that, but he doesn't have a job.

143 **I:** Who else do you know, among your neighbours, or your classmates' parents or relatives?

144 **S:** Most of the unemployed people I know, most of them are unemployed because they drink alcohol, that's why, the majority... I do not know any people who do not have a job and are just like other people, but simply without jobs. I do not know any such people, I think. The majority of those who do not have jobs, drink. But there is one exception, my aunt's husband... My godmother, I think, she has a job... yes, she works. But anyway, they do very well.

145 **I:** The ones with the collective garden...

146 **S:** Yes. Her husband, even though he drinks, at least he does something, [which] is good, because there are [people] who don't do anything. It is absolutely terrible. Shabby home. These social workers, when they enter [such homes], it makes them wrinkle their noses. It is terrible. Or like [some things] they show on TV ... so many famous people are forgotten [or]

disabled, it is terrible. The state doesn't take care [of them] properly. It is still young as a state, it [can't] take care of everything yet. That is why people are cheerless and disappointed with life sometimes.

147 **I:** When [people] encounter [them], how do people treat these unemployed people?

148 **S:** How do they treat them? They feel pity for them.

149 **I:** Pity?

150 **S:** Yes. For example, a while back, a woman would come to my grandma; you could see from her swollen face that she drank a lot. She asked for two *litas* [€0.6] and my grandma gave them to her, she really felt sorry for her. And especially those who haven't become unemployed recently, but who have not found a job for a long time: I feel pity for these people most of all, that they are not lucky in life, that they cannot live well and have all that ... I have. Other people, for example, my family members, well, I don't know... Because I do not live with my parents, I live with my grandparents, both my grandparents are pensioners. Thanks God, they get good pensions, more or less, compared to others. So, are they considered to be unemployed? But they are retired people. How do they look at them [the unemployed]? First of all, they call them lazybones, like I do. [He is laughing.] I agree with their opinion. Maybe they made us get used to the idea that they are lazybones, so they think the same as I do. People always think the same way that adults do – their grandparents or parents.

11 Euro-Islam, Islam in Europe, or Europe Revised through Islam? Versions of Muslim Solidarity within European Borders

Schirin Amir-Moazami

So far, Islam has been mostly excluded from the identifications and self-representations of Europe. However, over the course of recent decades the 'Muslim other' has become internal to Europe, and its relation to the imaginary of Europe as a non-Muslim (Christian, secular) space is widely debated. Apart from the divergent normative approaches to European forms of Islam, the establishment of Muslim networks and organizations at both the national and the European level has also empirically forged a European basis both of and for Islam.[1] The very fact that Islam has de facto become an integral part of European societies is therefore crucial to the question of how Muslim solidarities could be conceptualized within Western European borders. This raises the question of how arrangements of nation, state and religion can be approached, or even re-conceptualized with regard to a 'distinct' religious minority knocking at the doors of European states, requesting de jure recognition as full members of European societies.

This chapter will thus tackle the central topic of this volume on solidarity from the perspective of a religious minority within European borders, and thereby try to bring into the discussion forms of solidarity that potentially challenge the secular foundations of European societies. It aims to look into the ways in which Islam is currently 'imagined' in relation to 'Europe', and

---

1 An interesting development in this respect is, for example, the European Council for Fatwa and Research, founded in 1997 and headed by Yussuf al-Quaradawi. By issuing *fatwas* (religious opinions), the council aims at responding to the particular needs of Muslims in Europe, instead of letting them depend on the *fatwas* of the *ulema* (scholars) in Muslim majority societies (cf. Caeiro, 2004).

vice versa. The notion of solidarity as a structural guideline seems to be promising for this purpose, as it allows us to depart from any pre-constituted idea of how Islam in Europe should ideally look, and potentially opens the path to various forms and shapes of solidarity in relation to both 'Islam' and 'Europe'. I will structure the analysis by addressing some of the key questions inspired by this volume: What versions of Muslim solidarities are reflected in projects of European forms of Islam? How are these related to, combined with or detached from solidarities with European societies? Although this investigation will be primarily theoretical in nature, one possible means of approaching the concept of solidarity from the perspective of Islam within European borders, at least in a schematic way, is to operate with a three-fold distinction between 'Muslim solidarity' (implying a particularistic component of solidarity), 'universal solidarity' (which attempts to subsume specific bonds with Islam under a universal framework), and 'plural solidarity' (which attempts to combine different group affiliations within a plural setting, including solidarity with Islam and with Europe).

I will proceed by focusing on three different and representative approaches articulated by Muslim scholars residing in different European societies (namely Germany, Switzerland and the UK):[2] Bassam Tibi, Tariq Ramadan and Tariq Modood, respectively. These three scholars all define themselves as Muslims, but what they mean by this self-identification sometimes sharply differs, as do their conceptualizations of Islam within European borders. The first position, condensed in the notion of 'Euro-Islam', legitimizes only one model of Islam, oriented towards an 'enlightened European system of values' and in harmony with 'secular constitutions', as its most important proponent, Bassam Tibi, has put it (Tibi, 2000, 36). In this case, solidarity is meant to be abstracted from any group affiliations, and appeals only to universal categories of human reason. If deemed legitimate at all, religious forms of solidarity should, accordingly, be confined to a purely 'private' domain.

The second type aims at combining theological arguments with reflections on how Muslim traditions can fruitfully be re-contextualized within non-Muslim (i.e., European) societies, without being absorbed by dominant secular norms. Here, the bonds with the sacred sources of Islam as much as with a global Muslim community *and* solidarity with European societies do not a priori stand in opposition to each other; this approach, by contrast, seeks to reconcile them. The main concern here seems, however, to be that of

---

2 Since this chapter is mostly preoccupied with the various perspectives and conceptions of solidarities articulated by Muslims within Europe, I will not go into details about contextualizing their positions within the national public spheres in which they interact and articulate their views.

finding possible paths for Muslim solidarity with Europe (or rather with individual European countries in which Muslims have settled) as a subsidiary question, which emerges from a more important one: How can Muslim forms of social life and practices find an adequate place and representation within European societies, while continuing to be related to an Islamic 'discursive tradition' (Asad, 1986, 1993)?

The third approach can be read as a direct counter-argument to the first. At the same time, it complements the second approach through a critical reflection on the normative foundations of European societies vis-à-vis religious plurality. From a political theory point of view, it contributes to the topic by suggesting how Muslim forms of solidarity could be incorporated into European contexts beyond a strictly 'private' level within a universal framework, most notably by questioning the often taken-for-granted and secularly-founded 'neutrality' of liberal democracies. This position chooses to acknowledge that the historically-shaped arrangements of state, nation and religion in Europe could and should be opened up by the active presence and participation of Muslim minorities. Solidarity is not understood here as a one-way process – in other words, as a request for Muslims to establish bonds and bounds with Europe – but as something that would appeal to the majority societies, inviting them to reflect critically on their normative foundations in order to increase the likelihood of establishing bonds with differing forms of religion.

This chapter raises the question of how the combination, fusion or disconnection of 'Europeanness' and 'Muslim solidarities' can be intelligibly approached from a plural point of view, without falling into the trap of construing one of them as a pre-constituted body of norms and values. It shall contribute to a deeper understanding of the partly contradictory and conflicting developments of constructions of Muslim solidarities in Europe (which seem to be more complex than might at first sight be expected), with reference both to the notion of a gradual submergence of Muslim traditions in Europe, and to their fundamental difference from European societies.

Bassam Tibi: longing for a 'Euro-Islam'

The first approach to be scrutinized is that of a 'Euro-Islam'. In the course of its usage, this term has taken on a multiplicity of meanings depending on the specific viewpoints and positions of the authors who have used it (the media, scholars, politicians, etc.); however, there seems to be an increasing consensus over the core of its content, as well as a common frame of reference that characterizes this notion. This is at least evident within the German context, where the term has flourished in the past decade.[3] Not accidentally, Bassam Tibi, one of the 'founding fathers' of the concept, was based in Germany for a long time. It is important to note at the outset that this political scientist, a Middle East specialist, started his academic career with a number of well-founded studies on the emergence and spread of 'Islamic fundamentalism' in the Middle East (1991; 1992). Since the late 1990s, Tibi has tended to shift his focus onto Islam in Europe, and it seems that the roles of the German media and politicians in promoting and supporting him as an expert in this domain should not be underestimated. While his previous books had an academic profile in terms of their style and the methods and theoretical frameworks used, his more recent publications on Islam in Europe (1998; 2000; 2005) address a wider audience, including academics and non-academics, and are written in accessible style. Tibi mainly bases his arguments on speculations, personal assessments and references to studies conducted by other scholars. This becomes obvious when we consider, for example, the fact that he puts himself in the centre of his analysis, frequently appealing to self-representations like the 'liberal cultural Muslim' (2000, 247), or 'Islamic enlightener' (2000, 249). Moreover, he structures his analysis around small anecdotes, things that he has experienced himself, and mixes these with a shorthand usage of socio-political concepts, such as 'Enlightenment', 'communitarianism', 'multiculturalism', etc.

His shift from being a scholar to being a public intellectual has lead to a number of critiques within academic circles (Abdallah, 1998; Salvatore, 1999 [1997]). Although he is perhaps not particularly sophisticated in academic terms, Tibi is nonetheless a very important figure for our current purposes, not just because he has gained a broad credibility and respect among German politicians and the media, but also because his notion of Euro-Islam has now become commonplace.[4] With his profile as an established university professor who constantly reasserts his own personal background as a 'secular Muslim', while blaming the rise of publicly committed and organized forms of Islam in Europe, Tibi has become one of the most visible and well-received 'experts'

---

3   A German scholar who offers an alternative interpretation of the implications of the rise of a 'Euro-Islam' is the political scientist Claus Leggewie (2002). Leggewie differs from the mainstream usage of the term in Germany, particularly in his emphasis on the impact that the presence of Islam in Europe potentially has on the secular foundations of European nation states.

4   Tibi has also acted as a political adviser in several cases in which Muslim practices were discussed, the most prominent example being the question as to whether teachers should be allowed to cover their heads while teaching in state schools. In this case, Tibi was quite successful in convincing the public that the headscarf was a 'post-Qur'anic invention' (*Der Tagesspiegel*, July 16 1998), and 'imported under the influence of Islamism from Arabic countries' (Tibi, 2000, 45).

on Islam in Germany. The effects of his public presence and publications can be assessed, for example, when we consider that some of the notions introduced by him have by now become part of everyday speech and integrated into the political agenda of various parties in Germany. This holds true for the concept of Euro-Islam, as well as for notions like *Leitkultur* (leading culture), as will be shown below.

The ingredients of Euro-Islam

Tibi's approach to Euro-Islam is two-fold. On the one hand, it is anchored in a positive evaluation of the achievements of the European Enlightenment. On the other hand, he calls for an adaptation of Islam to the normative standards of Western societies. His central idea is that Europe can and should be a major driving force in reforming Islam, both within European borders and worldwide. Tibi grounds his research in what he calls a re-evaluation of the positive achievements of 'Western civilization', asserting that Europeans should stand up for their liberal achievements and protect them against external influences (i.e., 'Islamic fundamentalism'). Universal values, he argues, are the only basis for the fruitful co-existence of non-Muslim Europeans and Muslim immigrants. However, Tibi rejects a delineation of the coordinates of the universalist ethos that he tries to protect or to revitalize, other than including within it 'democracy' and 'human rights', whose content is also far from unequivocal.

By calling this a 'limited universalism' (1998, 91) Tibi attempts to provide a nuanced picture of his own commitment to abstract universalism. He does this mainly by criticizing the expansionist tendencies of 'European' universalism, in colonial times as well as the present day, referring to these as 'Euro-arrogance' towards non-European 'civilizations'. However, on closer inspection, Tibi himself quite obviously reconstructs somewhat narrow dichotomies between Europe and non-European (i.e., Islamic) borders. Moreover, while arguing against a physical domination of what he calls 'pre-modern' societies, as occurred during colonial times, he nonetheless seems to support an ethical imposition of Enlightenment ideals.

Thus, although asking for a binding value system, Tibi does not hesitate to appeal to the concept of 'civilizations', and this quite in a Huntingtonian fashion, dividing the world into 'modern' (enlightened) and 'pre-modern' hemispheres, and openly denouncing 'immigrant cultures' as 'backward' (1998, 95). Moreover, in falling back on abstract universal values, Tibi simultaneously brings into focus the notion of a European *Leitkultur* (leading culture), which should serve as a concrete guide for immigrants wishing to

190

adapt to 'modern' norms and technologies. The term *Leitkultur* has, interestingly, been taken up by conservative politicians in Germany, who have used it in order to emphasize national borders vis-à-vis immigrants, while inviting *Ausländer* (foreigners) who already live in Germany to follow specifically 'German' cultural patterns. In the first instance, this actually appears to be a simple misinterpretation of Tibi's intentions, especially when we consider his critique of what he calls the German *Abstammungsideologie* (ideology of the descent) (1998, 92). Due to the particular history of the comparatively late formation of the nation state in Germany, Tibi argues, German society was still based on the belief in blood, considering foreigners to be 'foreign' however long they had lived in Germany, and even if they had acquired German citizenship. However, as far as the second implication of *Leitkultur* is concerned, the difference between his own usage of the *Leitkultur* paradigm and that of conservative politicians has become less clear-cut, not least because of the 'old paradox' inherent in universalistic claims, since they are always anchored in particularistic visions of the world.

Tibi, indeed, quite outspokenly joins the proponents of a German *Leitkultur* on the issue of multiculturalism. While re-assessing German citizenship norms, Tibi also extensively attacks the politics of multi-culturalism. In his view, Germany has a particular affinity with what he labels the 'multi-kulti ideology' (e.g., 1998, 50), due to its bad conscience about the Nazi past. Tibi's discrediting of multiculturalism actually reflects a broader trend, both in Germany and in other European countries (in particular in France), which also constitutes the core of his argument.

Instead of anchoring his rejection of multiculturalism in any systematic analysis of the various implications of this concept, he simply subsumes the ideas implicated in multiculturalist approaches under the term 'relativism' or 'neo-absolutism' (1998, 95) and denounces them as lacking any binding values:

> The culture relativist attitudes of multiculturalists unintendedly lead to an affirmation of the communitarian neo-absolutism of the migrants of pre-modern cultures ... the communitarianism is an expression of the co-existence of 'communities', who live without a leading culture and according to their own norms. Neutrally put, in the case of the immigrant cultures we are dealing with pre-modern cultures, who claim absolute validity for their own ideas. (1998, 28)

The main objections that Tibi puts forward to the politics of multiculturalism are that they might undermine 'European' values and achievements; and that they would unavoidably play into the hands of fundamentalist groups, whom he denounces as openly rejecting all the key ideas embodied in human rights principles. The only suitable alternative, according to Tibi, is to prescribe 'integration'. A political strategy that went beyond the recognition of individual rights would contradict the Enlightenment tradition of abstract universalism. For Muslims to become truly European, or to become members of European nation states, means to follow these principles and, at least on a public level, relinquishing their religious affiliations.

What is interesting about Tibi's consistent rejection of multicultural politics is not only the argument that multiculturalism is to be blamed for leading to violence and religious fundamentalism, which has by now become almost the consensus view in Europe (cf. Gilroy, 2004), but also his assumption that Germany had practised, or even institutionalized, multicultural politics. This view simply does not correspond with empirical realities (cf. Amir-Moazami, 2005).

Tibi further displays his distaste for multiculturalism, and thereby also the particularistic implications of his universalistic claims, when he refers to France, and in particular to its tradition of citizenship and *laïcité*, as the only acceptable model for the successful 'integration' of Muslims into European settings (1998, 214f.). The main reason for his sympathy with the French model is that it is the only country in Europe that has successfully protected, or rather reinforced, secularism vis-à-vis Islam (1998, 228f.). It is important to pause here for a moment, because it is a particular version of secularity that constitutes the core of Tibi's appeal to Enlightenment ideals, and which he argues Muslims in Europe should adopt.

Tibi's notion of religion, coupled with the classical secularization thesis, is anchored in a functionalist approach, according to which processes of modernization are characterized by a functional re-orientation of society, which has led to a substantial decrease of religion. Accordingly, religion constitutes no more than a societal sub-system, distinct from other fields, such as the economic, political or educational spheres (cf. Luckmann, 1991 [1967]). The key phrase here is 'the individualization of religion', which is rooted in a particular post-Enlightenment concept of religion as standing in semantic opposition to the transcendental ideas of reason, individual autonomy and humanity (cf. Casanova, 1994; Asad, 1993; 1999; Koenig, 2006). However, when appealing to notions like secularity or *laïcité*, Tibi avoids embedding his priorities within the broader discussions surrounding these concepts. Far from being defined once and for all, the terms 'secularization', 'secularity' and 'secularism' have become increasingly contested, in both political and academic settings (Casanova, 1994; Asad, 2003). In particular, the privatization thesis, which Tibi tries to strengthen in his writings, has been roundly criticized and questioned on both the empirical and the normative levels.

While taking such contested concepts for granted, or simply equating secularity/*laïcité* with the successful separation of political and religious spheres, Tibi makes his priorities clear when he refers approvingly to France's restrictive policy vis-à-vis religious symbols (i.e., the Islamic headscarf) (Tibi, 2000). The kind of secularity of which he is supportive is one which does not start with the capacities and freedom of the individual, but which attempts to regulate the content of speech and behaviour in public life. This understanding of secularity, or rather of *laïcité*, is thus not characterized by the goal of abolishing religion in political or public institutions – as it claims to do – but rather of regulating religious, and in particular Islamic practices, in order to ensure that they take on a particular shape, i.e., that they conform to the secular norm. Instead of being characterized by the alleged functionalist distinction between different sub-systems, the outcome of the headscarf case in France in fact offers a quite remarkable example of an intervention of an external actor (i.e., the state) in the religious and personal sphere by attributing binding meanings to a religious symbol (the headscarf), and by authoritatively marking out the boundaries of correct and incorrect religious practices according to the secular credo. Instead of respecting the alleged neutrality of the public sphere, what occurs here is a regulation of public life according to secular standards (cf. Bowen, 2004; Asad, 2005).

From this point of view, the main task for Muslims in Europe is to reform Islam in order to make it fit for contemporary requirements worldwide. Euro-Islam, as conceptualized by Tibi, would escape the traps of traditional authority in which Islam is supposedly still mired in Muslim-majority contexts, and favours the normative settlement of Muslims in European societies. However, Tibi does not simply invoke the notion of reform, but also introduces the Christianity-based notion of 'reformation'. In his vision of Euro-Islam undergoing the process of a reformation similar to that undergone by Christianity in the early modern period, the central component is secularization, which he associates in the first instance with Islam's relinquishment of its alleged political ties (1998, 244). In reaching his conclusion that Islam is inherently tied to politics, Tibi argues – as do many Western scholars who deal with Islam – that Islam is linked to the political establishment (cf. Salvatore, 1999 [1997]). This argument also points to a familiar dichotomy between Christianity and Islam. While modern Christianity is represented as a religion that has effected a separation of church and state institutions, Islam is supposedly still mired in politics, especially at the state level. This argument can easily be challenged by reference to countries such as the UK, but also Germany, where church and state institutions are constitutionally bound together in various respects.

Tibi couples his promotion of this particular type of Islam with a critique of the existing versions of organized forms of Islam in Europe, and in particular in Germany, openly de-legitimizing most established Islamic organizations and movements as tendentiously promoting the 'ghettoization' or 'ethnicization' of Islam. The main problem with this assessment is that Tibi fails to give his observations any empirical basis, apart from associatively drawing on examples that are mostly taken from the press. Only rarely are his results empirically grounded or based on first-hand research that could give more credibility to his critical evaluation of Muslim groups in Germany or Europe. The repetition of existing knowledge in a field that is characterized by a lack of data and by a complex social and political dynamic obviously leaves a question mark over his conclusions. Moreover, given the fact that representatives of the younger generation of Muslims, mostly born and brought up in Germany, have gained senior positions in most Muslim organizations, it seems important to give more serious consideration to recent developments and to look carefully at intergenerational shifts and dynamics in Muslim discourse and action.

Tibi's approach also mirrors a much broader and quite frequent assessment within the academic literature regarding Islam in Europe. In one way or another, Muslims have been asked to position themselves vis-à-vis the requirements of modern societies or vis-à-vis modernity *tout court,* as set out in the integration paradigm (cf. Teczan, 2003). One of the most frequent hopes underlying such investigations, both among politicians and among many academics, is that European versions of Islam might prove to be major driving forces in the reformation of the worldwide Islamic tradition, as the critique of orthodox interpretations of Islam voiced by practising Muslims in the West might influence Muslims in Islamic societies.

The interesting point about Tibi is that he defines himself as a Muslim while condemning not only orthodoxy, but also Muslim practices and forms of social life that do not fit into his own liberal vision of Islam. Tibi shares his idea of Euro-Islam with many other Muslim intellectuals in Europe who favour a notion of Islam that withdraws from the public stage to the privacy of personal belief.[5] Similarly to Tibi, these people have recently had great

---

5   All across Europe, we can see the emergence of public intellectuals with Muslim backgrounds who tend to blame Islam for the failure of Muslims to integrate with European societies. Prominent examples include liberal feminists like Fadela Amara, who founded the 'Ni Putes Ni Soumises' (Neither Whores Nor Submissives) movement in France (Amara, 2003); the sociologist Necla Kelek, who wrote a book about the phenomenon of arranged and forced marriages within Turkish Muslim communities in Germany (Kelek, 2005); and Ayyan Hirsi Ali (Ali, 2005), a politician of Somalian background previously based in the Netherlands, but now in the US.

public successes, because they speak with the 'voice of the Other' while adopting liberal rhetoric, and openly accuse the majority of Muslims of an inability to become as 'modern' as they consider themselves to be. While more or less reinforcing predominant images of Islam, these intellectuals are largely applauded in the public sphere as the prototypes of 'liberated Muslims' who have been able to integrate themselves into European society. Although I would never dare to deny his Muslimness, Tibi's discourse reveals a certain kind of self-alienation that seems to have become a precondition for Muslims in Europe today if they are to be heard in public arenas. (On the issue of exclusion/inclusion more generally, see Chapter 6 in this volume).

Although the notion of solidarity does not emerge in Tibi's writings, we can find several indicators of the type of solidarity that he seems to favour. Looking, for example, at his affirmative approach to abstract universalism and his longing for a *Weltbürgertum* (cosmopolitanism), one would expect Tibi to be interested only in 'universal solidarity'. However, as he admits, the universal framework of references is not formed in a vacuum, but rather has a clear geo-political location, which is 'Western civilization'. Indeed, the whole concept of Euro-Islam, at least the version outlined here, indicates that there is a civilization from which Muslims can and should borrow in order to give up their own universalistic claims, which are embodied, for example, in the transnational *umma* (Islamic community). If solidarity with a religious group on a particularistic level is therefore at all relevant here, it is reduced to the very preliminary grounds of the individual believer, who is allowed to aspire to religiosity within a distinctive and purely private domain. Every form of Muslim solidarity that goes beyond this, and is based on shared values or traditions in public life, is suspected of being tied to authoritative structures or provoking segregation. Tibi actually calls for Muslims in Europe to solidarize with his notion of a secularized Islam, and embrace his idea of an 'enlightened liberal' Muslimness.

Tariq Ramadan: Muslim solidarities as a basis for European solidarities

Tariq Ramadan is a Swiss-based Islamologue and philosopher with a wide audience across Europe, especially in French-speaking European countries. Although one could devote book-length investigations to portrayals of Tariq Ramadan, or to attempts at situating him in the contexts in which he interacts as a scholar and Muslim preacher,[6] my focus here is primarily on the content

---

6　The main interest of scholars who have conducted research into Ramadan has been his capacity to 'mobilize' large numbers of Muslim young people, especially in France. This is often associated

of his discourse and, more concretely, on his conceptualization of Islam in Europe, or 'European Islam', and the notion of solidarity that emerges.

Although Ramadan at first oriented his sermons and books towards the Muslim community in particular, the large popularity that he has gained, especially among Muslim youths (organizations and individuals alike), has turned him into a figure of wider public interest, and especially of suspicion for the French authorities and the media (Fourest, 2004; one public denunciation of Ramadan is described by Salvatore in Chapter 4 of this volume). Ramadan's substantial public success has encouraged him to address the non-Muslim majority as well, while not giving up his perspective as a committed Muslim intellectual. This is also apparent in the shifts in the content of his writings. Especially in his more recent publications, one can observe a move from the claim of a simple 'loyalty' on the part of Muslims to the European societies in which they live, to the establishment of more affective and deeper bonds with these societies.

Europe: Dar al-da'wa

Central to Ramadan's thought is the attempt to overcome the dichotomy between *dar al-harb* (the abode of war) and *dar al-islam* (the abode of Islam), regularly invoked by both Muslim and non-Muslim scholars and politicians to describe the geo-political divisions between non-Islamic and Islamic spaces (cf. Kepel, 1994; Tibi, 1998). On the one hand, Ramadan argues – using Islamic sources –that these notions are 'post-Islamic' conceptions, which, in the contemporary world of interdependence, interactions and globalization, are even less appropriate than they were during the post-Prophet era. On the other hand, he emphasizes that all Western European countries legally provide conditions that enable Muslims to practise their religion, sometimes more thoroughly than certain Islamic societies. Even if the representation of Islam in the European public sphere is often characterized by a hostile attitude, Ramadan argues, the categorization of Europe as per se hostile to Muslims – and thus *dar al-harb* – is inadequate and counter-productive. Ramadan does

---

with his 'charisma' (e.g., Mohsen-Finan, 2002, 210). Another focus of interest has been his status, which reflects a wider shift in the structures of Islamic authority in European societies. Having both a classical training in Islamic sciences and a university education in philosophy, Ramadan represents a new type of Muslim leadership in Europe. Although he is not tied to the *ulema*, he is widely recognized as a religious authority, especially among young Muslims who were born and raised in Europe. This particular status has particularly preoccupied scholars with an interest in the structures and transformations of Muslim religious authorities within European borders (e.g., Frégosi, 2004).

not go into details about the counter-concept *dar-al-Islam*, but from what he goes on to write, it becomes evident that he does not consider this as an adequate term either, for it would imply the goal of transforming Europe into Islamic societies, to which Ramadan clearly does not subscribe.

Trying to avoid both concepts, what Ramadan offers is a third and alternative approach, which he subsumes under the notion of *dar al-da'wa* (abode of invitation to God). Although the implications of *da'wa* are certainly much more complex, Ramadan purposely tries to reduce it to a quite simple message, asking Muslims to:

> remind the people around them of God and spirituality; and – when it comes to social issues – they must be actively involved in supporting values and morality, justice and solidarity. [They must bear] witness to their faith before humankind. (2004, 73)

Relating his conceptualization of *dar al-da'wa* primarily to an ethical commitment to Islam, Ramadan attempts to overcome the ideological abuse of this term by some Muslim scholars, as well as by non-Muslim commentators in Western Europe who tend to associate *da'wa* with 'propaganda' or 'proselytism', and hence identify it as the driving force behind the effort to 'Islamize the West'.[7] Although, with his invocation of *da'wa*, Ramadan addresses Muslims *and* non-Muslims, he clearly has distinct objectives with respect to these groups. It seems that he uses *da'wa* in the context of non-Muslims not so much in a missionary spirit, with the goal of conversion, but rather with the idea of a rectification of negative representations of Islam within European public spheres.

Ramadan's conceptualization of *da'wa* can be placed within the reformist Salafi tradition, which emerged in the late 19th and early 20th century. While *da'wa* was initially understood as an activity to be conducted under the aegis of clerics, reformist thinkers – of whom Ramadan is one – claimed it to be the duty of every Muslim. This shift most notably paved the way for laypeople to become involved in the process of the acquisition and circulation of Islamic knowledge (cf. Mahmood, 2005; Roest Crollius, 1978).

Characteristically, Ramadan combines his emphasis on the importance of *da'wa* with a belief that European Muslims must accumulate a deeper religious knowledge. This, according to him, is the most important step in fulfilling

---

7 At one point (2004, 240), Ramadan also argues explicitly against the over-simplistic association of *da'wa* with proselytism: 'The notion of da'wa is often understood as the expression of the inherent Islamic inclination to proselytise and its desire to convert. However, the notion conveys rather the idea of presenting and expressing the message of Islam, because conversion, which must be a free act, is a matter entirely between God and the human heart.'

da'wa appropriately. Adequate faith, he argues, can only be attained on the basis of an adequate knowledge of the sacred sources: in the case of Islam, these are the Qur'an and the Sunna (traditional Muslim law). Ramadan has two different aspects in mind: first, knowledge as a tool for investigating and 'understanding' Islamic dogma; and, second, knowledge as part of the development and cultivation of certain pious emotions. In this perspective, faith, instead of being a hindrance to the accumulation of knowledge, constitutes its necessary starting point, as does knowledge for faith: 'There is no true faith without understanding. For Muslims, this means understanding both the sources (the Qur'an and the Sunna) and the context in which they live.' (2004, 80)

Ramadan's call to approach Islam cognitively in order to better 'understand' it and to cultivate faithful behaviour should also be understood as a critique of blind imitation, or the non-reflexive emulation of religious practices, which is often associated with the first generation of Muslim immigrants to Western Europe. Ramadan thus invokes a 'discourse of authenticity', blaming Muslims' detachment from religious sources for misinterpretations and deviations. Ramadan considers 'ignorance' of 'genuine' Islam to be one of the main reasons for the crisis that Muslims are experiencing on the global and European levels.

This argument recalls the dominant contemporary Islamic discourse, which, again, emerged from the Islamic reform movement at the end of the 19th and beginning of the 20th century, and was successively diffused by Islamic movements. *'Ilm* (knowledge) and the corollary notion of *tarbiya* (education) became the key terms for the goal of the social and moral reconstruction of the individual, as well as for the Muslim community, which was deemed to be in decline (cf. Mitchell, 1988; Shakry, 1998). From this perspective, the dissemination of a 'pure' Islam, detached from all traditional deviations, would re-establish the glorious state of past Muslim civilizations.[8] It is in this vein that Ramadan tends to identify various problems in the Muslim community (especially the unsatisfactory condition of Muslim women), not only in Muslim majority countries but also in the European context of migration. These problems occur as a consequence of a lack of appropriate knowledge. In this regard, Ramadan is part of a wider trend among young

---

8 The leading figures of this discourse were Jamal ad-Din al-Afghani (1838–1897) and Muhammad Abduh (1849–1905). Abduh is of particular importance in understanding the genealogy of Ramadan's discourse, since he combined reforms in the educational domain with the idea of a renewal of Islamic thought and practice. The distinction made by these scholars between 'scripture' and 'custom' has become a model for the discourse on authenticity, which has continued to the present day.

Muslims in European contexts (or vice versa), who have started to return to the scriptural sources of Islam in order to overcome 'traditional' deviations, and most notably prohibitions, associated with their parents' generation (cf. Mandaville, 2001; Nökel, 2002; Amir-Moazami and Salvatore, 2003).

In common with other Muslim reformist thinkers, Ramadan calls for an improvement in educational provision for Muslims in Western contexts, placing emphasis on the necessity of expanding the system both at the primary level (through the provision of basic religious instruction) and at the higher level (by the establishment of adequate professorships in the education of imams at universities (2004, Chapter 6)). His concern for Islamic education is driven by his aforementioned belief in the necessity of adequate knowledge of religious texts, and by a resolve to maintain Islam's status as a 'discursive tradition' (Asad, 1986), even in contexts in which it has a minority status. Here, Ramadan is in open opposition to Tibi. Although Tibi also believes that imams should be provided with a better, European-based education, he wants young lay Muslims in Europe to increase their secular knowledge, rather than their Islamic knowledge. For Tibi, the driving force behind the reform of Islamic traditions should be a detachment from Islam and an attachment to secular norms. Ramadan, on the contrary, contends that the driving force should be a return to religious sources, and an intensified cultivation of adequate religious knowledge.

However, Ramadan does not limit his call for the accumulation of knowledge to Islamic sources. He extends it to the study of the European institutional settings and arrangements in which Muslims live and interact. This point brings us closer to his version of a European Islam. While Ramadan appeals to a universal notion of Islam with regard to *da'wa*, he is simultaneously aware and supportive of its localized implications. He therefore seems to link two major goals: an increased understanding of the European, and increased understanding of the national contexts in which Muslims live and interact.

Ramadan links the idea of an adequate re-contextualization of Islamic sources to non-Islamic contexts. In this sense, his commitment to a Muslim discursive tradition should not be misunderstood as an attempt to conserve a tradition, or simply to transplant it into a new, non-Muslim setting. Instead, it represents an active and critical engagement with this tradition. This is most clearly apparent in his emphasis on the importance of *ijtihad*: the Islamic principle of original reasoning from within the tradition (Ramadan, 1999). He does not interpret Qur'anic verses in an absolute or timeless manner, but always in relation to the concrete settings in which Muslims live. On the other hand, Ramadan suggests a selective appropriation of what 'Western culture produces, in order to promote its positive contributions and resist its destructive by-products at both the human and the ecological level' (2004, 76). The main foundations for the fruitful involvement of Muslims in European settings, according to Ramadan, are their active engagement with the Islamic discursive tradition, and a contextualized understanding of its sources.

Ramadan does, however, not go so far as to indicate more concretely the shifts and transformations in Islamic discourses and practices that might result from these efforts at a re-contextualization. Moreover, he tends to avoid addressing more closely the question of who is the legitimate interpreter of the texts, and who has the power to shape, circulate and transform discourses, and hence the very question of religious authority. It is not clear to what extent Ramadan attempts to renew Islam, or prefers to stay within the consensus of established orthodoxy. This ambiguity has led scholars like Khadija Mohsen-Finan (2002, 211) to conclude that Ramadan 'wants to combine strict obedience to the teachings of Islam with civic commitment.'

What is clear, however, is that Ramadan considers it necessary for Muslims to establish a sense of belonging to Europe, not only because of his desire for an appropriate re-contextualization of Islam, but also in order to demand rights in the name of their status as citizens. Contrary to Tibi, Ramadan does not see any contradictions between a contextualized commitment to Islam along these lines, and the secular constitutions of European societies. On the contrary, he assumes that these things can form the basis for the harmonious co-existence of Muslim and non-Muslim citizens.[9] It is, however, obvious that Ramadan's interpretation of secularity differs sharply from that of Tibi. Ramadan understands secularity as a vehicle for freedom of conscience. His interpretation is grounded in the principle of fundamental rights, according to which the freedom of religious expression is essential. Such freedom envisions respect for religious practices and expressions, in both private and in public arenas, as far as these are not in contradiction with other elementary rights. For Ramadan, secularity constitutes a principle that favours the pluralization of religious expressions in public life, and not one that delimits or controls them. Secular constitutions are therefore, at least in principle, evaluated positively because they constitute the basis on which demands for participation by diverse religions can be made. In other words, the central issue, once again, concerns the interpretation of certain laws, rather than the

9   His simultaneous commitment to a Western philosophical tradition is also displayed in his religious teachings and public sermons and, to a lesser extent, in his publications, where he freely combines references to such sources as Montesquieu, de Tocqueville and Rousseau with quotations from the Qur'an.

laws themselves, which might constitute a hindrance to Muslims' attempts to practise their religion in European spaces in accordance with Islamic requirements.

What Ramadan does is to expand the possibilities for public forms of religious expression by taking up, and to a certain extent re-interpreting, tools and norms that are anchored in European societies. This politics of re-description challenges the dominant understanding of secularity, which mostly asks Muslims to limit religious expressions to the point of invisibility. With his call for a constant effort to re-contextualize Islam's sources in European settings, Ramadan does not consider Muslims only in terms of their 'presence' in Europe: he asks for their active involvement as citizens. In contrast to Tibi's position, Ramadan's conception of citizenship for Muslims implies both duties (in particular loyalty and identification with the constitutional order of the society in which they live) and rights (to representational structures: 'Muslims really are *citizens*, and they too have the right, within the framework of the national legislation, to be respected as *Muslims*' (2004, 100) [original emphasis]). Unlike Tibi, who promotes an abstract concept of the citizen, Ramadan has a more concrete and situated citizen in mind, while also appealing to a civic model of membership criteria. According to his interpretation, Muslims can and should be full members of European societies, while remaining openly and publicly confined to Islam. He favours what Mohsen-Finan (2002; 2003) has neatly called 'faith-based citizenship'. Religion is, for Ramadan, a basic component of European societies, rather than an obstacle to active membership.

In contrast to Tibi, the approach offered by Ramadan is situated within a context of reform activated from within the Islamic tradition (i.e., the sources), rather than a mere internalization of Enlightenment philosophy, or Islam's retreat from the public stage. He thus mounts a robust challenge to the idea of the gradual integration of Muslims into European societies, and to the goal of building a separate community in order to be protected from the temptations of Western societies, as some other orthodox thinkers have suggested.

> From the Islamic point of view, adapting, for the new generations, does not mean making concessions on the essentials but, rather, building, working out, seeking to remain faithful while allowing for evolution.' (2004, 85).

It is important to remember that Ramadan's approach to Europe as a Muslim, and his conception of how to be a 'European' Muslim, should be understood as contradicting some basic assumptions of liberal secular thought. One example of this may be found in the idea of the 'politics of conventions', as

Saba Mahmood has framed it (2005, 148), to which self-declared, practising and publicly committed Muslims like Ramadan have committed themselves. Mahmood uses this term in order to characterize the self-willed obedience of what she calls 'pious' Muslims to religiously prescribed conventions, which she juxtaposes with concepts of autonomy that underlie most liberal approaches, including even those that admit the social embeddedness of the self, but which are ultimately guided by the goal to liberate it from social conventions:

> Such a criticism turns upon an imaginary of freedom, one deeply indebted to liberal political theory, in which an individual is considered free on the condition that she acts autonomously: that her actions be the result of her own choice and free will, rather than of custom, tradition, transcendental will, or social coercion. (Mahmood, 2005, 148)

Contrary to this conception of freedom and autonomy, the Islamized self, as propagated and experienced by thinkers like Ramadan, 'looks to a different set of strategies and horizons than a subject for whom the principal ideals and tools of self-reference reside outside of herself.' (Mahmood, 2005, 151).

In consequence, the type of agency that Ramadan ideally attributes to Muslims in Europe should not be understood as a confident resistance to (religious) authority – as it is predominantly conceptualized and desired by scholars like Tibi – but rather in terms of an active engagement with authoritative discourse, which might at times be empowering but at times also very restrictive. Mahmood has convincingly described this notion as the 'politics of piety', and this also lies at the heart of Ramadan's approach to Islam. As we can see with Ramadan, public piety, instead of merely being directed towards the inside of the believer, also has a political implication, in that it openly challenges secular assumptions of a gradual disappearance of faith from the public agenda.

'Muslim solidarity' is conceptualized here in terms of a two-fold and interrelated inquiry. On the one hand, it means a boundedness with the local and transnational Muslim community, in particular through spiritual conduct and respect for the basic norms inscribed in the religion, while working with and re-working the sources. This is to be achieved mainly through the constant accumulation of theological knowledge. On the other hand, it implies a commitment to the constitutional foundations of secular European states, which – according to Ramadan – goes beyond mere loyalty. Such solidarity should emerge from a feeling of being 'at home', in terms of Muslims' identification as Europeans (or members of European nation states), and also of being represented as Muslim citizens. Rather than causing an obstacle to their existence in, and co-existence with, Western European societies, the commitment to Islam (and a coherent and continuous attempt to contextualize it according to Ramadan's schema) opens up the path to solidarities that are understood as pragmatic, and also to emotional identifications with the non-Muslim European context. Accordingly, a strengthening of the faith, through both the accumulation of knowledge and appropriate moral conduct, constitutes the necessary starting point for a fruitful interaction and engagement with non-Muslim majority societies.

The final approach to be analysed can actually be read as an attempt to make the idea of public piety more concrete, and to institutionalize – within a framework of other minority requests – a version of 'faith-based citizenship'.

Tariq Modood: multiculturalism extended to the field of religion

UK-based political theorist and sociologist Tariq Modood is as a key figure in this approach. Modood is one of a few self-declared Muslim thinkers (though clearly not outspoken to the same extent as, for example, Ramadan) who critically engages with the political implications of the Muslim presence in non-Muslim European nation states. Although defining himself as a Muslim, Modood is probably less concerned than Ramadan with Islamic discursive traditions. Nonetheless, his argument is based in the first instance on a political theoretical point of view. He does not have very much to say about how Islam should ideally look in Europe, but focuses on how European nation states could adjust to the presence of a religious minority that has so far not been incorporated into the European self-understanding.

His concern with the presence of Islam in Europe is based on a critical engagement with the politics of multiculturalism, and his most recent publications (2005, 2007) are the fruit of a long inquiry into matters of race, ethnicity and religion in the UK and elsewhere in Europe. Contrary to Tibi, for whom multiculturalism does not appear to be much more than a metaphor for previous failures in the political management of cultural plurality, Modood offers a nuanced and multi-levelled reflection vis-à-vis theories of multiculturalism. His central question is not whether multiculturalism is a good or a bad thing, but rather which version offers a potential for coming to terms with the existing multicultural reality of Western European nation states.

Categorizing possible approaches to the challenge of multiculturalism into five different ideal types – the 'decentred self', the 'liberal state', the 'republic', the 'federation of communities' and the 'plural state' – Modood prioritizes the 'plural state'. He contends that this form of multiculturalism is the one most likely to incorporate differences, including different forms of belief, while at the same time not giving up equal citizenship as the basis of the political order. What distinguishes Modood from Tibi, and other proponents of a republican model of citizenship, is his open objection to notions of abstract universalism, as spelled out in the equality (i.e., sameness) paradigm:

> Racial equality cannot always mean that our public institutions and the law itself must treat everybody as if they were the same – for that will usually mean treating everybody by the norms and convenience of the majority. (2005, 108)

The main objection to abstract universalism, as proffered by Tibi and others, is a well-known argument by other theorists dealing with politics of multiculturalism or plurality as a whole (e.g., Young, 1990; Taylor, 1993) that this scheme is based on an alleged ethical blindness of the liberal public sphere, which on closer analysis turns out to be a mere construction. Questioning the presumption of a distinction between the 'ethical' and 'political' cultures of a given nation state (as famously put by Habermas in his reply to Taylor, 1993) on the grounds that it ignores the ethical and non-neutral character of political cultures, Modood stresses that liberal democracies do not provide a natural mechanism for integrating minority positions into the dominant political culture. Contrary to Tibi, Modood thus acknowledges that any public space, policy or society is structured around certain kinds of understandings and practices that prioritize some cultural values and behaviours over others, and that no public space is culturally neutral. He thereby takes the issue of power seriously into account into his approach.

In common with Ramadan, he argues for an 'ethical conception' of citizenship beyond the idea of the abstract self, one which explicitly accounts for supposedly 'private' matters such as family or community ties. Working from the assumption that the individual is shaped by 'the social order constituted by citizenship and the publics that amplify and qualify, sustain and critique and reform citizenship' (2005, 140), Modood aims not at the deconstruction of the nation state, but at the integration of difference in order to 'remake the nation state' (2005, 140). This is quite an interesting argument, as it goes beyond the 'friendly co-existence' of different 'cultural units' that underlies most other approaches to multiculturalism, and explicitly accounts for the dynamics that the incorporation of cultural plurality necessarily brings about at the national level. This is most clearly apparent in Modood's explicit treatment of the issue of religion and secularism. It is this that makes his approach to multiculturalism far more intriguing and original than those of most other theorists, who seem to take the secular condition of nation states for granted while excluding 'religion' as a legitimate category for plurality claims (cf. Koenig, 2007; Amir-Moazami, 2007). By laying bare the 'cultural impregnation' (Habermas, 1993, 181) of principles like secularity or neutrality, which are often taken for granted as pre-given categories, Modood requests that these should be opened up to the new cultural and religious constellations in society generated by processes of immigration.

With regard to his conceptualization of multiculturalism as an option for the 'plural state', which constantly reforms itself by actively accounting for cultural differences, the most interesting part for our present purposes is his analysis of the politics of multiculturalism in relation to secularism. In this context, Modood questions one of the most central claims within liberal thinking (including liberal approaches to multiculturalism): that the state is, or even should be, decoupled from religious matters. He combines this argument with another doubt concerning the widely held assumption that Islam is, by definition, tied to politics. This seems to be particularly important, since the assumption that Islam is inherently embedded within politics, and therefore excludable from the public sphere, is widespread among proponents of multiculturalism. This must be related to the self-assessment of Western societies as being rooted in the Enlightenment philosophy of the separations of spheres, which is responsible for the notion of 'religion' itself, as a distinctive and distinguishable domain (cf. Asad, 1993; Koenig, 2007). Modood claims:

> The distinction, on the one hand, between the practical and reasonable nature of politics and, on the other hand, between the totalizing and dogmatic nature of religion is in effect a distinction between politics and ideology. (2005, 146)[10]

This potentially dislocates the notions of the legitimate boundaries of the public sphere, as most openly manifest in the enduring hostility of broad sectors of European societies towards the active presence and participation of publicly committed Muslims in public spaces. Modood proposes one of the central critiques of public spheres theories: that the involvement of power is not thoroughly taken into account, and that the fact that certain groups, actors or individual voices are not captured in an idealized public sphere, as an open and equal site of rational argument and discourse, is often overlooked. He also argues within a post-structuralist perspective, essentially claiming that

---

10 In support of this argument, Modood posits that a radical version of secularism does not prevent a radicalization of religious groups or movements: on the contrary, it often encourages it. Evoking historical examples like Nazism, Stalinism and Communist China, Modood observes that various historical experiences indicate that secularism is by no means free from ideology or repressive politics (2005, 150).

the 'public–private' distinction is a specific technique for secular-liberal governance. Instead of promoting a radicalization of secularism as an adequate answer to the challenges that are generated by the emergence of 'public forms' of religion, Modood claims that a linkage between religious and political spheres not only reflects an empirical reality, but can also be re-read as a fruitful way of enhancing the democratic potential of political orders and social peace.[11] He concludes that the 'goal of democratic multiculturalism cannot and should not be neutrality, but rather inclusion of marginal and disadvantaged groups, including religious communities, in public life.' (2005, 147) Although Modood does not go into details about how this should happen, his critical re-reading of liberal assumptions of multiculturalism makes clear that the version of the 'plural state' he has in mind should go beyond simply protecting Muslim minorities within a separate unity, and should incorporate Muslim rationalities and practices on an institutional level, as implied in the idea of a constantly (self-)reforming nation state.

What Modood fails to do, however, is to make his assumptions more concrete. For instance, he hardly gives any examples of how such an incorporation of public Islam would look on a practical level, nor does he seriously take into account the conflict that this might entail (i.e., claims by religious groups that stretch the boundaries of equal citizenship). It seems that this lacuna stems in the first place from the limited focus offered by Modood, engaging as he does only marginally with Muslim thought and social practices in Europe. Although Modood clearly goes beyond Tibi's assessment of Muslims as simply having to adapt to 'European' norms, in particular the call to secularize and resign from the public stage, he does not engage to the same extent as, for example, Ramadan with Islam as a 'discursive tradition.'

At certain points, it even seems that Modood, like many of his colleagues, interprets the demands by Muslims for participation in the name of their religious identities in terms of a swift 'coming out' of Muslims, encouraged by various transnational or local 'events' (like the Rushdie affair, or September 11th), but not by a coherent transmission of Muslim traditions. Such an assessment, however, questions his own normative assumptions about an active participation of Muslims in all domains of society in the name of their collective ties.[12] Modood takes Islam seriously enough to require a move

11 Here, Modood takes up an argument that was first developed at length by José Casanova in his well-known study *Public Religion* (1994).
12 To bring the religious affiliations of European Muslims down to the level of the politics of identity in fact mirrors a more widespread argument among scholars dealing with Islam in Europe (cf. Amir-Moazami and Salvatore, 2003). One of the most central conclusions is that young Muslims in Europe have been characterized by 'believing without belonging', as famously put by Grace Davie (1994).

towards a critical self-assessment of the secular foundation of liberal states, but he does not go further in setting out in more detail how Islam could become an integral part of them. Moreover, although Modood offers a more innovative approach to multiculturalism through his recognition that cultural and religious plurality affects national self-understanding and, in the longer run, also transforms the normative premises of 'recipient societies', he does not necessarily avoid one of the central dilemmas inherent in theories of multiculturalism. This is because his assumptions are also based on a certain tendency to objectify community ties, and entail the risk of constructing 'religious units' under the label of a common cultural, political or religious identity (cf. Caglar, 1997).

Relating this to the concept of solidarity, we can introduce a little caution, pointedly spelled out by Jodi Dean (1996, 27):

> When solidarity requires that members be 'recognized as', their concrete particularities will always be excluded. Because flight is preferred to dialogue and critique, fragmentation tends to leave the basic assumptions of the dominant group intact.

While Modood, indeed, does not in the first place necessarily emphasize the internal dynamics of religious groups that are to be promoted within a 'plural state', his goal is nonetheless precisely that of going beyond a notion of multiculturalism, which – while trying to cope with the articulation of cultural or religious particularities – tends to 'domesticate' differences by managing a consensus based on a specific secular norm. With his call to critically revise the secular foundations of European nation states securely taken for granted in most multiculturalist approaches, Modood fills an important gap in the field of Islam in Europe. I see in his critique of the unbalanced effects of neutrality or, more generally, of abstract universalism a potential for exposing the contradictions inherent in discourses on equality and neutrality. Both represent contested and still largely unfulfilled norms, which often serve as instruments of social control and hegemonic politics towards minorities that make demands. In this sense, we could argue that Modood promotes 'solidarity with difference', instead of supporting the (Enlightenment) idea of 'solidarity with sameness', which, in one way or another, always brings us back to the issue of power, so tightly related to mechanisms of exclusion: Who has the power to solidarize with differences, or to decide that difference should be erased from public life in favour of one single, univocally shared solidarity, based on humanity?

Conclusion

Over the course of this chapter, a relatively wide scope of approaches to the question of how Islam should ideally look in European landscapes, and in consequence a variety of implications of solidarity, have emerged. The proposed versions range from the retreat of Muslims from a particularistic framework of references towards a universal (yet Western) scheme of bonds, through an openly committed pious Muslimness that appeals to a critical yet coherent reflection upon the theological tools of Islam, to those that incorporate multiculturalism in order to open up the scope of expression of potentially contradicting and conflicting world views.

While the first approach lies in a tradition of thought that seeks to expand the category of solidarity to encompass principles of egalitarian difference and to express universal ideals of accountability (cf. Honneth, 1990; Habermas, 1989–1990), the second and the third approaches are related to a scholarly discourse that looks for a concrete and historically specific understanding of solidarity (cf. Fraser, 1986; Rorty, 1989; 1995). In the first approach, we could argue, a specifically Muslim form of solidarity emerges merely in terms of a criticism of certain forms of exclusion that contradict the leading ideal of equality. Analyzed, for example, through the lens of Richard Rorty's (1995) conceptualization of the term, one could even argue that Tibi (along with a number of other proponents of 'Euro-Islam') represents a tradition that Rorty has framed in terms of 'objectivity', understood as a counter-concept to solidarity. While solidarity, in Rorty's interpretation, implies a necessary commitment to a community, tradition or life narrative, which through locality and context cannot be universal, 'objectivity' implies the commitment to bonds with 'humanity' understood in the abstract. Reading Tibi in this way, we could argue that in his view, solidarity is legitimate only on the basis of universal values or in terms of 'affectional solidarity' (cf. Dean, 1996, 24), which arises from intimate relationships of love or friendship within a clearly distinguishable private domain.

In the second approach, there is a more explicit reference to particular identities, which builds up a relatively strong sense of 'community'. It offers an alternative to universalistic understandings of ties connected to 'humanity', and understands Muslim solidarity as both an engagement with an inherited Islamic discursive tradition, and the cultivation of practices related to this tradition. However, it is not a static version of the Islamic tradition that thereby emerges, and thus is is not also a notion of solidarity that necessarily starts from an essentialist idea of the community. It is rather a notion of tradition, which potentially embodies transformations through the efforts of a constant re-working. This becomes obvious in the emphasis on the importance of *ijtihad*, which points to the reforming and transformative potential of Islamic traditions, led from 'within' the tradition. It also emerges as a consequence of the call for Muslims to settle as citizens within the European countries in which they live. There is an appeal to a reflexive kind of solidarity with European spaces as much as with Islam, understood as both a 'natural' belonging and as a commitment to be cultivated. Despite clear appeals to particular identities and specific forms of solidarities, there is thus also a commitment to intersubjective ties, which understands the Muslim 'we' in terms of a process that is shaped by specific contexts.

The third type of argument, which I label 'plural solidarity', challenges the very idea of a unique European identity into which Muslims should be integrated, or from which they should be excluded. Rather than merely tackling the question as it has been conventionally framed – how Muslims position themselves vis-à-vis the normative requirements of Western European societies, and whether they are on their way to becoming truly European – this brings to the fore the question of how European societies can cope with and adjust to the presence of Muslims, as well as the challenges deriving from the increasing cultural and religious plurality within European borders. From the exposure of the particularity of the universal emerges an understanding of solidarity, which stems from the recognition, rather than merely toleration, of difference. In this sense, the often taken-for-granted idea of a European solidarity that mainly constitutes itself through the non-European 'other' is thrown into doubt. Situated and concrete identities emerge in place of the abstract identity of the citizen acting in a universal public sphere. Because of this appeal to the situatedness of the self, Muslim solidarity seems to be taken for granted as a starting point for renegotiating European secular spaces and for a critical engagement with a basic presupposition of liberalism. Solidarity might arise from the efforts of both sides to respect each other, for which the recognition of religious difference – and hence of specific, locally shaped forms of solidarity – is crucial. Accordingly, the active involvement of Muslims in European societies should not (and does not) lead only to transformations in Muslim thought and social practices, as anticipated and prescribed in the first approach, and to a lesser extent also in the second approach. It should also lead to transformations in European public spheres, insofar as they accept and incorporate a pluralist conception of solidarity, and on this basis cultivate solidarity with Muslim demands to establish representational structures, instead of offering a one-way notion of integration, i.e., solidarity with a pre-given and static political order.

Trying to situate these different viewpoints more explicitly within the wider public spheres in which they are articulated, it is quite obvious that the version of Euro-Islam offered by Tibi has hitherto been the one most frequently propounded in European public spheres, at least if we consider the mainstream public discourse on Islam. Ramadan's approach, which, while expressing solidarity with the constitutional orders of Western Europe, refuses to reject his commitment to a Muslim community, is clearly less widely accepted. Yet this has not prevented him from becoming one of the most prominent figures with whom pious young Muslims in European societies, who have started to similarly consider themselves 'Europeans', can identify without having to give up what is sacred to them. While Ramadan could fit into an expanded notion of solidarity, understood as a plural commitment to diverse and dynamic community logics, he will clearly continue to draw suspicion from public authorities and the media for propagating 'double talk' (as Salvatore points out in Chapter 4 of this volume). Similarly, though to a lesser extent, Modood's suggestion of a critical revision of the secular foundations of liberal states in order to prepare the way for plural solidarity is definitely a marginalized argument.

In other words, while all these scholars have similar profiles – Muslim intellectuals with the power to speak publicly – it is also quite clear that they do not have the same ability to shape and circulate versions of European Islam. In other words, the ideal of free speech and the power of any religious group to enter the public sphere – a situation from which Muslims in Europe benefit – does not automatically imply 'being heard', since the public sphere is 'not open equally to everyone because the domain of free speech is always shaped by pre-established limits' (Asad, 1999, 180). Similarly, while 'Europe' is located at the centre of Muslim self-positionings (however critically it might be conceived of), Islam has to date been excluded from the self-representations of Europe and the narratives through which these representations are constituted (cf. Asad, 2003). If this continues to be the case, then the whole idea of solidarity with regard to Islam in Europe seems to remain a rather one-dimensional concept: Muslims are asked to solidarize with European norms, while Europe is far from thinking about solidarity with Islam or, more generally, with plurality that affects shared norms and values, and that goes beyond a friendly co-existence with the 'abstract other' (Žižek, 1998). This brings us back to the issue of power, which we cannot ignore when locating these different approaches in the wider public spheres and which is, of course, also involved in notions of solidarity, which cannot be detached from mechanisms of exclusion.

However, the concrete outcomes are certainly more plural and open-ended than they may at first sight appear to be, just as the relationship between discourse and power is never clear-cut. The relatively broad spread of approaches to European Islam also indicates that at least a certain type of Muslim (i.e., the educated intellectual) has started to participate in the process of shaping ideas of how Islam could and should look in Europe, and also how Europe could be possibly re-read in the light of the presence and involvement of Islam within European borders. Even the more 'self-alienated' version, offered by authors such as Tibi, clearly also indicates an empowering effect, not least because it challenges orthodox discourses. Although it shows that certain Muslims in Europe have now become co-opted through a caricaturist appropriation of dominant paradigms of secularism and integration, it also makes clear that Europe has become a space for ongoing debates about Islam's place within Europe, in which some actors take up and revitalize dominant ideas, and others show more reflexively that the content of both Islam and Europe is contested, conflictual and compassionate.

Acknowledgements

I would like to thank Nathalie Karagiannis and Mika Hannula for their helpful comments.

References

Abdallah, L. (1998), *Islamischer Fundamentalismus, eine fundamentale Fehlwahrnehmung? Zur Rolle von Orientalismus in westlichen Analysen des islamischen Fundamentalismus*, Berlin, Das Arabische Buch.

Ali, A. H. (2005), *Ich klage an. Plädoyer für die Befreiung der muslimischen Frauen*, Munich, Piper.

Amara, F. (2003), *Ni putes, ni soumises*, Paris, La Découverte.

Amir-Moazami, S. (2005), 'Buried alive: multiculturalism in Germany', *ISIM Newsletter*, **16**.

Amir-Moazami, S. (2007), *Politisierte Religion: Der Kopftuchstreit in Deutschland und Frankreich*, Bielefeld, transcript.

Amir-Moazami, S. and Salvatore, A. (2003), 'Gender, generation, and the reform of tradition: from Muslim majority societies to Western Europe' in J. Nielsen and S. Allievi (eds), *Muslim Networks: Transnational Communities in and Across Europe*, Leiden, Brill, 32–77.

Asad, T. (1986), *The Idea of an Anthropology of Islam*, Washington, DC, Georgetown University.

Asad, T. (1993), *Genealogies of Religion: Discipline and Reasons of Power in Christianity and Islam*, Baltimore and London, Johns Hopkins University Press.

Asad, T. (1999), 'Religion, nation-state, secularism' in P. van der Veer and H. Lehmann (eds), *Nation and Religion: Perspectives on Europe and Asia*, Princeton, N.J., Princeton

University Press, 178–192.

Asad, T. (2003), *Formations of the Secular: Christianity, Islam, Modernity*, Stanford, CT, Stanford University Press.

Asad, T. (2005), 'Reflections on *laïcité* and the public sphere', *Social Science Research Council: Items and Issues*, 5.

Bowen, J. R. (2004), 'Muslims and citizens. France's headscarf controversy', *Boston Review*, February/March.

Caeiro, A. (2004), 'The social construction of shari'a: bank interest, home purchase, and Islamic norms in the West', *Die Welt des Islams*, 44, 3, 351–375.

Caglar, A. S. (1997), 'Hyphenated identities and the limits of "culture"' in T. Modood and P. Werbner (eds), *The Politics of Multiculturalism in the New Europe: Racism, Identity and Community*, London and New York, Zed Books, 169–185.

Casanova, J. (1994), *Public Religions in the Modern World*, Chicago and London, University of Chicago Press.

Cohn-Bendit, D. and Schmid, T. (1992), *Heimat Babylon*, Hamburg, Hoffmann und Campe.

Davie, G. (1994), *Religion in Britain Since 1945: Believing without Belonging*, London, Blackwell.

Dean, J. (1996), *Solidarity of Strangers: Feminism after Identity Politics*, Berkeley, CA, University of California Press.

Fourest, C. (2004), *Frère Tariq: Discours, stratégie et méthode de Tariq Ramadan*, Paris, Grasset.

Fraser, N. (1986), 'Toward a discourse ethic of solidarity', *Praxis International*, 5, 4, 425–429.

Frégosi, F. (2004), 'L'Imam, le conférencier et le jurisconsulte: retour sur trois figures contemporaines du champ religieux islamique en France', *Archives de sciences sociales des religions*, 125, 131–146.

Gilroy, P. (2004), *After Empire: Melancholia or Convivial Culture?*, Oxford, Routledge.

Habermas, J. (1989–1990), 'Justice and solidarity: on the discussion concerning Stage 6', *Philosophical Forum*, 21, 1–2, 32–52.

Habermas, J. (1993), 'Anerkennungskämpfe in einem demokratischen Rechtsstaat' in C. Taylor (ed.), *Multikulturalismus und die Politik der Anerkennung*, Frankfurt am Main, Suhrkamp, 147–196.

Honneth, A. (1990), 'Integrität und Missachtung. Grundmotive einer Moral der Anerkennung', *Merkur*, 12, December, 1043–1053.

Kelek, N. (2005), *Die fremde Braut*, Cologne, Kiepenheuer & Witsch.

Kepel, G. (1994), *A l'ouest d'Allah*, Paris, Le Seuil.

Koenig, M. (2007), *Religionspolitik in Europa*, Frankfurt, Campus.

Leggewie, C. (2002), 'Auf dem Weg zum Euro-Islam? Moscheen und Muslime in der Bundesrepublik Deutschland', speech held on the occasion of the presentation of the manual 'Der Weg zur Moschee – eine Handreichung für die Praxis' at the Representation of the State of Hesse, Berlin, 14 May.

Luckmann, T. (1991 [1967]), *Die unsichtbare Religion*, Frankfurt am Main, Suhrkamp.

Mahmood, S. (2005), *Politics of Piety: The Islamic Revival and the Feminist Subject*, Princeton, N.J. and Oxford, Stanford University Press.

Mandaville, P. (2001), *Transnational Muslim Politics: Reimagining the Umma*, London, Routledge.

Mitchell, T. (1988), *Colonizing Egypt*, New York/New Rochelle/Melbourne/Sydney/ Cambridge, Cambridge University Press.

Modood, T. (2005), *Multicultural Politics: Racism, Ethnicity and Muslims in Britain*, Minneapolis/Edinburgh, University of Minnesota Press & Edinburgh University Press.

Mohsen-Finan, K. (2002), 'Tariq Ramadan: voice of a new religiousness' in W. Shadid and S. van Koningsveld (eds), *Intercultural Relations and Religious Authorities: Muslims in the European Union*, Leuven, Peeters, 208–214.

Mohsen-Finan, K. (2003), 'La mise en avant d'une "citoyenneté croyante"': le cas de Tariq Ramadan' in R. Leveau, K. Mohsen-Finan and C. Wihtol de Wenden (eds), *De la citoyenneté locale*, Paris, Institut français des relations internationals, 87–96.

Nökel, S. (2002), 'Die Töchter der Gastarbeiter und der Islam: Zur Soziologie alltagsweltlicher Anerkennungspolitiken – Eine Fallstudie', transcript, Bielefeld.

Ramadan, T. (1999), *Etre Musulman Européen*, Lyon, Tawhid.

Ramadan, T. (2004), *Western Muslims and the Future of Islam*, Oxford and New York, Oxford University Press.

Roest Crollius, A. R. (1978), 'Mission and morality: al-amr bi-l-ma'ruf as expression of the communitarian and missionary dimensions of qur'anic ethics', *Studia Missionalia*, 27, 257–284.

Rorty, R. (1989), *Contingency, Irony, and Solidarity*, Cambridge, Cambridge University Press.

Rorty, R. (1995), *Solidarität oder Objektivität? Drei philosophische Essays*, Stuttgart, Reclam.

Salvatore, A. (1999 [1997]), *Islam and the Political Discourse of Modernity*, Reading, Ithaca.

Shakry, O. (1998), 'Schooled mothers and structured play: child rearing in the turn-of-the century Egypt' in L. Abu-Lughod (ed.), *Remaking Women: Feminism and Modernity in the Middle East*, Princeton, N.J., Princeton University Press, 127–169.

Taylor, C. (1993), *Multikulturalismus und die Politik der Anerkennung*, Frankfurt am Main, Suhrkamp.

Teczan, L. (2003), 'Das Islamische in den Studien zu Muslimen in Deutschland', *Zeitschrift für Soziologie*, 32–33, 237–261.

Tibi, B. (1991), *Die Krise des modernen Islams: eine vorindustrielle Kultur im wissenschaftlich-technischen Zeitalter*, Frankfurt am Main, Suhrkamp.

Tibi, B. (1992), *Islamischer Fundamentalismus, moderne Wissenschaft und Technologie*, Frankfurt am Main, Suhrkamp.

Tibi, B. (1998), *Europa ohne Identität? Die Krise der multikulturellen Gesellschaft*, Munich, Bertelsmann.

Tibi, B. (2000), *Der Islam in Deutschland: Muslime in Deutschland*, Stuttgart and Munich, Deutsche Verlagsanstalt.

Tibi, B. (2005), *Mit dem Kopftuch nach Europa? Die Türkei auf dem Weg in die Europäische Union*, Darmstadt, Wissenschaftliche Buchgesellschaft.

Young, I. M. (1990), *Justice and the Politics of Difference*, Princeton, N.J., Princeton University Press.

Žižek, S. (1998), *Ein Plädoyer für die Intoleranz*, Vienna, Passagen.

12 European Solidarity with 'the Rest of the World'[1]

Nathalie Karagiannis

Solidarity with 'the rest of the world'

The fate of dilemmas is that they cannot be fully resolved; the origins of any dilemmatic construction must be sought in the impression that the question it poses is one of obligatory choice between two options, neither of which is self-evident. The refusal of this obligatory choice entails showing that the dilemma qua dilemma does not hold. In this respect, this chapter does two things: it uncovers a dilemmatic construction that remains implicit in the texts overviewed (and, therefore, makes a dilemma explicit), and it rejects the dilemma as the wrong way of putting the issue.

The dilemma in question concerns, on the one hand, European solidarity – that is, solidarity within Europe – and, on the other hand, the solidarity of Europe with 'the rest of the world'. It is posed in the usual either/or form: *either* solidarity within Europe *or* solidarity of Europe with the rest of the world. It starts out from the assumption that the question: 'Can solidarity in Europe exist and be enhanced while also aiming to achieve solidarity outside Europe?' must receive a negative answer.

Until now, however, the dilemma has remained implicit in the two main places in which it appears: EU policy discourse[2] and political-philosophical discourse. The reasons for this implicitness range from neglect to uneasiness, but this chapter is not centrally concerned with them. Rather, its central

---

1 I would like to thank Steffen Mau, William Outhwaite and Herwig Reiter, who gave helpful suggestions on an earlier version. This chapter was previously published in *European Societies*, 9.1, pp. 3–21, under the title 'Solidarity within Europe/solidarity without Europe'.
2 For practical reasons that have to do with the discourse examined, but also for reasons that have to do with the construction of a political whole, I use 'Europe' and 'EU' interchangeably.

concern is the relative indeterminacy of 'the rest of the world', and the relative indeterminacy of the time for action, which this implicitness allows. The chapter ultimately argues that these indeterminacies can be reduced by, first, inserting the solidarity of Europe with the rest of the world into a particular realm, that of the social; and, second, articulating the relevance of the historical, colonial past of Europe to the future political project of Europe.

Regarding, first, the discourse emanating from the EU institutions: social policy and humanitarian aid have long been considered two totally separate areas. In this sense, the dilemma has, for a long time, remained implicit because the separation between those areas was not challenged. Generally speaking, however, resort to dilemmatic constructions seems to be one of the most efficacious rhetorical tropes of political discourse. Second, the theoretical discourse on Europe has also, for a long time, neglected or refused to treat the two solidarities simultaneously. As a rule (that is, with exceptions), the result was that thinkers who chose to write or talk about Europe did not consider it relevant to talk about Europe's relations to the 'rest of the world'; in a similar fashion, those thinkers who chose to focus on Europe's relation to the 'rest of the world' were not interested in the internal construction of Europe and, at the same time, were considered not to be interested in Europe, and were thus relegated to the periphery of European affairs.[3]

Conceptually, both of these strands of discourse treat the same dilemma, though they both pretend not to. After acknowledging that there is a wide variety of usages of solidarity in both discourses, it is possible to see that this variety deploys in various ways the dichotomy of solidarity *within*, and solidarity *of* Europe *with the rest of the world*. In each case, taking a closer look at the rather ambiguous and multiple understandings of the concept of solidarity helps to uncover the implicit dilemmatic constructions.

The usual understanding of solidarity is 'that which holds society together'; it is either needed because there are differences that must be overcome, or it exists as the product of the idea of a homogeneous whole. At first sight, then, the justifications for solidarity cover opposite poles. It could, for instance, be advanced that solidarity within Europe is needed because there is so much diversity within Europe that it would not otherwise (i.e., without solidarity) hold together; and it can be advanced that solidarity within Europe exists as the reflection of a relatively homogeneous society. Keeping this great flexibility of the concept in mind, the following definition can be proposed:

---

3 A good example of the first case is a recent volume that brings together the contributions to the debate on Europe initiated by Habermas: Levy, Pensky and Torpey, 2005. An example of the second case can be found in any academic department of European studies.

solidarity is a recurrent specification of social bonds with a political view. In other words, it brings together, without disentangling them, a (often a posteriori) description of a certain *social* reality at a certain time, and a (often a priori) *political* project (Karagiannis, 2006). Such a definition does not include connotations of a wilful distortion of social entities, or of an undercover political agenda: it merely brings together the social and the political in a way that is general enough to cover the manifold usages of solidarity. Thus, historically, solidarity has been used for, and come to mean, situations that vary markedly, either sustaining the established order or challenging it, either promoting generality or specificity, either acknowledging inequality or assuming equality.

This chapter is an application of this definition, and a way of practically thinking through the opportunities and pitfalls of the concept: just as the social and the political are blurred in the usages of the concept that is overviewed here, so too are 'is' and 'ought', or the descriptive/static and the normative/dynamic modes. However, it is argued, the central dilemma examined in this chapter is posed in categories that do not neatly overlap with one of the two sides of the concept: the social versus the human, and Europe versus the rest of the world, are encountered in both 'is' and 'ought' modes. Finally, while it would be tempting to map the social onto Europe and the human onto the rest of the world, a close reading of the various solidarity discourses lead us to a paradoxical conclusion that keeps these clearly distinct.

Society or humanity?

Solidarity within Europe is epitomized by the 'unique European Social Model' (European Commission, 2000). Solidarity of Europe 'with the rest of the world' is mainly entrusted to humanitarian policy: that is, urgent operations. The first type of solidarity is thus exclusively concerned with the internal element of the EU, while the second, geared towards the outside, aims at catastrophe relief in the humanitarian domain (and much earlier, when it was still used by development discourse,[4] at structural economic changes). The dilemma that is made explicit and criticized in this chapter resides in the interstice between these two areas of solidarity – as it were, the social and the humanitarian – and can be formulated as follows: either Europe creates and strengthens its *social* solidarity (its society), or it creates and strengthens its

---

4   Development policy's use of 'solidarity' has progressively receded in favour of humanitarian policy, since the former has been reconstructed on the basis of a shift of responsibility from the former colonizer to the former colonies.

human solidarity (or solidarity in the name of humanity or humanity); it cannot do both.

In EU documents concerning the social and relations to the rest of the world, the concept is understood in various ways. A helpful distinction can be made between the static and the dynamic modes of representing solidarity. In the static mode, solidarity belongs to 'the values and interests' of European society(ies),[5] to quote the draft constitution (European Commission, 2004, Article I-3, Objective 4).[6] Although a value is not the same thing as an interest, we can, for our purposes, assume that the very fact that solidarity is so self-evidently understood to be a European interest turns it into a value. Another way of speaking about solidarity in this mode, also found in the draft constitution, sees it as one of the 'fundamental characteristics of the society composed by the member states' (European Commission, 2004, Article I-2).[7] Overall, the static mode is one that purports to rescue a dwindling solidarity, and for this reason, it can be called pragmatic.

By contrast, in the dynamic mode, solidarity is something that is aimed at, something that must be achieved. Underlying this mode is the assumption that solidarity is not yet, or not fully, there. It is seen as an objective (European Commission, 2004, Article I-3),[8] but it is also seen as the means to something else: a bringing together of means and goals in terms of 'the commitment to solidarity' and 'solidarity as the commitment to x or y', which can be found in almost every text about solidarity. Insofar as solidarity remains a principle, this mode can be called normative.

Unfortunately for the elegance of the argument, but significantly regarding the implicitness of the discourse, the dilemma described earlier does not lie in this distinction: each mode does not neatly correspond to one of the two areas examined. By contrast, both modes can be found in both broad policy areas: this points to the similarity of the understandings of the concept used in the policy mainly concerned with solidarity within Europe, and in the policy mainly concerned with solidarity with the rest of the world. Thus we find the concept's ambiguous oscillation between what is (as a core value, an *acquis*) and what ought to be (as a challenge) in both cases. On the one hand, Title

5   I will come back later to the use of singular or plural with regard to European society.
6   Here, solidarity is understood as solidarity with the rest of the world.
7   Other characteristics are justice and tolerance. The values of the EU are respect for human dignity, freedom, democracy, and so on, and they are said to be common to all member states.
8   'Objectives of the Union': the third objective aims, among other things, at greater economic, social and territorial cohesion, and at greater solidarity among member states. It is immediately clear that cohesion is different from solidarity in an implicit way that has to do with the subject covered; cohesion should come about, presumably, across the whole of Europe (its *one* society, its economy and its territory), whereas solidarity should exist between member states.

IV of the Charter of Fundamental Rights, containing the fundamental rights associated with the socio-economic existence of European citizens, is entitled 'Solidarity', and the Commission, writing on the Social Agenda, refers to 'the vision that binds us together' (European Commission, 2004a). Similarly, one of the objectives of the same agenda five years earlier had been the promotion of solidarity (European Commission, 2000, 4.3.1. (23)). Moreover, in a brochure explaining humanitarian aid to the public, the European Commission's Humanitarian Aid Office (ECHO) writes: 'Humanity and solidarity are among the core values of the European Union, which is why the bloc is one of the largest humanitarian donors in the world' (2005, 2). The EU Commissioner for Development and Humanitarian Aid, Louis Michel, accordingly talks of solidarity, in this context, as being a 'major political challenge' (Michel, 2004).

At the same time, and again in both policy areas, the chronological-conceptual 'rescue' of solidarity precedes its pursuit: this is the challenge for humanitarian and social assistance alike, the latter of which also exists in a weaker version in which solidarity is depicted as a means. Regarding humanitarian policy, there is, first of all, an understanding of solidarity as the means for fostering a better life for the people who receive the aid.[9] However, solidarity as an instrument is pernicious: before the ECHO was set up,[10] the low visibility of the EU's aid had been strongly problematized (European Commission, 1991),[11] with the EU going on to acknowledge quite explicitly that 'Humanitarian assistance ... became a key element of the EU's international presence' (European Union, 2004, 1). The same phenomenon is encountered with regard to social policy's solidarity, in particular in earlier versions of the struggle against economic globalization.

The epitome of the oscillation between the pragmatic and the normative can be found in the balance that European texts try to strike with regard to their appeal on the one hand to reasonableness and rationality, and on the other hand to emotions. It is most clear in the case of humanitarian aid, in which emotions are mobilized. For example, ECHO's posters claim:

9 In ECHO (2005, 1), one reads: 'For many, international solidarity provides the only hope for survival'. Compare this with page 8 of the same document: 'Respect for the humanitarian space is essential for the delivery of humanitarian aid – the only hope for survival for millions of crisis victims around the world'. This reveals the metonymy: solidarity is the same thing as humanitarian aid. In European Union (2004, 6), one reads: 'Above all, humanitarian aid *expresses* the European Union's solidarity with the world's most vulnerable people'.
10 ECHO itself is presented as 'an instrument of solidarity' in ECHO, 2003.
11 '[I]nternational and European public opinion is rarely aware of what the Community is doing to aid the victims of disasters and fighting' (European Commission, 1991, 1), and thus the Commission 'acts more as a banker than a partner' (European Commission, 1991, 2).

'Solidarity is at the heart of Europe!' (ECHO, 2003b), which is also evidently a positioning of this solidarity as central, just as in the case of its characterization as a core value. It is striking that the most explicitly material solidarity of the two is the one that appeals so strongly to emotions. However, this materiality is reinforced by the fact that the aid's implementation, resting 'on fundamental *principles* of impartiality, non-discrimination, independence and neutrality' (ECHO, 2005, 4), strongly appeals to reason and reasoned principles that allow the values and emotions to act efficiently. The case of the concept of solidarity in social policy is more complicated. Despite its constant position in the social 'values' that confront economic 'necessities',[12] the texts have managed to turn it into a reasonable, reassuring device: accordingly, everything that ought to be maintained in the framework of the famous 'European social model' and everything that ought to be 'modernized' (European Commission, 2000, 20), changed or cut down, depend on 'solidarity', and are hence decided on the basis of solidarity.

Despite this great conceptual affinity, the two 'substantive' solidarities have remained unconnected. Very recently, however, an attempt at (re-)connecting these two areas has been made via the promotion of the European Social Model to the rest of the world.[13] In a recent seminar, the EU Commissioner for Employment affirmed that 'solidarity should be viewed in a global context' (Špidla, 2005, 3). Going on to borrow the emotional register from humanitarian aid discourse, he added: 'The challenge has been to place social development at the heart of all policies' (Špidla, 2005, 3). Indeed, on the website of the International Affairs division of the Directorate for Employment, Social Affairs and Equal Opportunities, the 'social dimension of globalization' is the central theme. Referring to a report by the World

---

12 'In the past, social policy has enabled the European Union to manage structural change while minimizing negative social consequences. In the future, modernizing the European social model and investing in people will be crucial to retain the European social values of solidarity and justice while improving economic performance.' (European Commission, 2000, 6)

13 The impulse for such a passage from one solidarity to another has certainly come from the outside (the 'global'), since the EU based its whole discourse of uniqueness on the development of something different inside. It is nevertheless interesting that the EU responds to such an impulse with its own example, which results in a variety of levels of the 'social world'. The references to 'one society' formed by the member states co-exist with references to a slightly different 'one European society', to the different social systems of the member states, and to the idea of a global 'community' in which charity – one of the expressions of the existence of a society – occurs. '[W]hile strong parallels could be drawn, it was also of course important to recognize the rather different political contexts of the EU and the global community. The global community too often involved fragmented charity for debt defaulters. Within the EU, in contrast, the Lisbon strategy involved a cooperative effort by member states which enjoyed sovereign equality...' (European Union, 2005, 12).

Committee on the Social Dimension of Globalization, the site insists on the importance of the regional level for social policy.[14] The other side of the coin is a concern with the effects of globalization within the EU, in a way that tends to see the outside and the inside as co-extensive. The fact that this is presented as a vision with a long history should not lead us to neglect the novelty of a rather positive approach to diversity within the EU[15] and to immigration (European Commission, 2000, 11).[16]

That both EU policy discourses share the same ambiguities with regard to their use of the concept of solidarity – that both envisage it as, at the same time, already existing and something that must be brought about, a goal and a means to achieve goals, rational and emotional – is an indicator of the two policies' similar understanding of what solidarity is. However, this similarity is left unacknowledged, clearly to the detriment of one solidarity, namely 'human' solidarity with the rest of the world. This is most evident in the most general European texts such as the draft constitution or the Charter of Fundamental Rights, where there is an oscillation between a solidarity belongs, first, to the social realm, and second, to the present; and a solidarity that belongs to the realm outside Europe – not characterized as social or otherwise – and in an indefinite time, between the past of a value and the future of an interest. This wavering expresses an implicit dilemma. To avoid making the dilemma explicit, the EU institutions recently opted for an attempt to merge the two solidarities, but this merging again appears to privilege social solidarity over humanitarian solidarity. Why?

One of the reasons for this is that the 'unique European social model' has been 'marketed' in such a way as to fulfil internal and external purposes. European solidarity in the social arena has wilfully served for the passionate and absurd pursuit of European identity.[17] However, the most important reason for this is that the definition of social solidarity (and of its context) is much more precise than that of humanitarian solidarity. The former is social, and it is defined by opposition to the economic domain, although their

---

14 'The WCSDG also highlights the importance of a strong social dimension in regional integration if it is to be a stepping stone towards a more effective social dimension of globalization.' (European Union, 2005a)

15 'The EU must also ensure that it exercizes its external policies in a way which contributes to maximizing the benefits of globalization for all social groups in all its partner countries and regions.'

16 'While the essential role of the member states' social systems in creating a cohesive society must be recognized, they now face a series of significant common challenges ... this calls for a reflection on the role of immigration as part of a strategy to combat these trends (demo pressures).'

17 Balibar (2003) fruitfully proposes that one should see European agency as having priority over an elusive European identity. For a similar accent on the multitudes of Europe and the definition of borders, see Wagner, 2005.

common development is advocated.[18] The latter is asymmetrically distinguished from the former: it is implicitly advocated in the name of 'humanity', and is much broader than social solidarity. Similarly, as we shall see in the next section, whereas the term 'European societies' designates a fairly precise entity, 'the rest of the world' remains indeterminate.

However, the issue is not only one of comparable precision. In the case of the solidarity of 'humanitarian aid', we can also point out that it is explicitly defined against the political, and that it is clearly translatable into material terms: this apolitical solidarity, the EU says, is mostly about giving money to others (ECHO, 2005, 4). It is only apparently a paradox that, claiming the highest moral grounds, solidarity concerning 'humanitarian aid' is basely material. We can ultimately observe two different trajectories for the two solidarities: if the first starts by pointing at differences (between European societies, welfare states, etc.) and ends up pointing at commonality (the European Social Model, European society), the second claims to originate in the most evident common feature – humanity – and ends up pointing at 'otherness': poverty, catastrophe and calamity, fates that are relegated to Europe's past. Both are old understandings of solidarity – the first privileging the keeping together of the group, the second privileging the bringing together of differences – but it is clear that they differ in motivational force, in the 'sacrifices' they demand and in the degree of morality in which they are steeped. Thus, the two solidarities' descriptions of social ties differ so crucially that they end up portraying different future polities.

Europe or the rest of the world?

Onto the dilemma, posed by the European institutions' texts, concerning social solidarity and human solidarity, or society and humanity, can be mapped the dilemma concerning Europe and the 'rest of the world'. This question is implicitly or explicitly posed by thinkers on Europe.[19] It is within the context of a debate on Europe's place in the world, cosmopolitanism and republicanism, that this dilemma emerged; it should immediately be noted that this debate addressed the relations between Europe and the USA. Although a book has recently been published that brings together all the

---

18 '[T]he objectives of employment, solidarity and social inclusion cannot be separated from the globalized economy, where the competitiveness and attractiveness of Europe are at stake' (European Commission, 2004a, 4).

19 The chapter does not review Eurosceptic views, since the debate in which these views are expressed concerns the passage from the national to the European level, which is beyond the remit of this paper.

contributions – including invited ones – to this debate (Levy, Pensky and Torpey, 2005), I look closely at just four contributions: two by Europeans, Jürgen Habermas and Jacques Derrida; and two by Americans, Richard Rorty and Iris Marion Young. These were immediately available to the general, Anglophone public.

It seems an uncanny coincidence that Habermas's article 'Why Europe needs a constitution' first appeared in the autumn of 2001. In this article, Habermas was arguing for a constitution for the European Union that would, both as a means of convergence and as a symbolic result, crystallize a political project for Europe. The broader argument was that European integration already expressed a tradition that is distinct from the Anglo-American model,[20] but that this distinctiveness has not been made clear enough and could, thus, not sufficiently mobilize the European people.

In this text, there are two main uses of the concept of solidarity, both of which refer to what I have called 'solidarity within Europe': social solidarity and civic solidarity. In the section of the article that is entitled 'Globalization and social solidarity', solidarity is seen as a 'formative background' that is provided by 'the political tradition of the workers' movement, the salience of Christian social doctrines and even a certain normative core of social liberalism'(Habermas, 2001, 4). Habermas invokes this tradition of social solidarity because he believes that for normative arguments in support of the maintenance and enhancement of a European social welfare to be truly effective, they must appeal to some already existing tradition.

Civic solidarity appears a few pages later, when Habermas argues that European nation states do not have a communitarian understanding of themselves. Thus:

> a civic, as opposed to ethnic conception of 'the nation' reflects both the actual historical trajectory of the European nation states and the fact that the democratic citizenship establishes an abstract, legally mediated solidarity between strangers. (Habermas, 2001, 8)

This 'civic solidarity that provides the cement of national societies' (Habermas, 2001, 8) is a 'striking innovation' produced jointly by democracy and the nation state. The reason why Habermas invokes this 'solidarity between strangers', the product of a 'painful process of abstraction' (Habermas, 2001, 8), is in order to argue that there is no reason why one more

---

20 'With a view to the future of a highly stratified society, we Europeans have a legitimate interest in getting our voice heard in an international concert that is at present dominated by a vision quite different from ours.' (Habermas, 2001, 6)

step in such a process of abstraction could not be taken, from the civic nations to the European one.[21]

Even though Habermas clearly intends to keep the social and the political (or 'civic') apart, in both concepts of solidarity, he offers a description of a social reality and tradition with a political and normative view. There is no mention, in this text, of the solidarity of Europe with 'the rest of the world'. However, he does mention how Europe and European countries relate to their outside, in the section: 'Sharing a political culture'. There, Habermas talks about 'the well-taken – and only too deserved – critique of our aggressive colonial and Eurocratic past; the critique of Eurocentrism itself emerges from continuing self-criticism' (Habermas, 2001, 11). (A little bit later, in the same section, he invokes again solidarity within Europe, the 'solidarity among strangers' that has historically been based neither on 'assimilation' nor on mere 'co-existence'. Although there is no direct conceptual link – apart from a 'moreover' – the next phrases address the challenges of immigration and multiculturalism.)

The same conceptual categories re-appear in a text that was published two years later. The article, written by Habermas and co-signed by Jacques Derrida, was entitled 'February 15th, or what binds Europeans together', alluding to the day of the massive demonstrations against the largely Anglo-American war in Iraq. Its main purpose was to bolster the argument that had been made earlier, wrapped up in a call for a common European defence policy, but the context was now that of the war in Iraq and the 'war on terrorism'; the accent on the incompatibility of the US and the European worldviews was much stronger.[22]

Solidarity within Europe, in its civic guise, and in stark contrast to the goal of competitiveness vis-à-vis non-Europeans, is mentioned in the context of the need for the enhancement of citizens' political motivation: 'The population must, so to speak, "build up" their national identities and add to them a European dimension' (Habermas and Derrida, 2003, 293). Repeating, in slightly more moderate terms, the argument of the previous article, the main author adds: 'What is already a fairly abstract form of civic solidarity, still largely confined to members of nation states, must be extended to include the European citizens of other nations as well' (Habermas and Derrida, 2003, 293). Social solidarity is referred to later in the paper, when, attempting to

---

21 The second reason is that he sees the conditions for such a step (civil society, public sphere, political culture) as sourced in the empirical depths of the first process of abstraction.

22 For instance: 'For us, a President who opens his daily business with open prayer, and associates his significant political decisions with divine mission, is hard to imagine' (Habermas and Derrida, 2003, 296).

define an elusive European identity, Habermas writes that an additional characteristic is the Europeans' preference for 'regulations on the basis of solidarity' (Habermas and Derrida, 2003, 295). Interestingly, towards the end of the article, solidarity is turned into an existing ethic: presumably, a tradition that can normatively be relied upon for the future.[23]

As in the previous article, there is no mention of the solidarity of Europe with the rest of the world. The article deals twice with Europe's 'other': once, briefly, regarding Europe's internal diversity (which we can place close to the earlier article's brief reference to immigration and multiculturalism) (Habermas and Derrida, 2003, 294); and, in the second instance, with a more substantial discussion of colonialism.[24] Thus, despite the text's central focus on the outside of the EU, 'outside' in this context is mainly understood as the relation of Europe to the US or, in other words, relations within the West. What seems problematic here is the casting of the rest of the world either in a present that is only very remotely relevant to the constitution of the European identity (very brief excursions into immigration, which are unconnected to colonialism, as if they were happening suddenly), or in a past that is definitively over, like colonialism. Pointing this out is not equivalent, for the purposes of this chapter, to making an anti-Eurocentric critique: rather, our attention should be drawn to the erasure from the relevant present of Europe of solidarity with the rest of the world. Rather than cancelling the dilemmatic construction, this erasure sustains it.

To digress slightly, we could note that, more than a decade earlier, Derrida had written a well-known text, originally a newspaper article, called *The Other Heading* (1992). In it, Derrida explicitly refers to the question of the 'otherness' of Europe, which he considers intrinsic to the European spirit, and in effect, though in other words, connects solidarity within Europe and solidarity of Europe with the rest of the world. Starting by considering himself an 'over-acculturated, over-colonized European hybrid' (Derrida, 1992, 7),

---

23 'In the context of the workers' movements and the Christian socialist traditions, an ethics of solidarity, the struggle for "more social justice", with the goal of equal provision for all, asserted itself against the individualistic ethos of market justice that accepts glaring inequalities as part of the bargain.' (Habermas and Derrida, 2003, 296).

24 'Each of the great European nations has experienced the bloom of its imperial power and, what in our context is more important still, each had to work through the experience of the loss of an empire. In many cases this experience of decline was associated with the loss of colonial territories. With the growing distance of imperial domination and the history of colonialism, the European powers also got the chance to *assume a reflexive distance from themselves*. They could learn from the perspective of the defeated to perceive themselves in the dubious role of victors who are called to account for the violence of a forcible and uprooting process of modernization. This could support the rejection of Eurocentrism, and inspire the Kantian hope for a global domestic policy.' (Habermas and Derrida, 2003, 297)

he suggests that '[Europe] advances and promotes itself as an advance, and it will have never ceased to make advances on the other ... to colonize and to colonize itself' (Derrida, 1992, 49).[25]

On the contrary, it is striking that colonialism, not to speak of the solidarity of Europe with the rest of world, would barely get a mention in a volume bringing together all the contributors to this debate. Two US writers are exceptions. Richard Rorty should be briefly mentioned, not least because he has previously been interested in solidarity (Rorty, 1989) and because his own piece, published in a German newspaper on the same day as the article by Habermas and Derrida, was entitled 'Humiliation or solidarity? The hope for a common European foreign policy' (Rorty, 2003). However, he only explicitly refers to 'the solidification of the European Union into a powerful independent force in world affairs' in the last paragraph. So the question in the title expresses another dilemma than the one between solidarity within Europe and solidarity with the rest of the world: a dilemma between the humiliation to which the Europeans would be subjected if they did not follow the anti-Bush impetus of the February 15 demonstrations, and the solidarity that Europeans must show among themselves in order to resist that humiliation. Solidarity of Europe with the rest of the world is never mentioned. However, when repeating Habermas and Derrida's invitation to dream a cosmopolitan dream, Rorty mentions that this 'idealistic self-definition [of Europeans] would be responded to around the world, in the United States and China as well as in Brazil and Russia' (2003, 4). Europe – a future cosmopolitan vision born in Europe – is represented here as a call for responses elsewhere in 'the rest of the world'; as an example to be followed.

By contrast, Iris Marion Young does not read Habermas and Derrida's Europeanism and cosmopolitanism as co-extensive. Her criticism of their intervention argues that the latter was a 're-centring of Europe' rather than 'the invocation of an inclusive global democracy' for which Young herself hopes. She thinks that 'the call to embrace a particularist European identity' (2003, 1), as she calls Habermas and Derrida's call for a European political identity, 'means constructing anew the distinction between insiders and outsiders' (2003, 2).

Thus, Young is the one who most explicitly poses the dilemma, even though – following the usual division of labour between thinkers on Europe and thinkers on the global condition – solidarity within Europe holds no real

25 Derrida already poses the question of the newness and oldness of Europe and its critics, wondering: 'Is there then a completely new "today" of Europe beyond all the exhausted programmes of *Eurocentrism* and *anti-Eurocentrism*, these exhausting, yet unforgettable programmes?' (Derrida, 1992, 13).

interest for her, despite a mention at the very end of her article. Regarding the solidarity of Europe with the rest of the world, rather than *imagining* the perspective of colonized people, as Habermas and Derrida suggest, Young asks Europeans to talk to formerly colonized people. Rather than seeing colonialism as an uprooting process of modernization, as Habermas and Derrida propose, she proposes to see colonialism as 'a system of slavery and labour exploitation' (Young, 2003, 3). In other terms, where Habermas and Derrida speak to the Europeans' imagination, she speaks to their potential for communication and action; where they describe, she denounces. Much of her reasoning – see the quotes above – tends to the conclusion that if Europe puts an accent on itself – on redefining itself, as Rorty says, or on forging a political identity for itself, as Habermas says –the inevitable outcome is the neglect of the rest of the world.

Despite this main and consistently followed line, however, there are two important discrepancies. Around the middle of her text, Young asks: 'Surely invoking a European identity inhibits tolerance within *and* solidarity with those far away?' (Young, 2003, 2). If we choose to understand 'tolerance within' as what we have called 'solidarity within'– however minimalistically understood – then it is clear that, at this point, Young collapses the dilemma: solidarity within and solidarity of Europe with the rest of the world are directly analogous, and one does not inhibit the other. The parallel problem is, of course, to know to what degree Young misinterprets Habermas and Derrida's 'political identity'. More drastically, at the end of the article, Young suggests that Europe's 'solidaristic culture', along with its many other privileges,

> position[s] European states and citizens well *to take the lead* in the project of strengthening international law and peaceful conflict resolution, and instituting mechanisms of global redistribution. (Young, 2003, 4)

Here, the dilemma is again collapsed, but the other way around: given that Europeans know solidarity within, Young says, then they should be the leaders of solidarity with the rest of the world. The paradox of 'taking the lead' and 'being solidary with' is not discussed; the idea that solidarity, rather than being the classically understood pact among equals, more often than not actually rests on unequal foundations is not touched upon (Karagiannis, 2006).

Global, social, political

The dilemma – implicit or explicit – is the wrong way to formulate the issue: first, because it rests on two fundamental indeterminacies; and second, because, in the current circumstances, European solidarity within Europe goes hand-in-hand with European solidarity towards Europe's outside. Third, the concept of solidarity is both a description of a social situation and the articulation of a political project.

The two indeterminacies on which this dilemma is based concern the notion of 'the rest of the world' and the articulation between Europe's colonial past and its political future. Regarding 'the rest of the world' (an expression used mainly by EU policy discourse and by Rorty, in the examples given above), it has been noted that, in the theoretical debates on Europe, it has mainly meant the USA, or other economically competitive areas of the world. The reduction is all the more problematic given that, although setting Europe apart from the rest of the world may seem an ambiguous move, usage of 'the world' underlines the commonality of the space or experience shared by Europe and others (Karagiannis and Wagner, 2006). Even if 'the rest of the world' is extended – as it should be – to all regions, and particularly those that should be favoured by redistribution, it remains relatively indefinite when compared to solidarity within Europe. This is because a general, worldwide solidarity does not say anything about the nature of the solidaristic link other than a laudable ethical propensity. In order for this link to become substantive and, hence, meaningful, it must be translated into social terms, just like the solidarity of Europe's social affairs. Only when solidarity with 'the rest of the world' can become a *social* solidarity – as it has been alluded to by policy rather than theory discourse – will it have any serious impact on the weaker areas of the world and on the self-definition of Europe.

Concerning the articulation between Europe's colonial past and the future of its political project, the step to be taken is rather straightforward. Making Europe's history relevant to its future seems unproblematic for most thinkers and policy makers; there is no reason why this general principle should not apply to Europe's colonial experience. Immigration and multiculturalism in Europe are evidently a product of European imperialism and colonialism, and the only viable way forwards for a future European polity is the acknowledgement of the richness and diversity that this history has produced for the making of Europe.

Under current circumstances, solidarity within Europe goes hand-in-hand with solidarity with the rest of the world. Assuming that the latter solidarity is understood as making Europe part of a common 'world', that is as 'global solidarity', then this solidarity makes no sense unless it attributes egalitarian responsibility – that is, a responsibility that, based on historical ties of interdependence between poor and rich countries, renders the latter responsible for the former's welfare today – to the rich areas of the world like Europe, the USA and Japan. This leads us to see the relevance for global

227

solidarity of a solidarity of Europe with the rest of the world . However, Europe, perhaps contrary to the USA or Japan, has no direction as such, unless a stronger sense of cohesion and 'univocity' can be summoned: unless there is a solidarity within Europe that can actually produce a globally responsible Europe. The point here is not so much to render Europe distinct from other international entities such as the USA, as Habermas would argue, but, quite simply, to bring about rapprochements between aspects of Europe that are considered separately. Arguments that consist in pointing out that there must realistically be a trade-off between solidarity within and solidarity with the rest of the world miss the point made earlier regarding the 'unique European social model': institutionalized internal solidarity builds up Europe's character, as it were, towards the outside, just as 'humanitarian' solidarity also serves as a mirror for Europeans themselves. Such arguments perpetuate a dilemmatic construction that cannot be sustained in the light of the similarity in the usages of the concept of solidarity, as I hope to have shown. In other words, solidarity is not a scarce resource; it is as expandable as the political will for it.

In general terms, the concept of solidarity simultaneously fulfils a descriptive function (that can be brought close to the pragmatic mode of the policy discourse) and a normative function. The first serves to describe social situations (or social bonds). The second serves programmatically to announce a political project. Thus it is important to note that when – as is usually the case –solidarity within Europe is referred to, the reference to a singular Europe pre-empts its solidarity. Logically, Europe would not need solidarity, if it were one. On the other hand, the solidarity of Europe with the rest of the world is also characterized by constitutive ambiguity: if 'the world' were indeed one, then Europe would not have to be solidaristic with any of the other parts of the world.

This confusion between what there is and what there should be was traced in a more detailed manner in the discourse emanating from EU institutions, but can also be found in the theoretical discourse. From this perspective, internal solidarity has centrally been thought of as being defined by the same qualities as the solidarity that used to characterize the nation state. In these terms, European solidarity only involves taking a further step in largeness or in abstraction. If this were the case, then in what sense would solidarity be a characteristically European feature? The contention, here, is that the strategy of solidarity theorists within Europe – expressly to ignore a dilemma with which they implicitly work – has resulted in a conceptualization of solidarity within Europe as a solidarity deprived of specific qualities of its own (since it emulates national solidarity) and a solidarity of Europe with the rest of the world as being somehow distinctly European. This unlikely conclusion has paradoxically been made possible by, first, the relegation of the solidarity of Europe with the rest of the world to the historical (and only occasionally relevant) and cognitive (imagination) realms; by, second, retaining solidarity within Europe as a normative and political project; and concomitantly by, third, collapsing the distinction between social and civic solidarity into the latter term, which makes of the 'social' an unalterable entity that has the same characteristics under different polities.

By contrast, critiques of such theorizations of Europe, rather than ignoring the dilemma, have articulated it in the form of a pro-global-South argument, which is simultaneously, it is claimed, a critique of the Eurocentrism of the previous authors. The main strategy here is to posit solidarity within Europe as globally irrelevant: irrelevant to the solidarity of Europe with the rest of the world, and irrelevant to global solidarity in general, whatever this term may precisely cover. At the most, it is a solidarity *without* Europe that is advocated. 'Eurocentrism' and 'anti-Eurocentrism', to use Derrida's terms, are, however, ultimately, fundamentally alike in that they illustrate very vividly that solidarity is a recurrent specification of social bonds with a political view. Whether they aim to fix the place of the social or, on the contrary, turn the whole world into a 'social' world, they unavoidably use it with a political project in view.

References

Balibar, E. (2003), 'Europe: vanishing mediator', *Constellations*, 10, 3.

Derrida, J. (1992), *The Other Heading: Reflections on Today's Europe* (transl. P.-A. Brault and M. B. Naas), Bloomington, IN, Indiana University Press.

ECHO (European Commission's Humanitarian Aid Office) (2003), *ECHO and its Greek Partners*, Brussels, European Commission.

ECHO (European Commission's Humanitarian Aid Office) (2003a), *Palestinian Territories: Solidarity with the Victims*, Brussels, European Commission.

ECHO (European Commission's Humanitarian Aid Office) (2003b), 'Solidarity is at the heart of Europe!' (poster), Brussels, European Commission.

ECHO (European Commission's Humanitarian Aid Office) (2005), *European Humanitarian Aid: Values and Principles*, Brussels, European Commission.

European Commission (1991), 'Commission decides to set up a European Office for Humanitarian Aid', press release, 16 November, Brussels, European Commission.

European Commission (2000), 'Social policy agenda', Communication, COM 379 final, Brussels, European Commission.

European Commission (2004), 'Draft Treaty for a European Constitution, Charter of Fundamental Rights', Brussels, European Commission.

European Commission (2004a), 'The social agenda (until 2010)', Communication, Brussels, European Commission.

European Union (2004), 'Humanitarian aid: introduction', http://europa.eu.int/scadplus/leg/en/lvb /r10000.htm

European Union (2005), 'Promoting Social Development for All', seminar, Brussels, 13–14 January.

European Union (2005a), 'The social dimension of globalisation', http://europa.eu.int/comm/employment_social/international_cooperation/globalisation_front_en.htm

Habermas, J. (2001), 'Why Europe needs a constitution', *New Left Review*, 11, September–October.

Habermas, J. and Derrida, J. (2003), 'February 15, or what binds Europeans together: a plea for a common foreign policy, beginning in the core of Europe', *Constellations*, 10, 3.

Karagiannis, N. (2006), 'Multiple solidarities: autonomy and resistance' in N. Karagiannis and P. Wagner (eds), *Varieties of World-Making: Beyond Globalization*, Liverpool, Liverpool University Press.

Karagiannis, N. and Wagner, P. (2006), 'Globalization or world-making' in N. Karagiannis and P. Wagner (eds), *Varieties of World-Making: Beyond Globalization*, Liverpool, Liverpool University Press.

Levy, D., Pensky, M. and Torpey, J. (eds) (2005), *Old Europe, New Europe, Core Europe: Transatlantic Relations After the Iraq War*, London, Verso.

Michel, L. (2004), 'It is not the impossible which gives cause for despair, but the failure to achieve the possible', http://europa.eu.int/comm/commission_barroso/michel/index.en.htm

Rorty, R. (1989), *Contingency, Irony and Solidarity*, Cambridge, Cambridge University Press.

Rorty, R. (2003), 'Humiliation or solidarity? The hope for a common European foreign policy', *Dissent Magazine*, Fall.

Špidla, V. (2005), 'Promoting social development for all', speech, Brussels.

Young, I. M. (2003), 'Europe and the global south: towards a circle of equality', www.openDemocracy.net

Wagner, P. (2005), 'The political form of Europe, Europe as a political form', *Thesis Eleven*, 80.

Index